To Napier C[...]
with gratitude. without the encouragement
of yourself, Scallop, and Shell, this
book would have not come about.

With warm regards,

Howard

1 February 1988

Developmental Time, Cultural Space

Developmental Time, Cultural Space

STUDIES IN PSYCHOGEOGRAPHY

Howard F. Stein

UNIVERSITY OF OKLAHOMA PRESS : NORMAN AND LONDON

Library of Congress Cataloging-in-Publication Data

Stein, Howard F.
  Developmental time, cultural space.

  Bibliography: p. 211
  Includes index.
  1. Ethnopsychology.   2. Environmental psychology.
  3. Ethnic relations.   4. Psychoanalysis.   I. Title.
  GN502.S74   1987   155.8   87-5088
  ISBN 0–8061–2070–3 (alk. paper)

An earlier version of chapter 1 was previously published in *The Journal of Psychoanalytic Anthropology* 7 (1) (Winter 1984): 23–73. © Copyright 1984 by the Association for Psychohistory, Inc. An earlier version of chapter 2 was previously published in *The Journal of Psychoanalytic Anthropology* 7 (3) (Summer 1984): 269–92. © Copyright 1984 by the Association for Psychohistory, Inc. An earlier version of chapter 3 was previously published in *Ethos* 4 (4) (Winter 1976): 403–38. Copyright © 1976 by the American Anthropological Association. An earlier version of chapter 4 was previously published in *The Psychoanalytic Quarterly* 46 (1977): 650–83. Copyright © 1977, by the Psychoanalytic Quarterly, Inc.

Dedicated to the

COMMITTEE ON INTERNATIONAL RELATIONS,

GROUP FOR THE ADVANCEMENT OF PSYCHIATRY

1986

Contents

Illustrations

Preface

This book explores cultural space as a metaphor of developmental time. It examines how developmental themes rooted in growing up in the human body and in a family context are subsequently played out in cultural images and intergroup relations. Building on the pioneering work of Sigmund Freud, William Niederland, Erik Erikson, Weston La Barre, Vamık Volkan, Lloyd deMause, Henry Ebel, and many others, I postulate that the insights from depth psychology and human development are indispensable to advancing our understanding of people's sense of self and sense of place in the world. Numerous cultural and historical examples illustrate this point of view. Special attention is devoted to exploring the shared psychodynamics that are involved in group boundaries, that is, the identification of "What is inside, and what is outside?" and "Where do we begin, and where do we end?" It is my hope that this book will help answer the question "What are boundaries about?"

The discoveries of science have long challenged our cherished assumptions about ourselves, our place in nature, and our very understanding of what we take to be reality itself. This book is no exception. In documenting how much we take to be "outside"—out there—that is in fact deeply symbolic of processes and meanings that take place inside ourselves, this book will be unavoidably disorienting. But at the same time the patient reader will find himself or herself reoriented to a world long forgotten.

This book proposes the thesis that, in large measure, human beings construct the world they inhabit *from* the body and the family *outward to* society and nature. I argue that cultural space symbolizes and bears the heavy burden of fantasies, anxieties, and conflicts deeply embedded in the developmental time of infancy, childhood, and adolescence. I propose that to understand human perceptions of the world, of themselves and of other groups, it is necessary to turn our everyday assumptions inside out, so to speak. I argue that locations in space are in fact locations in time; that migrations in space are in fact migrations in time; that "place" and "thing" and "group" are symbols in space; and that their referent is the unremembered vicissitudes of developmental time. Outer battles wage personal or shared inner struggles. In displacing our attention onto natural or social objects outside ourselves, we both protect ourselves from the anxieties they represent and render ourselves vulnerable to what we will not allow ourselves to see.

In a sense, the goal of this book is to help us to reclaim or retrieve what we have put outside ourselves—to be able to say "I" or "we" instead of "them" or "it." In the introduction and five subsequent case-study–oriented chapters, I attempt to show that, whether as individuals or as groups, human beings tend to cast the identity of their "who-ness" with their emotion-laden "where-ness," thus merging "who am I" with "where am I," binding self and place. In our nuclear age such distortions have become among the most dangerous threats to our species' survival. It is my hope that many of the discoveries in psychogeography will help us understand why intergroup and international problems have been so refractory to solution—and, by extension, to help us reach more humane solutions by recognizing the psychological contribution to such problems.

Readers of this book, many no doubt having grown up during the "sexual revolution" and women's liberation movements of the 1960s and early 1970s, may well find many of my interpretations, especially those of the cultural-political cartoons, to be "sexist" and "male chauvinistic." At most, perhaps, readers will concede that themes of castration fears, homosexuality, and military aggression are quintessentially male preoccupations. Indeed, most political cartoonists are males. The official patriarchal imagery and structure of the Judeo-Christian West notwithstanding, successful cartoonists and popular artists, like successful leaders, offer images in which large groups of people if not entire nations can recognize themselves in what feels like a shared self-portrait.

The unconscious logic of primary process is irrational; under its dominion we can imagine human bodies, social groups, and the universe to be anything. The unconscious and its contemporary manifestations do not abide by our current ideological fashions about how modern people ought to visualize themselves. In fact, it does not abide by shared conscious logic at all, but rather by shared unconscious logic. At times these images may seem skewed toward one sex or the other. Their power, nevertheless, lies in their ability to resonate with our shared unconscious wishes, fantasies, and dreads. And when a set of images (representations of shared unconscious fantasies) becomes widespread, the interpreter of that culture—or any other culture—can begin to suspect that he or she has at least a rudimentary glimpse into the emotional core of the age. Boyer (1979), Dundes (1985), and Hook (1979) have discussed both psychoanalytic theories of folklore, mythology, ritual, and the use of psychoanalytic methodology in making interpretations of culture.

Only a moment's reflection confirms that one need not be sexist to recognize that male or female symbols can come to represent whole groups. Virtually every Russian-founded city has its shrine at which has been built a statue of a mother figure, benefactress, protector; it serves, or at least once served, as a collective image, a focal point of the imagination of males and females, adults and children alike. Americans have a not dissimilar symbol in the Statue of Liberty, often called Lady Liberty or Miss Liberty. During the "Liberty Weekend" ceremonies in July 1986, celebrating the completion of the yearlong restoration of the statue, Americans openly described the statue as a maternal symbol and the ritual of rededication as one of American rebirth. One does not need to be a committed Freudian to see sexual symbolism in the exuberant fireworks exploded over and near Lady Liberty at night or in the parade of boats large and small around her during the day (e.g., Primal Scene, incest with mother, orgasms, spermatazoa aswarm in the uterine sea, newborn infants in the broken water beneath the mother). Now, it is true that the French designer of the statue was male and that his fantasies certainly played a role in his creation of the statue (purportedly modeled from his mother's face and his fiancée's arm or body). But the rededication-rebirth ritual was a *national* enactment by males and females alike. My point throughout this book is simply that the conscious rules of logic and supposed rationality do not apply to our understanding and interpretation of group fantasies, myths, folklore, and the like. This book is about the unconscious, primary process logic that governs—outside our awareness and control and access—our perceptions of "bodies" of various kinds (organisms, groups, natural formations) that occupy cultural space.

The product of an attempt to integrate perspectives from anthropology, psychoanalysis, group dynamics, psychohistory, and family dynamics, this book will, I hope, be useful to social and behavioral scientists of academic persuasions interested in the application of psychoanalytic insight to understanding human behavior and to problem solving in clinical, corporate, and diplomatic activities.

This book has benefited from many sources. The Maurice Falk Medical Fund, Pittsburgh, Pennsylvania, supported my ethnographic research among white ethnic Americans from 1967 to 1972, work which became the foundation of my subsequent work in ethnicity and nationalism. In the mid-1970s the Spencer Foundation and Nashville University Center, Nashville, Tennessee, supported a continuation of this work, and its expansion into a historiographic exploration of Russian and Jewish identity, during the mid-1970s while I taught at Meharry Medical College, Nashville. During the early and mid-1980s I have served as Ittleson Consultant to the Committee on International Relations of the Group for the Advancement of Psychiatry, American Psychiatric Association. Five years of discussions and work on a monograph have persuaded me of the utility of a psychogeographic view of group identity and intergroup conflict. This book is gratefully dedicated to the members of the Committee on International Relations.

In 1983 and 1984, I was invited by Karel F. J. Niebling and Napier Collyns to lecture on psychogeography to senior executives of Shell International Petroleum Maatschappij B.V. at the Harvard Conference Center, Mont-Pèlerin, Switzerland. The invitation confirmed my belief that such a framework was not only intellectually interesting and promising but immensely practical for understanding group identity formation, intergroup problem formation, and conflict resolution. Upon leaving the conference and returning to the United States, I found myself driving my car out of the way to pump gas from a Shell service station. I discovered that I was dealing with my grief over the loss of that "peak experience" by identifying with a company I knew far better in fantasy than in fact. If I had to leave Shell behind, I could at least in some small way also take it home with me and take it inside (which I symbolically did in fueling—nourishing—my automobile with its gasoline).

It was the impetus of these invitations that led me to formalize this work on psychogeography, culminating in chapter 1 of this book. The material for the original paper was enriched by discussions I had with Vamık D. Volkan, M.D.; Henry Ebel; William D. Grant; and Margaret A. Stein. I am especially grateful for Lloyd deMause's encouragement at the publication stage of this paper. To George A. De Vos goes my unflagging gratitude for his encouragement in the mid-1970s that I publish my unorthodox interpretation of the history of the relationship between czarist Russia and Western Europe; in this volume that paper now appears as chapter 3.

The primary sources for chapter 4, an exploration of the dynamics of Judeo-Christian relations, are twofold: the first is that I was born and have grown up as a Jew; the second is the transforming influence of a chapter entitled "The Immortal People," by Weston La Barre in his *The Ghost Dance*, published in 1970. My originally published paper was dedicated to him.

In 1983 a widening awareness of my writing on group identity and intergroup conflict led to an invitation to participate in the Second Annual Erik Erikson Symposium on the Psychology of the U.S.-Soviet Relationship, held at the Esalen Institute in October. Most recently I was invited to present a paper on the group psychology of adversary relationships at an all-day conference on "Psychological Aspects of the Nuclear Arms Race," held at George Washington University on April 26, 1985, and organized by Physicians for Social Responsibility of Greater Washington. These invitations have greatly accelerated my work in psychogeographical analysis and have greatly catalyzed my attempts to synthesize ethnographic research in contemporary cultures, psychoanalysis, family studies, and international relations. Chapter 5 grew out of my presentations at the Erikson Symposium and the Physicians for Social Responsibility conference.

My work over the past eight years as research associate of the Institute for Psychohistory (New York) and as editor (since 1980) of the *Journal of Psychoanalytic Anthropology* has given me the opportunity to formulate, test, and revise my ideas on psychogeography.

I gratefully acknowledge the editorial suggestions made by Robert Coles, M.D., and Weston La Barre, who read an earlier manuscript of this book. I likewise wish to thank John N. Drayton, Editor-in-Chief of the University of Oklahoma Press, for his helpfulness and encouragement.

My wife, Margaret, diligently typed and scrupulously edited this volume. I owe much to her tenacity in bringing this book to fruition.

HOWARD F. STEIN

January 1986

Developmental Time, Cultural Space

Introduction

There is nothing mysterious or esoteric about psychogeography: it is part of our everyday experience of ourselves and our world. The close fit, if not fusion, between one's sense of self ("who-ness") and one's sense of place ("where-ness") can be seen throughout the range of the imagery of large groups such as nations to smaller groups such as corporations and medical departments, and in the personal symbolism of individuals as well. The term "psychogeography" refers to people's shared psychological representation or "map" of the natural and social world, the developmental antecedents of that map, the group dynamics which forge and revise that common map, and the consequences in group and intergroup action of living according to that map.

Many Oklahoma wheat-farming and cattle-raising families whom I know inextricably link their sense of self, their family, their farm, and their beloved land. One son says, "We always have the farm to fall back on; I'll try college, but I can always go back and help Dad on the farm." Other farmers say, "The land is us; we're the dirt." With the onset in the early 1980s of the now-chronic depression and crisis in the midwestern farming economy, the sense of threat to farmers and their families portends not only the loss of a business or of land as a commodity but of a whole way of life—a disruption of one's very sense of place and belonging in the world.

In the late 1960s and early 1970s, I conducted field research among Slavic-American families (Slovak, Ruthene, and Polish) in the "Steel Valley" area of western Pennsylvania. I learned that many of the immigrants had transposed their original local environment of feudal estate–home–village–church–tavern onto the New World neighborhood of the steel mill–home–church–ethnic fraternal society–bar. A new place came to recapitulate old and familiar meanings; e.g., the steel mill, emotional successor to land and estate, was often described by Slavic millworkers as a stingy, depriving, even murderous mother (Stein 1980c; Stein and Hill 1979).

A friend born in California said that when he grew up he always knew his bearings from the moment he awoke in the morning, for the Pacific Ocean was constantly and visibly to the West. Now an Oklahoman, he says that for years he felt disoriented as he went about his daily affairs, for he had lost the Pacific Ocean as his reference point. Similarly, during a 1984 radio interview English conductor Neville Marriner, director of the Minnesota Orchestra, animatedly remarked that in Minnesota he was thousands of miles from the sea whereas in England he always knew where he was with reference to the sea. Plains dwellers have expressed a notable sense of claustrophobia when visiting the tall forests of the coasts; and others new to the plains may feel some initial discomfort with the wide-open spaces. Inhabitants of Manhattan Island, New York, segment their world into regions each of which has its emotional valence: Uptown, Midtown, Downtown, East Side, West Side, and so on (and woe be to any visitor to the city who brings with him or her the notion that "downtown" everywhere means the same place or ambience).

Clinics and corporations, too, have a spatial organization that performs psychological functions as well as strictly task functions. For instance, numerous medical clinics rigidly compartmentalize business and service functions, areas, and personnel—a polarity built into workers' very language, viz., "the back" (examining rooms) versus "the front" (business office–reception area; see Stein 1983d). Such place-names play an important role in people's emotional organization. They are never "merely" cognitive constructions which are affectively neutral. Rather, they are incalculably powerful condensations of feelings of safety versus threat, the sense of being at home versus isolation and alienation, the sense of continuity and cohesiveness versus discontinuity and fragmentation, and feelings of "goodness" versus "badness."

Many spatially mobile people—from foreign immigrants to executives climbing the corporate ladder by transferring to new locations—react to the jarring disparity between old self and new place by creating an at least temporary cult of the past. Experiencing the pain of dislocation and the grieving of the lost, they often scathingly criticize the deficits of the people and places in their new habitat to ward off feeling the full brunt of the hurt for leaving so much behind. No new hotel, restaurant, shopping mall, bluegrass band or symphony orchestra, office, or staff quite compares with that of which one feels now so keenly deprived.

I think, for instance, of a senior executive who moved to Oklahoma some years ago from a highly responsible position with a multinational corporation headquartered in an eastern city in the United States. Among his first words upon "touching down" in Oklahoma were a vow to make his new company "the IBM of the Midwest." A golf aficionado, he was promptly given a royal tour of the best country clubs in his adopted city. While being driven through one, he remarked that this must be their public golf course—to which his embarrassed hosts dejectedly replied that this was their prized private club.

With a tinge of paranoia one accuses the new environs of not being good enough, of being depriving, of setting up stumbling blocks—when in fact the people are simply being themselves. One externalizes one's own sense of inadequacy and dislocation. It is as if to say: "There is not something disturbing about *me;* rather, something is wrong with *them.*" The disgruntled "natives," feeling devalued and unappreciated, in turn disparage the "carpetbagging" outsider whose high culture they never wanted anyway, and they tenaciously reaffirm their psychogeographic identity far more stridently than if they had not been—or felt—insulted in the first place. In both cases, that of the newcomer and that of the settled, it should be noted, the psychological aim was to preserve the sense of goodness and wholeness inside and expel the sense of badness and fragmentation outside. In this book I explore, with deference to Freud, the psychogeography of everyday life in which our emotionally influenced maps become experienced as the outer territories in which we conduct our lives.

Human beings universally erect symbolic boundaries to provide inner cohesion by delineating where "we" end and "they" begin—and to make certain that the outside is kept at bay. Such markers are sometimes conspicuous, for instance, the Great Wall of China of antiquity and the Berlin Wall of today. They are often built into the very fabric of one's language. For instance, among Navahos, the word *indéh* signifies "the people," the Navaho themselves, while the word *indáh*, differing from the former by only a single phoneme, refers to "the enemy" beyond the boundary of Navahos (Boyer 1986). Armenians have the term *odar*, which unflatteringly condenses into a single image everyone who is not Armenian (Khantzian 1985:6); Jews likewise have a similar term, *goyim* (one which, although in official denotation simply means "nations," in connotation is unmistakably pejorative toward the outside world).

That nations and even whole continents are often perceived in terms of the morphology of the human body can be discerned from people's folklore about themselves and others. During periods of a shared sense of peril to boundaries if not to existence itself, groups commonly feel and represent themselves as tiny, threatened, helpless virtual islands in a dangerous sea, surrounded by adversary groups whose size and threat are correspondingly greatly enlarged (as one can discern from a number of political cartoons in the early and mid-1980s). The feeling state conveyed by cartoonists and by those who read and discuss the cartoons alike is that of the small infant if not fetus struggling for its life in a world of big, murderous adults. In one cartoon printed in the *Washington Post* on May 1, 1983, for instance, a grim President Ronald Reagan is depicted sitting at his desk. Behind him is an immense map of the world, one that dwarfs and virtually engulfs him. A tiny U.S.A. is tenuously connected to a slightly larger El Salvador: both are colored light. By contrast, El Salvador borders directly on a magnified Nicaragua, colored dark. To the right and above El Salvador–Nicaragua is an enlarged, engulfing island of Cuba, also dark. And above and to the right of Cuba, separated by only a narrow channel of water, are immense areas labeled U.S.S.R. and E. Europe, colored dark. A tiny light area on the left edge of E. Europe is marked W. Europe. The ominous image of the Red Tide, ready to swallow up the endangered body of the USA, could not be more vividly portrayed. Czarist Russia—and the Soviet Union, too—often described itself as a small, surrounded, and vulnerable child.

The United States has had a remarkably stable "body morphology" over historic time: The East is the front, the West is the back, the Northeast is the intellectual head, and the South is the vulnerable underside of the trunk. As one proceeds psychogeographically from east to west, one goes from what is felt to be the more civilized, domesticated, "tame" region to the "wilder," more rugged, aggressive part of the country. The Japanese attack on Hawaii during World War II (and the fear that the Japanese might attack California) and the Americans' dread of Communist invasion of the United States through Mexico and the Southwest are imagined as penetrations "from the rear" or attacks "from behind," where we feel most vulnerable. The Western Hemisphere, like historic Europe, is often imagined as a body such that the farther south one travels the more one moves from the realm of the abstract and intellectual to the realm of the sexual, sensuous, and "physical."

One need not look exclusively at relatively large-scale ethnic, religious, and national symbolism to recognize the operation of psychogeography in everyday life. People from "the city" and from "the countryside" (rural, agrarian) view one another with mutual envy and suspicion; each is "the outside," the repudiated, to the other. Within American biomedicine, although all disciplines are at least ideologically unified by the medical (microbiological) model of disease, each specialty— e.g., surgery, internal medicine, family medicine, psychiatry, pediatrics—jealously guards its border to ascertain that its own theories, methods, and practitioners are unique (not too similar to practitioners of other specialties,), that its members are fiercely loyal to their guild, and that others do not infringe upon its ideological territory. Certainly economic competition for patients, and struggle for political power, affects the intensity of this internecine strife, but it is by no means the entire picture.

From having worked some fifteen years in medical-education environments, I have long observed that although officially members of all clinical departments are welcome to participate if not present at one another's Grand Rounds conferences, one experiences some degree of uneasiness, even some sense of danger, at being "inside" the boundary of his or her professional competitors. Not altogether unlike the feeling we get when traveling in a nation which is the enemy of our own country, we not only feel like a stranger (even if an invited one) but fear feeling like the enemy. We become extravigilant, suspicious; we feel eerily that we are not quite supposed to be there. There is perceived danger not only in being regarded as the enemy but in becoming that enemy.

The opposite side of feeling endangered from without, if not also at risk for having violated one's group loyalties, when working or traveling in "enemy" territory, is the feeling of friendliness, security, even serenity when we live or work among those whom we have come to regard as colleagues or allies. We readily identify not only with individuals with whom we have had a good working relationship but more globally and abstractly with the organization itself.

Family metaphors and feeling states are built into the informal structure and language of even the most profit-minded organizations. One has only to listen "with the third ear," as Theodor Reik called it (1948), to discern these in organizational structure: "home office," "mother house," "satellite" clinic or office, "sister company," "parent corporation," and so forth. Not long ago, at a national conference on the family in family medicine, the chairman of the Department of Family Medicine of the University of Oklahoma introduced his faculty as "the Oklahoma Mafia"—with his implicit role as its "godfather." Familylike values and feelings come to be built into the very organizational style and structure—implicit or explicit—and heavily influence choices in even the most pragmatic, "hardball" decision making.

For instance, one corporate style of functioning places its highest priority on "keeping the family together," as one executive put it. Another manager remarked that group exercise may be conducted primarily to promote a sense of "unity" and "one family," and only secondarily for health benefit. To preserve family unity and to avert schism at all costs, ideas or persons who might be regarded as too radical or extreme (even if intrinsically good or profitable) may be well tempered in lower-echelon committee or conference structures to prevent divisiveness from reaching and confronting top-echelon decision makers. To ensure the continuity of family togetherness, no vote may be taken at such high-level meetings: only consensus would be the acceptable form of decision making (cf. Spiegel 1971).

Executives of another organization tend to think and feel about their corporation in terms of water and maternal imagery: a "cash cow" who is alternately generous, stingy, giving, withholding; "mother," "feminine"; or the Nile or Mississippi River with many tributaries all flowing into one, but also slow, enormous, fertilizing where it goes. In this organization family solidarity, personal loyalty to the company, the wish to preserve interpersonal harmony and avoid open conflict at all cost frame instrumental or "business" activity. Thus viewing one's organization as a mother and in terms of the content of mother's body has consequences in the everyday reality of corporate decision making. To understand how such an organization works, not to mention how one might intervene in such an organization as consultant, what I am calling a psychogeographic perspective is advantageous.

In this book I employ a particular imagery, that of psychoanalysis, in an effort to comprehend social, political, and historic matters. This imagery is of considerable value in helping us understand the dynamics of political struggles, social conflict, racial conflict, religious struggles, and international relations. It helps us comprehend the extent to which those phenomena are in fact heavily overdetermined by psychological forces. Whether these "groups" are professions, corporations, or nation-states, the underlying issues remain the same, for everywhere the geography of space recapitulates as it relocates the topography of the mind. From clinical decision making to international diplomacy, we unwittingly strive to solve the wrong problems, because we locate them in the wrong place. Surely *we* could not be the problem, or a part of it—surely the problem is wholly "out there."

This is not to assert that all aspects of these phenomena are reducible to unconscious fantasies or clinical metaphors; rather it is to identify these tendencies, to render them to more conscious awareness and scrutiny, and therefore to increase the possibility of controlling their effect upon the stage of history. As psychiatrist Robert Coles recently reminded me (personal communication, 1985), to argue that the geography of space recapitulates the topography of the mind is by no means to insist that this is all that goes on between international diplomats in Washington and Moscow and elsewhere. There are the material realities of tough economic rivalries and tensions with respect to access to markets, price advantage, possession of crucial materials, sea passageways, and the like. Still, the utility of a psychogeographic viewpoint when we are considering such realities lies in the awareness that unconscious forces often distort our perceptions and intensify intergroup conflict as a result. The seemingly straightforward pursuit of safe sea passageways for the transport of oil, minerals, and wheat, then, may be quickly transformed into the fear—if not group panic—that "our vital interests will be cut off" and that we may be rendered "impotent" or "emasculated" or that our outer alimentary canal will be unable to nourish our hungry mouths.

Events in reality—over which people often have precious little control—can unleash in social fits of rage all the unfinished business of human development. A psychogeographic perspective is offered in this book as a cogent part, if only a part, of the explanation. Man, the tragic animal who does not recognize the tragedy until it is too late, mistakes outside for inside, hopelessly conflates the two, and defends his error to the death. How can we solve our problems—medical, corporate, political—when we insist on mistaking both what they are and where they are to be found? This book is an attempt to help us understand why we are in this predicament and to suggest modest ways that our perennial problems of identity and boundaries might be differently addressed: by acknowledging, facing, and addressing those painful psychological issues that underlie and are symbolized in cultural forms.

Chapter 1 identifies and illustrates the scope of psychogeography in human affairs. It shows how body image, body feelings, and dimly remembered family relations become the template for feelings about, perception of, and action in the outer world. This chapter demonstrates the extent to which we, proud inhabitants of an ostensibly scientific modern age, blur the boundaries between inside and outside, and the often dire consequences of that blurring.

Chapter 2, based on my clinical work with a migrant population that had moved into the "Sun Belt" in the early 1980s, reveals that somatic, emotional, and familial problems which appear to be primarily symptoms of dislocation in space are in fact manifestations of conflict and arrest in developmental time. Culture is thus shown to be referent, symbol, target, repository, and focus of developmental issues displaced and exteriorized from their source.

Chapter 3, while manifestly a study of the identity conflict between the Slavophiles and Westernizers in nineteenth-century Russia, is likewise a tale of the chronic identity conflict between the West and Russia (and later the Soviet Union, its successor state). This chapter argues that what we perceive to be ostensibly cultural conflicts are rooted in shared developmental issues that render the cultural and intercultural conflicts unresolvable.

Chapter 4, a cultural and historical study, explores the persistent "symbiosis" (pernicious, to be sure) between Jews and Christians based in part on differing resolutions and symbolisms of the oedipal conflict of fathers and sons. I have concluded that, paradoxically, although both historic groups emphasize the theological and ritual boundaries which separate and clearly distinguish each from the other, they are also bound up within a single system of mutual mistrust and hostility.

Chapter 5 examines the apparently universal need in groups for what can be called "a good enough enemy." Enemies—not only in Soviet-American and Judeo-Christian relations—it seems, not only are hated but are indispensable for internal group stability, a fact which casts an ominous shadow on human adaptation. This chapter examines the historical case example of the psychology of Soviet-American relations and concludes that there exists a carefully crafted "fit" between these and other adversaries throughout human history. Can there be any exit from this endless process of creating, shoring up, extending, invading, violating, and revising group boundaries? This chapter, and the book, concludes that only as we are able to confront the painful unfinished business of developmental time *within* ourselves will we be able to forgo the compulsion to repeat it unknowingly on the dangerous stage of culture and history.

CHAPTER 1

The Scope of Psychogeography:
Who We Are in Terms of Where We Are

In my teaching since 1983, when I first began lecturing on the topic of psychogeography, I have tried to impress on interested listeners the ordinariness of psychogeography in our lives. I have searched for ways that might emotionally as well as intellectually engage others so that they might experience for themselves, and thereby have access to understanding more deeply, the role of psychogeography in all human beings' mode of relatedness to the world. Music has proved to be a rich "medium" for teaching about the "reality" of psychogeography, a reality that is immediately established and confirmed by the senses, thereby setting the stage for interpretation. I would wish others to recognize and to experience for themselves a psychogeographic style of thinking and feeling about human relatedness in the world, one that I have found to be compelling. With a number of long-playing records and compact discs I have used excerpts from the music of many nations—e.g., Bohemia, Russia, England, the United States, Germany, Austria, and France—to remind ourselves, albeit from only a single musical tradition (the "classical"), that psychogeography has been part of everyone's ordinary experience of group self-definition.

There is, for instance, *The Bartered Bride* of Bohemia's Bedřich Smetana—or is it Smetana's Bohemia feeling itself to be the bride bartered to Europe's monarchical plots? Then there was Modest Musorgski's operatic signature piece of czarist Russia, *Boris Godunov*—one that emotionally is as much the signature piece of its successor state, the Soviet Union, with its brutal violence, its "Kremlin intrigues," and its dread of invasion from any and all directions. One could speak of a similar symbolic significance associated with Vaughan Williams' *A London Symphony* or Benjamin Britten's opera *Peter Grimes* or Sir Edward Elgar's *Pomp and Circumstance* for conveying what it feels like to be a Londoner or an Englishman. Anton Dvořák's Ninth Symphony, written "From the New World," was the emotional architecture of a Bohemian composer longing for home and urging his American hosts to write music that embodies native elements (black, Indian) to remind them of *their* home—much as Americans mistakenly, though understandably, have taken the symphony to be homage to their adopted home, the United States, and renamed it "The New World Symphony."

Whatever the ubiquity of water symbolism, not all rivers and oceans feel alike to those near them. Johann Strauss's *On the Beautiful Blue Danube,* Vienna's official self-portrait, evokes a taste of raspberry, bittersweet chocolate, and whipped cream, and an age swirling with gaiety and yearning, an empire crumbling, and the presentiment of a world vanishing. Claude Debussy's *La Mer* and Richard Wagner's *Flying Dutchman* conjure very different images of the sea. Then, too, Musorgski's "Dawn on the Moscva" from *Khovanshchina,* Smetana's "The Moldau" from *My Fatherland,* and Wagner's evocation of the Rhine at the beginning of *Das Rheingold* all paint very different mental—and national—images of rivers.

My favorite comparison has been between depictions of the emotional landscape of American and Russian or Soviet composers. At the level of geographic reality the great plains of southwestern Russia and the Great Plains of the United States are remarkably alike: not only are they the "breadbaskets" of their respective countries, but even one major strain of wheat grown in the United States was originally brought by immigrants from south Russia. Still the emotional portrait of the *feeling* of the land revealed a vast difference: the foreboding, melancholy Russianness of Aleksandr Borodin, Pïtr Ilich Tchaikovsky, Musorgski, and even Sergei Prokofiev and Dimitri Shostakovich, as contrasted to the restless, energetic, even frenetic Americanness of an Aaron Copland, Leonard Bernstein, Walter Piston, or George Gershwin—whose *An American in Paris* "feels" quintessentially American.

In short, by playing and discussing recordings of excerpts

from this music, I have sought access to already familiar data of psychogeography. In using music to conjure images and feelings associated with the senses, I am persuaded from the outset that psychogeography has never been merely a matter of cognitive, intellectualized abstractions.

The Scope of Psychogeography

Psychogeography, the psychoanalytic study of spatial representation, is an approach that may help unravel why *who one is* comes to be experienced as indistinguishable from *where one is*, and in turn where and who others are perceived to be in relation to one's own. Psychogeography is a perspective, not yet another proposed discipline. The scope of psychogeography is the unconscious construction of the social and physical world.

Men and women fashion the world out of the substance of their psyches from the experience of their bodies, childhoods, and families. We project psychic contents outward onto the social and physical world and act as though what is projected is in fact an attribute of the other or outer. What we *attribute* to the world (verb) we subsequently take to be an *attribute* of the world (noun). Environment is heir to psyche (Stein 1983e). Unfinished developmental business is played and replayed on a stage of "reality" which we expect if not coerce to comply with our inner dramas. Fantasies about the body and the family are transmuted into descriptions of one's own group, other groups, shapes and features of the world. Projected outward, the fate of the body becomes the fate of the world.

Two complementary mental processes make human symbolic geography possible. The work of Kohut (1971, 1977) on "self-objects" has shown how people and other objects in the environment (actually, representations of them) are incorporated into the self and experienced as if they were parts of the self. Klein (1955), Kernberg (1975), and Hall (1977) have likewise studied how people take parts of themselves and "put" them into others, that is, perceive, experience, and treat persons and things in the environment as if they were extensions of the self. Unacceptable or unattainable parts or aspects of the self are both placed outside the conscious self and put into other people and things.

These two seemingly opposite processes are in fact dual aspects of a unitary psychological one: the continuous interplay between introjection (taking into oneself, incorporation) and projection (excluding or extruding from oneself, erecting a boundary between oneself and the outside and placing what is unacceptable outside). In both processes persons and things come to play a specific symbolic function: that of serving as repositories for aspects of the self that could not be integrated into one's psychic structure. The very developmental plausibility for a "psycho"-geography rests on the universal tendency to endow the world "out there" with one's psychic structure and in turn to depend on that world to complete and stabilize one's very self.

Consider the following news story on the eruption of Mount Etna (Sicily) and of subsequent attempts to divert lava by explosives. It begins with the following passage:

> "Our mother is the fire of Mount Etna, our father is the sea," said Enza Montepiano, a Catania University student, as she waved toward the hellishly glowing southern slope of the massive volcano. "Like any mother and father, sometimes they punish us," she added ruefully. [Schanche 1983]

This exquisite passage reveals not only how geography can be anthropomorphized but *familio*-morphized as well. This passage conveys both what parents are and what angry parents do. It further illustrates how concrete (not here metaphorical) thinking can function regressively in the mind of an otherwise (presumably) intelligent, rational university student.

In a series of papers and books in the psychoanalytic tradition of Freud and Paul Schilder (1950), Fisher discussed Rorschach approaches for assessing "body-image boundaries" (1963, 1970, 1973; Fisher and Cleveland 1956, 1958), and TAT (Thematic Apperception Test) analyses for examining the relationship between body "landmarks" (e.g., heart, skin, stomach) and central cognitive processes (1970, 1972, 1973). Fisher concludes that "the body scheme is a source of cues which

have persistent selective effects on how the world is interpreted. The body scheme plays an active directive role in
adaptive behavior. It seems to consist to an important degree
of a system or sets or intents expressed as body feelings"
(1972:105). According to Fisher:

> The body scheme, considered as a series of landmarks with differ-
> ential sensory prominence, may be conceptualized as a represen-
> tation in body experience terms of attitudes the individual has
> adopted. These are experiences coded as patterns of body aware-
> ness (e.g., involving muscle, stomach). . . . the individual's body
> scheme contains landmarks which reiterate to him that certain things
> are important and others are not. [1970:356]

Fisher has also ingeniously employed a number of geographical images (islands, rivers) as a means of measuring
body-image feelings. He developed a Rorschach scoring technique for identifying "barrier responses" and "penetration responses" (1963; Fisher and Cleveland 1958) in the perception
of body boundaries. In the preface to his book *Body Experience in Fantasy and Behavior,* he writes of the experience of
the body as a "psychological object" (1970:vii) that "a man's
body is, after all, synonymous with his existence. It should
come as no surprise that his perception of its attributes colors
his experience of life" (1970:viii).

The significance of Fisher's work for the study of psychogeography in group representations lies in the fact that individual psychological structure may find expression at another
level in the structure of group representations. For example,
the contemporary American "wellness" or "fitness" movement with its musculoskeletal, cardiovascular, and dietary obsessions (see Stein 1982f, g, i) represents a toughening up, a
masculinizing of the physical body (of females and males alike,
an aesthetic that highlights the body as an aggressive instru-
ment and downplays heterosexual intimacy). Similarly it represents a toughening up and masculinizing of the "body politic" and "national will" as we become preoccupied with the
solidity and security of the American national boundaries and
identity. Paralleling the "wellness" movement in America are
attempts to forestall immigration; efforts to secure taut "cor-

porate identities"; renewed depictions of the Soviet Union as a ruthless, toothy "bear" and voracious "evil empire"; and further attempts to strengthen our "military muscle" (see Stein, 1982a, 1985b). Often it is through a collectively hammered out and shared group fantasy of a national body scheme that the world of international group relations is perceived and conducted.

I am here reminded of a statement by La Barre that "psychoanalysis has been the only psychology which has ever taken seriously the human body as a place to live in, as it has been alone among psychologies in being interested in the actual symbolic content of thought" (1951:159). Extending a formulation of Freud's, Bion writes that "the psychotic's castrations are worked out on his mental skin—i.e. on the ego" (1955:222). What Bion argues for the individual ego holds also for the individual participating in group behavior and group representations. From the small ad hoc therapy group to the historic cultural group, all shared conflicts are worked out on its members' "mental skin"; i.e., conflict may be experienced and represented as group castration, penetration, an ulcerating wound, etc. This "membrane" is the experienced group-psychological boundary between inside and outside and serves as the shared representation of the members' egos. All *maps* are heir to this psychological function.

Psychogeography begins with the experience of selfhood in a human body within a family context and proceeds outward to encompass the world. Schizophrenia and international relations, hypochondriasis and cosmology are alike psychogeographic phenomena. Metapsychologically speaking, the psychogeography of spatial representations and relationships is metaphor for developmental and generational *time* (see also chap. 2). The issue of *boundaries* takes us to the heart of psychogeography. Symbolic group boundaries have the quality of dreamlike condensations. Through boundaries we express anxiety over body integrity or cohesion versus disorganization, maleness versus femaleness, pleasure versus unpleasure, animateness versus inanimateness, security versus danger, symbiosis versus emotional separation (representational differentiation), id versus superego. How these *all* are resolved finds ultimate expression in the delineation of inside from outside: What and who are to be included in the group, and what and who are to be excluded from it. What philosophers call the fallacy of misplaced concreteness is heir to the unconscious allocation of the inner world to the outer.

The study of psychogeography begins with the still-radical Kantian assumption that reality is not neutral, that is, simply "there" for the seeing. In doing psychogeography we study how and why we mediate reality with the contents of our psyches. Culture is not automatically adaptive to, or even accurately perceptive of, the real social and physical world. As Winnicott wrote: "The place where cultural experience is located is in the *potential space* between the individual and the environment (originally the [maternal] object)" (1967: 370–71; emphasis in original). What is allowed to inhabit that space later in life is prefigured by the child's early relationships. Only slowly, reluctantly, over recent historic time have we grudgingly come to notice, and perhaps later to accept, that what is "there" is far different from what we had assumed and needed to be the nature of things. *Spatial "otherness" is largely projective* (La Barre 1972; Devereux 1980; deMause 1982a), which means that reality testing is a far greater (and more recent) achievement than we might imagine. To understand representations of spatial morphology, we must turn to the topography and structure of the mind.

To date, scholars have been more accepting of official cultural texts (e.g., religious dogmas and liturgies, folklore) than of lay or popular culture as guides to a group's understanding of reality. However, with the publication of such journals as the *Journal of Psychohistory,* the *Journal of Popular Culture,* and the *Journal of American Culture,* the latter is coming to be recognized as a legitimate index to group fantasies. Examples of these sources include newspaper accounts of news, editorials, cartoons, and the relative space assigned to topics within a fixed number of pages; television and radio news accounts; and themes in television, radio, and film programming, etc. Ebel, for instance, draws our attention to the degree of anxiety stirred up in people when the morning news-paper prints a map with black arrows moving across it, and a caption informing the reader that "our vital interests are being cut off" three thousand miles away. The event seems somehow very tan-gible—even if it later turns out to be a false alarm—because that arrow is being experienced as either a castrating-knife about to lop off one's reproductive organs *or* a violating phallus about to pierce the maternal abdomen *or* both of these fantasies at the same time. [Ebel 1980b:2]

The reader who permits oneself to be carried away with one's imagination—that is, one who does not try to read too carefully—can obtain a remarkably accurate reading of the current psychogeography group fantasies simply by perusing the daily newspaper or, to supplement this, listening to the type and amount of fantasy language evoked in *ordinary* busi-ness and professional meetings (see deMause 1979; Stein 1980f; Schmidt 1982).

Any thorough discussion of human ecology and the prob-lem of adaptation must include examination of the extent to which perception of the environment is "polluted" with pro-jections, externalizations, and displacements from the human psyche. It is concluded that psychogeography is not a frivo-lous, esoteric, or superfluous matter with respect to the real world of public policy but is instead one of dire urgency, since human beings act on unconsciously motivated perceptions of themselves, others, and the world.

Geographical and geopolitical issues have always been in-fused with psychological images and bear the emotional bur-dens of these associations. Consider the following "free asso-ciations": Italy as a boot—is the island of Sicily an extension of southern Italy or independent? Florida as an erect—or flac-cid?—penis. Britain as an island fortress. Australia was long referred to in Europe as the continent "down under": not simply south of the equator but the dumping ground for Brit-ish criminals, another form of "beneathness." In Russian, the word *rod* which designates mother and family, likewise desig-nates nation. And according to a Latin aphorism: "Ex oriente lux, ex occidente lex" ("from the Orient comes light, from the Occident comes law").

A midwestern male friend recently asked me to define psychogeography. Following my explanation, he said with a twinkle: "If Russia attacked Turkey from the rear, would Greece help?" This double entendre discloses the speaker's fantasies (fear-wish) of anal sodomy and concern (fear-wish) lest it be painful (Greece=grease=lubricant)—all in the guise of international relations (in this case warfare). Each nation has its imagined role in the homosexual rape. The double meaning of "Greece" is the signal that declares, "This is a joke." It deflects attention from the speaker to international relations while permitting the discharge of aggressive fantasies with impunity. This joke also illustrates the principle of "triangles" formulated by Bowen (1978), according to which conflicts between two people or groups (e.g., family members, nations) often find temporary resolution through the recruitment of a third—outside—member. The resolution, however, is only apparent, for it is in fact collusion that escalates conflict, proliferates further triangles and enemy "camps." But then, to return to the joke, even if "Greece" tried to "help," it nonetheless would collude with "Russia" in facilitating the assault —therein fulfilling the displaced wish. In this joke, then, forbidden fantasies about the body and human relationships are simultaneously discharged and disguised—and dismissed as "only a joke" through the symbolism of international relations.

The human and nonhuman, animate and inanimate, environment bears the burden of developmental, psychosexual arrests or failures and regressions. And it is likewise one domain of human ecology that has been persistently neglected: for, if one is to discuss comprehensively the human ecosystem, surely one must consider the amount of psychologically dangerous "hazardous waste" that is endlessly deposited in the interpersonal and international as well as strictly geological environment.

Just as history is largely a mythology of past reality, a fantasy about *time*, likewise geography is largely a mythology of spatial reality, a fantasy about *space*. Material located within the unconscious, and derived from early caretaker-infant-family interactions and relationships, is symbolized in the preconscious and is consciously allocated to the external world of people and phenomenal nature. Superimposed upon reality, it is then taken to be reality itself rather than an interpretation. "Self" is thereby experienced as "other." People perceive and act toward other people, groups, and the phenomenal world *as though* they were one's own body or parts of the body, one's parental figures or parts of their bodies, and family members and relationships.

Human beings insist upon, psychogeographically speaking, possessing a mistaken identity. We first confuse our "whoness" with our "whereness," then invest that whereness in our very definition of whoness. The result is an inevitable *narcissism of place*, an affectively based "fallacy of misplaced concreteness" according to which deity, prophetic mouthpiece, and believer together proclaim, "I am *where* I am." Did not the heroes, ancestors, or gods reveal themselves *to us* upon our sacred mountain, or emerge from our holy river? Even in universalist religions—in which the mending of diverse self- and object representations is itself an advance—is not God on *our* side?

In *The Psychopathology of Everyday Life* (1901), Freud wrote:

A large part of the mythological view of the world, which extends a long way into the most modern religions, is nothing but psychology projected into the external world. The obscure recognition . . . of physical factors and relations in the unconscious is mirrored . . . in the construction of a super-natural reality. [1901:258–59]

The obscure recognition of physical factors and relations in the unconscious is mirrored in the *unconscious construction of social and physical reality itself*, one based upon the selection of what Volkan calls "suitable targets" for externalization and projection (1976).

It will be noted that Freud's topographic model (1900, chap. 7) that proceeds downward from the conscious to the preconscious and finally to the unconscious is itself a spatial representation of mental organization. The mind is hierarchically organized; one thus speaks of regression to lower levels of functioning. From another viewpoint, the spatial organization is metaphor for a temporal one (ontogenetic, developmental).

Loewald writes that topographic, formal, and temporal regression "are at bottom one and the same, since what is further back toward the starting point in the spatial model is earlier developmentally and simpler, less complex, in its form or representation" (1981:38).

A physician-colleague recently articulated in a single, unifying image an impression I had privately come to after working in the "wheat belt" of the American Midwest for seven years. Many colleagues, students, and patients had long referred to this region as "God's country," and although born and reared in the hilly, tree-laden area of western Pennsylvania, I too had come to love the endless monotony of wheat fields or snow-blanketed earth and to find a serenity (when tornadoes were not looming) in the sky that reached uninterrupted from horizon to horizon. But it took my colleague to fill in the missing psychogeographic features that gave moral, religious, and political meaning to the phrase. He remarked upon my return from a conference in New York:

You're in God's country here. Peaceful, quiet, decent. None of that crazy stuff you find Back East [a common phrase] or on the West Coast. God's country is right here in the center; Back East and everything to the West is the Devil's country. Broken families, drugs, hippies, weirdos of all kinds. Here you have some space to yourself, some privacy, not wall-to-wall people. I wouldn't want to go there. I wouldn't want my children to grow up there; it's not healthy.

Interestingly, although my colleague knows full well the realistic dimensions of the United States, when I asked him— and others—to describe the boundaries of "God's country," he tended to emphasize and enlarge "God's" territory and to collapse and reduce both "Devil's" territories (see fig. 1). For instance, Saint Louis, Chicago, Cleveland, Pittsburgh, New York, Baltimore, and Boston ended up seeming to be virtual suburbs of one another, and likewise for the major cities along the West Coast. It was as though "good" were enlarged in scope while "evil" was diminished and all were lumped together into a single cultural heap (that is, dedifferentiated) and finally excluded or extruded from the boundary of the "good" self: a vivid emotionally bipolar depiction of the world.

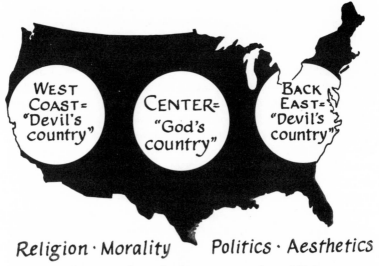

Fig. 1. Psychogeography and splitting: a view from Oklahoma.

This was for me a fairly convincing illustration of the importance of taking a psychogeographic approach to group identity.

Spatial metaphor is a symbolic representation of developmentally based and drive-derivative infused *memory*. Thus, somewhat like religion, psychogeography is a species of autobiography and is also experienced as true and necessary. It reveals the truths of childhood displaced and projected onto the screen of the real world. Just as "the lessons of history" possessed and diligently taught by every group are allegories of developmental time performed on the stage of group history, likewise all groups have lessons of geography and also are parables of developmental space in the imagination and the family.

Of special importance in discussing psychogeography are the following: (1) whether a spatial representation is metaphoric and recognized to be such or is experienced as concrete and literal (the symbol is the thing); (2) the extent to which the concrete representation is a product of regression from a higher personality organization or more or less constitutes the group norm; and (3) the extent to which the concrete

experience of the world is focal, that is, limited to encapsulated portions of the personality, or pervades the personality.

A distinction widely current in anthropological writings is
that between *instrumental* activities, which are held to be
task- and goal-oriented and related to reality (such as hunting
or growing food), and *expressive* activities, which are held to
be symbolic, highly subjectively motivated endeavors invested with personal meaning (such as religion and art). The
trouble with this compartmentalization is that it is misleading. The business of earning a living is heavily invested with
personal meaning, and even the most unconsciously driven
act has some goal with respect to imagined reality in mind.

Consider, for instance, Hitler's "Operation Barbarossa," the
massive eastward incursion into the Ukraine and the USSR as
an attempted undoing of the humiliating defeat of Germany
in World War I and an effort to feed mother Germany. One
may meticulously fashion an accurate map which one subsequently employs as a guide to make restitution for childhood's
hurts. Aspects of the expressive may not only contaminate the
perception of reality but govern instrumental activity as well.
The decision-making process and strategies adopted for im-
plementing goals are inseparable from self- and object representations, that is, from how the world is perceived.

Devereux, for instance, refers to the following:

The blurring of the frontier between reality and the imaginary.
Culture-historically, the existence of this dividing line is a relatively
recent discovery. In most primitive societies the dream is essentially consubstantial with reality. . . . The *fact* is that the primitive
acts realistically most of the time; the *trouble* is that he does not
know that he is acting realistically when he bandages a wound but
unrealistically when he tries to cure an illness by offering a sacrifice. . . . The Greeks were among the first to differentiate between
reality and the imaginary *as categories*, yet in practice they—and
Plato in particular—often treated certain of their cherished fantasies as real and treated as fantasies certain things they chose not to
believe—just as we do! [1980:227]

The more emotionally primitive the group-shared personality organization, the more fantasy is experienced to be real-

ity itself, and conversely. For instance, peasants regard the earth as the sacred mother and therefore cannot tolerate the thought of ravaging her by using the deep plow for cultivation—the very use of the shallow plow, and of the cycle of planting and harvesting, attests to no small amount of cultural individuation. The farmer, on the other hand, may revere the soil and still refer to the earth as "her" or "mother" but does so with a relatively consistent consciousness that such designation is metaphorical—for in other, practical aspects of his life he regards the earth and its fertility as an objective process apart from his imagination and therefore feels no reluctance to invent or use the deep plow.

To use a different example, to primitive peoples, the earth (or moon) *is* the mother, and the sun *is* the father. American Indians in Nevada object to strip mining on the grounds that the earth is their mother and that the sacred ground in which their ancestors are buried must rest undisturbed. The development of the "simile" and "metaphor" of Western poetry, however, rests on a painful recognition of an emotional separation and differentiation from the object of one's desire and imagination. Contemporary astronomers label a new comet— one which has not yet encircled the sun in a parabolic orbit— as "virginal." Mythologically, they are on firm ground in this designation, for a new comet is simply a female that has not been captured and impregnated by the father sun. While the nomenclature reveals a vestige of fantasy, it is clearly metaphoric and encapsulated, so that astronomers can go about their business of investigating this newly discovered celestial body (*Time* 1983b).

Members of groups imagine their group and other groups to be *human bodies* which protect and menace one another; groups can thus be born, mate, give birth, age, die, be male or female. In the group process of corporate, academic, medical, military, and religious committees (or organizations) alike, one commonly hears: "We've got to cover our ass . . . present a united front . . . protect the rear . . . guard our flanks . . . protect both our fronts . . . launch a frontal assault . . . conduct a two-front war. . . . They're bleeding us to death. . . . Make sure the enemy doesn't get a chance to come in the back door" (see Stein 1980f). While these expressive or symbolic statements take place in the context of instrumental or reality-directed activities, they convey what Bion (1959) termed the "basic assumptions" about what it feels like to be a member of a group (deMause 1977:11), which in turn adds impetus to the work, goal, or task-oriented behavior. As Bion (1959) emphasized, work (instrumental) and basic assumptions (expressive) do denote *not* two distinct types of groups or activities but rather two levels of the same activity. What deMause calls a "fantasy analysis" (1979) of a group's metaphors, similes, emotionally charged terms, body language—as revealed through a content analysis of political speeches, popular movies, political cartoons, press conferences, and newspaper and magazine articles—is a reliable index of the unconscious significance of group membership and group activity. An accurate "mapping" of group process would take into account that members feel their group to be a human body which experiences "itself" to be dependent in fusion or oneness with an imagined mother, in sexual activity, or in fight=flight (Bion 1959). In all group or cultural analysis what is called for is the careful explication of the *relationship* between expressive and instrumental functioning.

Sometimes this relationship in functioning shifts back and forth depending on the group's tolerance to stress. The more confused or regressed a group becomes while experiencing shared anxieties, the more the distinction shifts to portray reality as heavily burdened by primary process fantasy. For instance, as the conflict between the United States and the Soviet Union heated up beginning in the early 1980s, the "Russian Bear" motif has come to dominate newspaper and magazine cartoons and has even found its way into advertisements: see for instance, the voracious oral aggression of "the Bear" (fig. 2 in the following series of bear cartoons from newspapers); the Soviet Union as primal oedipal father who, armed with his hammer and sickle, is about to castrate the Americans from their vulnerable underside (fig. 3, in the body image of the USA, the North represents the upper part of the body, one associated with the brain, reason, and control, while the South is often depicted as the genital region,

Fig. 2. From *The Miami Herald*, September 4, 1983. Drawing by Kent Barton. Reprinted with permission of *The Miami Herald*.

one associated with sexual and aggressive impulsivity); the Soviet Union as untrustworthy, menacing "Mother Bear," while Poland as a small, domesticated, harmless offspring bear (fig. 4). I must here repeat a point made earlier that, although most American cartoonists are indeed male, the *group* folklore and fantasy they are articulating is not exclusively male.

This small series of cartoons illustrates different psychological meanings of the "Russian Bear" American image of the Soviet Union. In the first (fig. 1) is the theme of voracious oral aggression (with the tragic Korean Air Lines B747 becoming a literal body bitten into and squirting blood). In the second (fig. 3), the Russian Bear, partly anthropomorphized into a scheming Soviet official who hopes to castrate the USA by way of Latin America through the vulnerable undersides. The natural shape of northern Latin America is metamorphized into a Soviet hammer and sickle—our projection in the guise of the Soviet projection. In the third cartoon (fig. 4), the smaller, domesticated bear is Poland, while the toothy, agitated big bear is the Soviet Union as "bad mother." The cartoon also depicts an imaginary family scene with the father (the West) as friend of the endangered offspring, both against the mother.

In 1985 a widely printed advertisement encouraging invest-

You Might As Well Think About It ... He Is!

Fig. 3. From the March 25, 1984, issue of *The Sunday Oklahoman*. Drawing by Jim Lange. Copyright 1984, The Oklahoma Publishing Company.

Better Keep Your Eye on 'Mama'

Fig. 4. From the October 25, 1981, issue of *The Sunday Oklahoman*. Drawing by Jim Lange. Copyright 1981, The Oklahoma Publishing Company.

ment in U.S. Savings Bonds depicted the Russian bear as a patient in the dentist's chair. Uncle Sam was shown climbing onto the bear with his right foot in the bear's groin and with a pair of pliers as he moved to pull the bear's sharp teeth. The United States, perceiving itself to be the passive victim of Soviet aggression, here explicitly becomes the sexualized aggressor. Other cartoonists have depicted a tooth extraction as a form of castration. With these and other recent political cartoons a natural bridge, so to speak, can be built toward the more theoretical dimension of psychogeography, e.g., the projection of American fantasies, fears, wishes, parental images, and parts of the self onto the image of the Soviet Union.

In approaching psychogeography, one could legitimately ask: Why does one need the "psycho" to explain the geography? Why not "cultural" geography instead, since one is dealing mostly with group representations? I would reply to this demurral that, as in religion, the weight or authority of tradition or shared symbol systems does not, by itself, fully account for the acceptance and persistence (and change) in any beliefs (see Spiro 1967, La Barre 1972). For the authority of any tradition is itself contingent on the experience of these beliefs or perceptions as true. As Spiro argues for religion (1967), the source of the validity of cultural beliefs is twofold: (1) the motivation or predisposition to believe is based on the universal experiences of childhood and the particular experiences of growing up with specific caretakers; (2) one accepts the "reality" of beliefs because they are experienced as true. What is split off and/or repressed, that is, what cannot be accepted into consciousness as part of the self or gratified in direct human interaction, is "fulfilled" in the symbolism and ritual of religion—and psychogeography.

I wish briefly to outline in schematic fashion those bodily and familial precursors, so to speak, of later psychogeographic preoccupations, investments, and representations. They are human invariants because of the type of animal we are: at issue, whether in child rearing or in politics, is not *whether* we deal with them, only *how* we do so. As Erikson writes: " . . . ideological space-time perspectives . . . must alleviate what anxiety remains from the bodily ontogeny of each" (1974: 91). They underlie "the need to know where we come from and where we stand, where we are going, and who is going with us" (1974:91):

Psychogeographic Precursors

Upright posture or verticality/ Sitting down, crawling	Incorporating/Expelling or eliminating
Fusion-togetherness-	Holding on/Letting go

engulfment-belonging-loyalty /Separateness-differentiation

Inside/Outside (also self-object fusion/self non-self distinction)

Active-act upon/Passive-acted upon (i.e., locus of control)

Dependency/Autonomy

Cohesiveness/Disorganization

Male/Female

Sucking/Biting

Inclusion/Exclusion

Front/Behind/Flanks

Above/Below, beneath

Left hand/Right hand

Incest fantasy or act/Family exogamy (mating and marriage outside the family)

Animate/Inanimate

Existence/Nonexistence

Fantasy/Reality

Small/Large (i.e., relative size)

Psychogeography is a repository for any and all of these developmental issues, particularly when they remain unresolved. Psychogeography becomes symbol and stage alike for enacting them.

Historical Overview of the Concept of Psychogeography

A number of intellectually and clinically independent traditions have contributed to the development of the concept of psychogeography presented in this chapter. While they might be called precursors, it is in fact at their point of convergence that psychogeography is defined. Hall, an anthropologist, has written about the role of out-of-awareness cultural systems of distance regulation in intercultural communication, e.g., the preference of Arabs and other circum-Mediterranean peoples for close physical proximity even when discussing business matters, the discomfort this evokes among Northern European–descended Americans, and its consequences in misunderstandings and hurt feelings (1959, 1977).

Hall argues that culture is a largely out-of-awareness system based upon what he terms "extension transference," namely, a "common intellectual maneuver in which the extension is confused with or takes the place of the process extended" (1977:28). Later in the same work he parenthetically remarks (1977:234) that Klein's concept of projective identification (to be discussed later in this text) comes closest to his understanding of how the extension transference regulates inter-cultural transactions and therefore interferes with empathy: "People are in and remain in the grip of the cultural type of identification. Without knowing it, they experience the other person as an uncontrollable and unpredictable part of them-selves" (1977:239).

I believe the concept of projective identification, intro-duced by Klein (1946, 1955), to be crucial to our understand-ing of what, how, and why people invest unconscious aspects of themselves in space (i.e., spatial representations). From the outset I wish to add that the concept of projective identifi-cation is by no means universally accepted among psychoana-lysts (see Meissner 1980), despite my advocacy of its utility. Klein wrote, "Identification by projection implies a combina-tion of splitting off parts of the self and projecting them on to (or rather into) another person" (1955:311–12). She added that projective identification "underlies the feeling of identifica-tion with other people, because one has attributed qualities or attitudes of one's own to them" (1955:311).

The concept applies to the process of "externalization" wherein one allocates to another aspects of the self (Novick and Kelley 1970), rather than developmentally later "projec-tion" proper in which unacceptable drive derivatives are out-ered from the self to another to reduce the fantasied dangers that would arise from their expression (Volkan 1979:65). Using projective identification, "A participant interacts with others *as if* they were not themselves but someone else" (Zinner and Shapiro 1972:525). I hasten to add, following Searles (1960), that the inanimate environment can be used magically and that the nonhuman environment can be used to serve as a re-pository of the child's feelings (e.g., love, dependency) dis-placed from mother (1963). Thus human interaction with the environment can likewise be, to paraphrase Zinner and Shapiro, with it as if it were not itself but someone or some-thing else.

Relationships regulated by projective identification contain the following common threads:

. . . (1) that the subject perceives the object *as if* the object con-tained elements of the subject's personality, (2) that the subject can evoke behaviours or feelings in the objects that conform with the subject's perceptions, (3) that the subject can experience vicariously the activity and feelings of the object, (4) that participants in close relationships are often in collusion with one another to sustain mutual projections, i.e., to support one another's defensive operations and to provide experiences through which the other can participate vicariously. [Zinner and Shapiro 1972:525]

Once "whole objects, part-objects, drive representations, ego ideal, superego elements" (Zinner and Shapiro 1972: 526)—all aspects of the personality—have been ejected from the self, they are located within another person (or thing) at a safe distance from the self. The new object constitutes the basis for preserving a tie with what has been externalized. What has been cast out from the self *must* not be lost. It is instead embodied in someone or something else and is then experienced as an intrinsic part of their "nature": the process of attribution becomes structured as an attribute in the object. The function of projective identification is thus both defensive and restorative (Zinner and Shapiro 1972:526).

Furthermore:

In our conceptualization, "identification" (as in "projective identification") refers to the *relationship* between a subject and his projected part as he experiences it within the object. The subject's behavior in this relationship is directed by two principles. The first is that the subject interacts with, or relates to, that projected part of himself in the object as he would interact with the self-part were it internalized. . . .

The second principle governing behaviour of the projecting subject towards the recipient object is that efforts must be made to involve the latter as a collusive partner in conforming with the way in which he is perceived. [Zinner and Shapiro 1972:525]

Minuchin (1974), a family therapist, emphasizes the need to observe the seating and gestural patterns of a family in therapy, for space is a metaphor for interpersonal relationships; he takes this beyond assessment and begins to restructure family interaction by asking family members to change their seats or even to leave the room. Moreover, the therapist may not only verbally but physically (spatially) block communication. By observing a family's utilization of space, in the clinic or in the home (see Steinglass 1981), one can learn the role of closeness-distance, togetherness-separateness, etc., in its emotional economy and thereby begin to map for oneself the psychogeography of a family system (see Glenn and Dym 1983). In a classic paper Arensberg (1955) discussed the relationship between social structure and the spatial arrangement of Euro-American communities. And in an equally influential work Spicer (1971) elevated opposition and contrast between groups to an explanatory principle of ethnic and cultural identity.

In her influential book *Everything in Its Place: Social Order and Land Use in America* anthropologist Perin (1977) approached space utilization not only as an instrumental or utilitarian issue but as an expressive or symbolic one as well. Thus what one does with space follows from what he or she values. She writes:

> What have been thought of as singularly technical concerns in land-use matters I take to be value-laden, that is moral . . . land-use planning, zoning, and developmental practices are a shorthand of the unstated rules governing what are widely regarded as correct social categories and relationships. [1977:3]

In an appreciative essay on Alistair Cooke's *America* (Stein 1981a; see Cooke 1973), I have discussed the American cultural conception of space ("the wide-open spaces") in terms of such core values as freedom, mobility, exploration, and mastery. And in a related study German psychohistorian Raithel (1979) analyzed such spatial values and preferences as characteristics of what Balint (1959) called a "philobatic" personality, that is, one who develops weak object relations.

In a similar psychoanalytic vein is Erikson's path-breaking study of the Yurok Indians of the Klamath River in northern California (1963a). Here he brilliantly shows the connection between child rearing, an adult obsession with alimentary-canal cleanliness, the conception of the world, and the role of dams in salmon fishing. Another important precursor to studies in psychogeography is Klein. In her *Narrative of a Child Psychoanalysis* (1976) this pioneering child analyst described a therapeutic project conducted in England during World War

II. A child would enter the playroom she kept for play therapy, pull down a map of Europe, and begin to interpret current political and military events as though they were literal assaults upon the mother's body.

Human beings interpose a symbolic universe between themselves and the real world—termed by Hallowell a "behavioral environment" which is "culturally constituted" (1955). Because of this construction of reality we often apprehend what we have largely projected; what we perceive to be objective is filtered by the subjective. As a consequence, objective reality is suffused with unconscious issues. As is well known, Plato warned us of this in his parable of the cave in the *Republic*—only to prefer idealized abstractions to the palpable world. In our own time Walter Lippmann likewise referred to the fallacies and stereotypes of our "pseudo-environment": "It is to these special worlds, it is to these private, or group, or class, or occupational, or national, or sectarian artifacts, that the political adjustment of mankind in the great society takes place" (1922; quoted in Yankauer 1980:949).

It is to Geza Roheim (especially 1943) and Weston La Barre (especially 1951, 1968a, 1972, 1978) that we owe the formulation that all social institutions—not religion alone—build on symbolisms of the experience of growing up in a specifically sexually dimorphous body (that is, a species with two distinct types of body, male and female) within a family. The psychogeography of society is, so to speak, mapped outward from body and family, not—as most social scientists argue—inward from culture. Or, culture can teach us only what we are already eager to learn. The Mercator "projection" is only a historically recent one in the human evolution of projective cultural systems created to master the anxiety heir to childhood and child-rearing practices.

In the late 1970s the work of several scholars on the psychodynamics of the symbolism of place converged and goes by the name "psychogeography." Psychoanalyst Niederland had written of river symbolism (1956, 1957, 1959) and of the symbolism behind the naming of America (1971b) and of California (1971a). Both of the latter were fantasized as island paradises; early maps depicted each as surrounded by water.

"America" is a transmutation to the feminine of the name of Amerigo Vespucius: explorers and waves of immigrants alike imagined "her" to be a bountiful mother who would accept them into her welcoming embrace. Summarizing Niederland's work on psychogeography, Ebel writes:

Man's attempts to understand and envision the geography of his planet have always been contaminated by the projection onto land and ocean of primitive fantasies about the human body. . . . Only in the past few centuries have we succeeded in disentangling our fantasies from the actual shape of the earth to the point at which we are able to make accurate maps of its surface. But the older pattern still persists in a number of ways that may have real political consequences. . . . The land and ocean beyond one's immediate vicinity have always been seen as projections of our deepest needs and terrors . . . and this tendency has continued down to the present day. International distrust and hostility is based at least in part on the fact that "everyone living outside the 'known' borders is still considered 'barbarian.'" [1980d:5–6]

Both Volkan (1979) and Simos (1981) have employed a psychoanalytic group psychology to explain the recurrent inter-ethnic strife on the island of Cyprus. In "How Nations 'Use' Each Other Psychologically," Ebel (1980b) employs a psychoanalytically informed family-systems theory to international relations and identifies precisely what kind of system is operating: it is one in which groups *complement* one another by performing unconscious tasks or roles for one another. Contrary to the conventional view, groups do not act strictly autonomously of one another's influence. Rather, having shaped themselves to the needs of others—exactly as occurs within pathological families—they proceed to act out "their own" part, one piously disavowed by others. Ebel then applies his approach to Germany in the interwar period and during World War II. In a subsequent paper, entitled "Mitteleuropa" (1980c), he discusses the wealth of psychological tugs upon the identity from its location in the *middle* of Europe.

The studies of Binion (1976) and Stierlin (1976) are bona fide psychogeographic works which explore the group psychodynamics of Hitler's and Nazi ideology and policy with respect to the conquest (in the eastward expansion, reconquest), domination, and utilization of space. Erikson's pioneering studies of the Yurok and Sioux among North American Indians, and of German, Russian, and American national character (collected in 1963a) consider the relationship between bodily experiences in childhood, family dynamics, cultural values, and the meaning of space. I would add that, like La Barre (1968), Erikson (in his chapter "Toys and Reasons," 1963a, and in his subsequent book by that title, 1977) sees sexual dimorphism and fantasies based on sexual differentiation as prefiguring children's play and adult activity. Gorer and Rickman's brilliant and much-maligned work on Russian national character (1962) closely related long and tight full-body swaddling to the "featureless" and persecutory character of the Russian steppe.

From the late 1970s through the present, several colleagues of the Institute for Psychohistory, New York City, have studied pre–World War II international diplomacy and the conduct of the Great War (II) itself as a projection and displacement of family roles and interaction. Ryan (1980) and Szaluta (1980) emphasize the essentially "feminine" French and "masculine" German attitudes and roles: with tragic complementarity, Germany could not be stopped, and France could not help but be penetrated. Beisel (1980a, 1981, 1982a) expands the system of the "family of nations" to include the British and Americans. All these build, directly or indirectly, on the insightful though nonpsychological A. J. P. Taylor, who, in *The Origins of the Second World War* (1978), argued that Hitler and the National Socialists did not do their mischief alone, but that there was international collusion that permitted and encouraged Germany to escalate into warfare. Psychologically stated, they allocated their own disavowed aggressive impulses to the strutting Nazis, who acted out the sadistic role to the complementary masochistic role of the "Allied" nations, which in turn finally justified the latter's military action. Beisel, carefully examining libraries of political speeches and news accounts, goes to great pains to argue that the family metaphor is not a mere analogy (e.g., "like" a family), but that participants viewed themselves and their counterparts in diplomacy and warfare as specific family members (i.e., fantasy and function) all of whom played out their roles on the historic stage. He in turn attempts to trace the specific roles chosen and allocated to specific child-rearing experiences and family constellations.

In his psychohistorical studies of Zionism, Gonen (1975, 1978, 1980) demonstrates how the Zionist vision is a reclamation of and union with the mother, which in turn sows anxiety over fusion and oedipal anxiety over realizing the forbidden wish. In her work *Israeli Women*, Hazelton (1979) comes to similar findings.

DeMause writes:

What constantly startles *me* is how many things which I once considered "neutral objects" (i.e., I didn't much think about their meaning) are in fact highly concrete representations of inner objects or past events. The only place "neutral objects" exist is "out there" in the *ding an sich* world of reality; once the object gets actually perceived, becomes part of the inner world of the psyche, it quickly loses its neutrality. [1982b:220]

Metaphor, meaning, and memory are intertwined by projection.

As I review my own work since the early 1970s, much of it has been concerned, implicitly or explicitly, with psychogeographic boundary issues: e.g., Jewish-Christian (and, more broadly, Jewish-Gentile) relations (Stein 1978; see chap. 4 below), Russian-Western European perceptions (Stein 1976; see chap. 3 below), the relationship between the new Ethnicity and American culture (Stein 1979; Stein and Hill 1973, 1977a, b), the dynamics of us-them, inside-outside, opposition in ethnocultural identity (Stein 1980a, b), the contrast between physician–physician's associate and psychiatrist–clinical psychologist identities (Stein, Stanhope, and Hill 1981), and in a brief discussion of the proliferation of glass-mirrored and fully walled (windowless) buildings as spatial expressions of autistic encapsulation (Stein 1982c).

It is my present belief that eventually traditional social-role theory, labeling theory, and attribution theory will be seen as correct but part models of human cognition and interaction made more nearly complete by a psychodynamic-psychostructural approach to the division of labor, whether in a diadic doctor-patient relationship, family dynamics, or international relations (Stein 1982d, e, h, 1983c, f). As Niederland's (in Ebel 1980d) inclusion of *Homo monstrosus*, in a discussion of psychogeography would suggest, psychogeography is as much concerned with the imputed characteristics or features of human bodies and groups as it is with those of geological (whether terrestrial or in "space") structures. Its proper domain—whether its targets or containers are human or non-human, animate or inanimate—is the distribution of affect and psychic structure over space.

Human beings' *sense of placement in the universe* has suffered several major hammer blows in the past three centuries, among them (1) Sir William Harvey's dissection of the body, the discovery of the circulatory system, the beginning of the demystification of the human body, and the reclamation of the body from magical thinking and religious disparagement; (2) Charles Darwin's insertion of human beings into the animal kingdom (reawakening primal-scene fantasies among Victorians; see Irvine 1955) and the subsequent introduction of discontinuity and upheaval (later, catastrophism) into previously orderly evolutionary thinking; (3) Albert Einstein's work on relativity physics and Werner Heisenberg's work on quantum physics (culminating in the principle of uncertainty) which concluded that the measurer is always a part of the measurement (*not* that there are no universals apart from the observer but how the observer affects what is seen); (4) Sigmund Freud's discovery that persons are not always in conscious control of their very thoughts and perceptions, that what we see is largely what we need or wish to see; (5) the contribution of a large number of family and group theorists (e.g., Bion, Stierlin, Minuchin, Bowen, deMause) that not only are people involved in networks of relationships but often we are quite literally parts of one another and that the processes of separation-individuation are not only incomplete but reversible under conditions of considerable anxiety. Together these have affected our sense of who we are—and therefore have compelled some rethinking of where we locate ourselves in relation to each other and the world. The very *idea* of *psycho*geography is both an affront and an opportunity, for it suggests that we may be more remote from the *real* world than we had imagined.

Advances in psychogeography—that is, advances in perceiving people and things more realistically based more on empathy and less on projection—are possible only with the gradual diminution of splitting and projection and the increase both in the integrative capacity of the ego and in reality testing. According to deMause (1982a), improved child rearing is the principal source of this advance; i.e., psychogeographic change is rooted in psychohistorical change.

Adaptation: From Body to Family to World

Psychogeography cannot be considered apart from the problem of adaptation—that process of imperfect (or disastrous) fit between human population and environment. "Psycho"-geography is possible only in an animal who internalizes and symbolizes the environment. Internalization, language, and symbolism are Janus-faced processes: both blessing and curse, liberation from bondage to the outer or phenomenal world *and* a new bondage to the inner environment. One might say aphoristically that Homo sapiens are higher "apes" (hominids), who inherit primate acuity and depth perception that come with stereoscopic vision—only to swing precariously from limb to limb with *fantasies* of trees (or sugar plums) dancing in our heads. Big-brained, neotenous, familial animals, we specialize in learning as our principal adaptive modality, only to learn to specialize in fantasies which we mistake for the world. We than sacralize our motivated mistakes and frightened ignorance in taboo, idolatry, and ritual—and in methodology (for just as surely as there is but one right way to think, there is likewise only a single right way to do). Our hope lies in the fact that we are *beginning* to realize the extent to which the unconscious mediates commerce one with another and with the world.

To know that an extension of the body is but an extension, rather than reality itself, is quite an achievement. To "see" what is not there and misapprehend what is there is hardly adaptive. In our quest for peace of mind we teeter on the brink of self-made disaster: for what profiteth a species to gain its soul and lose the world (Stein 1983e)? Still, we often *think* that we can live by group fantasy alone.

How it *feels* to be a member of a human group is often expressed in the language of the human body. In the United States the state of Texas boasts its "bigness," while other states ridicule what their citizens take to be empty bravado. The Irish Catholics of the Republic of Ireland are well known for their emphasis on smallness and understatement, e.g., "the wee, little people."

Although this chapter will primarily discuss psychogeography in terms of representations of the human body and of the family, I hasten to add that, as the psychoanalytic, psychosomatic, and family-process literature has abundantly documented, the body and the family are themselves arenas *within* which psychogeographic representation and displacement take place. Such different clinical pictures as conversion hysteria, somatization (bona fide psychosomatic syndromes with or without actual tissue change), masked depression, somatic delusions and hallucinations, psychogenic pain, and the like are distinct body geographic pathways, so to speak, by which psychic conflict is channeled and represented. In this chapter I focus primarily on displacements and projections outward from body and family, and how participation in groups (e.g., cultural and small groups) puts this proclivity to use.

Unscrupulous politicians know they can mobilize their constituency by proclaiming that the "blood" of the group is being "polluted," that the "body politic" is endangered. Historically, such nations as Germany, the United States, Greece, Bohemia, Israel, and Russia not only have been geographically located at the center or middle of other groups and influences but have felt tremendous pulls and temptations exerted from all sides and have persistently had difficulty delineating what and where the boundaries of their identities are (cf. Ebel 1980c). How much "security" a nation needs derives from its sense of vulnerability.

"A poison spider is crawling up our leg." So began a radio

news commentator on the morning of May 11, 1983. He went on to sound a warning about the influence of communism in Central America and its threat to the United States. Whatever may *actually* be occurring in Latin America, politically and militarily, the commentator began by saying *what it felt like to him.* It illustrates zoomorphic thought, even more emotionally primitive than anthropomorphic thought.

If one considers the image more concretely and less meta-phorically, one perceives that Central America is our "leg" and that this poisonous menace is crawling northward (up the body toward the trunk) to strike and render impotent our vital organs. The spider commonly symbolizes a castrating female (see Adams 1981) who bites her victim with her vagina dentata once she has her victim within her grasp, immobilizes it, and then proceeds to devour it. Lore of the spider is commonly used to project internal aggressive fantasies and perceive them entirely from without. A self-fulfilling prophecy can easily be created, as outer reality is treated as though the con-tinent were in fact threatened parts of the body and the po-litical or social problems were in fact zoomorphized into a spider; i.e., the "spider" can easily be provoked into "biting," thereby appearing to confirm the group fantasy.

Not only do geological *features* and geographic *locales* sym-bolize the human body and the human family, but *natural and social events* come to represent the imagined and antici-pated vicissitudes of the body and the family. Actual physical cataclysm does not *necessarily* cause internal disorganization but rather becomes the referent or focus of inner chaos. It is when outer coincides with and bears the burden of inner that physical catastrophe is psychically most devastating. (This is, incidentally, why any psychodynamically valid theory of and treatment for "stress" must consider the human organism's perception of and available defensive organization to cope with environmental assault, and not merely the external agent itself; see La Barre 1971, Devereux 1955.) Succeeding world-destruction fantasies are world-*reconstruction* fantasies wherein the physical world (the body projectively) is reborn.

Animistic paleologic that sees in nature "signs" or portents is in fact projecting what it purports to perceive: an eclipse is no more an ominous portent than a rainbow is a heaven-sent harbinger. Yet, we protest, surely the rising and sinking island of Cyprus, or the vanished Atlantis, has *inherent meaning* (as opposed, for instance, to attributed meanings such as separation and merger). Likewise, the paleologic "post hoc, ergo propter hoc" ("after it, therefore because of it") links wrongdoings with earthquakes and lightning storms: I am guilty; therefore, this is punishment (or dire warning of the punishment to come).

I read a paper by Bedrosian entitled "Armenians in America: Reclaiming Pockets of Diversity" (1983). Read with an eye to body-language imagery, the paper reveals the following sequence:

. . . tenacious hold . . . distinctive . . . well-tempered identity . . . uniqueness in a world eager to file away the rough edges in any individual or group . . . lonely future . . . small . . . imminent extinction . . . swept . . . last vestiges . . . ancient . . . hidden pillars . . . heroism . . . out-numbered . . . smaller . . . begin to disintegrate . . . miniatures are magnetizing . . . the master of energies . . . never completely disintegrated . . . industrious and multi-talented . . . carrying a name whose "-ian" ending resembles an outworn appendage, an evolutionary relic . . . as the rivulet of tradition disappears underground, perhaps to dry up in the remotest reaches of the psyche . . . losing . . . failure to integrate and transmit this ethos . . . answered persecution with relentless fortitude and heightened cultural zeal . . . strong family ties built on high ethical standards . . . smaller . . .planted . . . sprout with recharged meaning . . . secret tongues . . . less visible, though fully potent magicians . . . disaster . . . speaking in "secret tongues" . . . small . . . close to ethnic ties . . . exposing . . . spark unassailable self-esteem . . . a many-chambered heart, channelling, integrating, and emitting sharp conflicts in a tiny minority . . . clannish protectiveness . . . supply the needed link . . . rooted . . . teeming . . . untapped cultural energy . . . rooted . . . "reclamation" . . . size. [1983]

Stated in terms of Federn's concept of "body ego feeling" (1952), Armenian-ness is here vividly portrayed as small, even tiny, vulnerable, old, even vestigial, but capable of recovering potent, even magical strength. In a manuscript of eleven double-spaced typewritten pages, size, cohesiveness, and ways of dealing with persistent threat to existence serve as recurrent and organizing images which convey *the psycho-geography of what Armenianness feels like* in the author's view. Although author Bedrosian did not explicitly say so, through her very choice of words she has shown how inter-twined, indeed interchangeable, are body perceptions and feelings, and perceptions and feelings associated with one's group. What is more—and this in turn takes us into political psychology or psychohistory—peoples act upon these feel-ings and perceptions in the social arena.

Family symbolisms and interactions are widely played out in group psychogeography. Usually at an out-of-awareness level, people tend to structure work relationships as though they were familial ones (Stein and Fox 1985). Every school-age child reads about the "family of nations" in history class. During the American Revolutionary War, "Mother" France protected the rebelling colonies against "Father" Britain—a special parental relationship between France and the United States that was permanently sealed by the gift from France of the matronly Statue of Liberty that greeted millions of immi-grants into New York Harbor.

While groups may or may not verbally acknowledge that they act in terms of a "family" of nations or cultures, they in fact often do so. Certainly, one psychological aspect of warfare consists of fathers' willingness to jeopardize the lives of their only partly beloved sons by sending them off to fight—and die—at their behest and in their behalf at the hands of others, and, reciprocally, of sons going "abroad" to seek and kill others' sons if not the fathers themselves. At this level one can interpret parricidal and filicidal, counteroedipal and oedipal issues displaced from the group onto the intergroup stage.

In the nostalgic quest for "roots" the individual often de-values his real family (and/or society) and looks elsewhere for a mythically "good" family. An origin myth falsifies and psy-chologically "corrects" painful family history, illustrating the process by which the "family romance" originates. Afro-Americans seek their idealized origins on the continent of Af-rica, Slovak-Americans in Slovakia, and so forth. One seeks reunion with a part of the family (and, at a deeper level, a more perfect part-object representation) from which one feels estranged. Conversely, one may radically distinguish between good and evil branches of the family, as, for instance, do Jews and Arabs who claim a common Semitic origin.

Family theorist Bowen (1978) coined the term "emotional cut-off" to describe family members to whom or about whom the remainder of the family never talks. They are members who are perceived to have violated the family's most sacred rules; they personify what good members of the family are constrained not to be (akin to Erik Erikson's concept of the "negative identity"). They are written off, discounted, disavowed, often disinherited, even killed to protect the family's good name. Still they are retained as perpetual negative examples for all to know about.

One sees identical behavior patterns in international relations. Whole governments and peoples are subject to being diplomatically "recognized" or not; nations "break off diplomatic relations" or "sever diplomatic ties" with one another and consequently treat these targets simultaneously as though they did not exist, were illegitimate, or were misbegotten menaces to the conduct of family life.

Just as families have members whom they appoint as sacrifices and proceed to sacrifice (e.g., drug addicts who comply by dying of overdose; see Stanton 1977), the international family likewise selects (sometimes remorsefully) family members who must be offered up "for the good of the rest of the family" or "to keep peace in the family." One thinks of the sacrifice of Czechoslovakia at the Munich Conference in 1938; Kren and Rappoport (1980) analyze the destruction of European Jewry during World War II as a sacrifice; the pre-Spanish Aztecs would go to war and collect immense numbers of prisoners whom they would offer as sacrifices. Whole groups, in their function as displaced and projected group-family members, fulfill themselves in their role as scapegoat intended to magically preserve the family integrity.

According to Koenisberg, Hitler's central fantasy is that "the country Germany is an organism, and this organism is in danger of being destroyed" (1975:51). His ideology devolves not from observation but from personalization of reality. Hitler projects his unconscious fantasy onto social reality

(1975:53) and magically discovers it there. What is "there" is not independent of his wishes and fears. Hitler's fantasy (that mother=land=Germany) can be broken into two major components, oedipal (conflict with the father for possession of the mother) and preoedipal (the wish to merge with the mother and recover lost narcissistic omnipotence). In both cases, what he could not accomplish in his *personal family* he sought in his *symbolic family:* to rescue and liberate the mother (land) from a debasing anal-sadistic father who forced her to capitulate to his sexual advances. The Jew within, and encircling foreign enemies without, represent this ever-menacing father against whom ruthless war must be waged. I would add that Hitler's strong identification with his mother, almost to the repudiation of his father, resulted in a psychosexually feminized identity for which Hitler compensated counterphobically through aggression against those from whom he feared homosexual attack. "Protection of the rear," Koenigsberg documents, is a theme Hitler obsessively reiterates in foreign-policy statements. In war the preventive strike averted the threat of attack from the rear; psychologically it represents defense against the passive homosexual position.

Whereas Hitler's first undoing of the past was riddance of the father, his second was restoration of his idealized preoedipal mother who died of breast cancer when Hitler was eighteen. If "The National Body = Hitler's Dying Mother" (Koenigsberg 1975:55), then this time Germany will not die. Koenigsberg documents numerous references to cancer in Hitler's imagery: cancer is a metaphor for the disease afflicting Germany. Radical surgery is required to eliminate malignant forces of disintegration within Germany. Through a resurrected Germany the death of Hitler's mother will be reversed. Since death is not natural, it must be the consequence of a malevolent, external agency against which heroic forces must struggle. The good must be separated from the bad, the healthy from the cancerous, the Aryan from the Jewish.

Moreover, as Binion (1976) and Stierlin (1976) argue, just as Hitler's *familial* role was to redeem and avenge his mother, his self- and group-appointed *cultural* role was to redeem and avenge the motherland. The urgent and geographically ever-expansive policy of *lebensraum* was symbolically a means of attempting to feed an insatiable appetite that was not only the mother's but also his own oral aggressive neediness. Psychogeographically, in this view Germany came to represent an organism caught up in the underlying contest of "devour or be devoured."

Yet despite Hitler's manic denial of death, the forces of destruction are destined to win, because in Hitler's "unconscious, the image of the mother (the country) and the image of cancer (the Jew) are inextricably bound. Thus insofar as Hitler is unable to relinquish his attachment to his mother, he must cling to her cancer as well. In perpetuating his love for her, he has no alternative but to love death" (Koenigsberg 1975:57).

I would add that the introjected dying mother creates an identity that is intrinsically despoiled. Radical surgery is futile for an incurable disease: it only postpones the loss. In Hitler the mother as redemption and the mother as death are fused, which consequence is a Wagnerian *Liebestod,* a redemption-through-death (and Hitler was an ardent Wagnerian).

Further, might a *person* (or rather the group representation projected on a person) be approached from a psychogeographic viewpoint? Consider the social role of the "leader" as not merely, or even primarily, a political one but a psychogeographic one. That is, members of a group allocate a considerable portion of their very selves to that leader, appoint him the executor of their will (and willfulness). Psychiatrist Lorant Forizs writes:

> When, within the realm of the social system, a concrete person begins to be treated as a leader upon whom the members begin to depend, in fact, he will be incorporated, internalized, not because he is a concrete person, but as a bearer of the role of the leader. This represents the new dependency target. With this statement we have just encompassed a quantum jump in abstraction from the concrete person to the role. [1980:252]

As a concrete embodiment of the Winnicottian "transitional object" (1953), now abstracted into a social role, the leader becomes "invested with attributes of relationships as seen in the relationships of the primary object" (Forizs 1980:252). *The leader embodies the group*, serving as repository and target of group fantasies. This view in turn stands completely on its head the traditional—and conscious—view that the leader leads, for it is the successful leader who best *follows* and fulfills his people's deepest wishes. What the ancient Christmas carol fervently states of the Christ Child is true of every leader: "The hopes and fears of all the years are met in Thee tonight." Leadership is a bona fide issue in psychogeography since it concerns the location and process of allocation of group fantasy (see deMause 1982a). The object of psychogeography can as much be a person (or group) as a geographic place.

This perspective takes us beyond the conscious boundary-maintaining strategies discussed by Barth in *Ethnic Groups and Boundaries* (1969). For "outside" is an externalized representation of and forum for "inside"; the "other" is "self"-contaminated, group-dystonic "self." Ethnic boundaries and the roles they contain operate according to the Wonderlandlike principle wherein inside is outside and outside is inside. Ethnic (and national) groups are profoundly important unconscious roles for one another.

Territorialism as Psychological Boundaries

If a single matter may be said to characterize psychogeographic preoccupations, it is that of *boundaries*. What and who are inside; what and who are outside? What and who are to be included; what and who are to be excluded? What and who are me-us-security-cohesion-goodness; what and who are not-me-them-danger-disintegration-badness? Universally, cultural content expresses and serves this boundary-definition process, while the defensive function and power of cultural content in identity definition prevents us from examining the process of identity formation.

Consider, for instance, the family-medicine movement and profession in the United States (formally founded in 1969), one with which I have been associated by both employment and affection. At national and local conferences, in departmental meetings, and in the literature of the field one finds a persistent attempt to define a "family-medicine concept," a conflict between being "reformative" or "radical" and "legitimate," both excitement and insecurity about being "the new kid on the block" (among medical specialties) or "the youngest member of the medical family," and an unabating anxiety over "borrowing" or "stealing" ideas, procedures, and models from other medical specialties and behavioral sciences, thereby ending up with "having nothing to call our own." The family-medicine identity is fashioned and reshaped through constant comparison with high-status orthodox biomedicine.

Although in official ideology family medicine aspires to a holistic, personalistic view of the clinical relationship and practice—one which would considerably differentiate family medicine from other, more procedure-oriented medical specialties—in practice family medicine uses them as its primary operant model. The result is often avowed ideological differentiation with underlying sameness based on tacit identification. Family physicians are lured in the direction of further internal subspecialization, e.g., sports medicine or geriatric medicine. The technological metaphor looms large: just as pediatrics has its neonatology units and ophthalmology has its laser-surgery, so family medicine now increasingly boasts of the "genogram" as an identifying procedure and of family therapy or family counseling as a standardized intervention. What might be termed a "family scan" could become as essential to the putative basic science of family studies undergirding family medicine as, say, a CAT scan is to the orthodox basic science of anatomy in internal medicine. This is not to impugn its potential utility for clinical assessment or intervention. Rather, it is to note that such utility is secondary to and derivative of the group boundary-making and -maintaining processes. The primary purpose or "function" of cultural (or, generically, group) content is often to serve as anxiety-allaying boundary markers: to notify those within and those without alike where each begins and ends.

Whether they are religions vying for souls or for theological truth, ethnic groups within a pluralistic society, nations in international diplomacy, or geopolitical units of some nation-state or empire, groups maintain a vigilant interest in their standing—both in their own eyes and as seen by others. It appears that many a city regards itself as one of a pair, usually one being of "high culture" and the other being "low culture," e.g., Dallas–Fort Worth in Texas, Tulsa–Oklahoma City in Oklahoma, Philadelphia–Pittsburgh in Pennsylvania, Leningrad-Moscow in the USSR, Amsterdam–Rotterdam in the Netherlands, and Weimar–Berlin in historic Germany.

Within the United States the geographic symbolism associated with being an Oklahoman was conveyed by radio newsman Jackson Kane. In response to the decision by the board of directors of Amtrak not to offer passenger-train service to Oklahoma, he wrote an editorial, "Where's Oklahoma?" Permit me to excerpt his reply in defense of Oklahoma's honor:

Amtrak's President, Alan Boyd, said it this way—"Oklahoma? Where's that?" . . . Where's Oklahoma, Mr. Boyd? It's at the *center* of this great nation of yours and mine. . . . It's at the *top* in oil and gas revenue, number one in winter wheat. . . . Oklahoma sits like a *crown* on the great plains. . . . Two majestic rivers cross *her* boundaries, and many smaller ones wind through *her* plains and hills toward their *wedding* with the Arkansas and the Red [rivers]. . . . she's the *home* of *great* Americans, Mr. Boyd. . . . She's a *growing youngster* among the states, stronger than most, and filled with the *pride* and *strength*. . . . She's the *future* of America, Mr. Boyd, as yet *unspoiled*, as yet *untouched* by the *diseases* of ennui and suspicion that *infect* your world. . . . Oklahoma, Mr. Boyd, is the *rising sun* to your *dying moon*, and perhaps that's why you wonder where she is. There's an old joke that Oklahomans, in their 1930's plight, found laughter in. The word Okie is no longer what it once was; fifty years ago it was less a badge of honor than a condemnation. The joke? Well they used to say . . . all the Okies have gone to California . . . and it raised the level of intelligence in *both* [emphasis in original] states. Where is Oklahoma, Mr. Boyd? She's right here . . . behind you, and comin' fast. [Kane 1983; emphasis added except where indicated]

The defense of self-image, self-respect, and honor has long preoccupied Oklahomans. The bullyish "bigness" of Texas looms massively to the south. The rural and religious conservative tradition digs in for a siege against the onslaught of cultural carpetbaggers from "back East" bureaucracy and godlessness and "West Coast" sensuousness and permissiveness. A defiant assertion of superiority is the product of reaction formation against the persistent feeling of inferiority. Feeling spurned by mainstream, official culture, one inverts one-downmanship into oneupmanship. Marks of shame become badges of pride. These illustrate the process which Devereux and Loeb termed "antagonistic acculturation" (1943), "where alien culture *means* are borrowed precisely in order to preserve certain indigenous *ends* more effectively" (Devereux 1980:313). Here categories of alien culture are used to shore up indigenous culture. Phrased in psychogeographic imagery, Oklahoma is a pure, young, strong, virginal female who is far from marginal in her own evaluation of her place in the American world: rather, she occupies both center and top; she is indeed a queen ("crown").

The sense of feminization engenders a compensatory protest masculinity, one which takes the priapistic form of "cowboy culture" in Oklahoma (see Stein 1987). In the final sentence Oklahoma is depicted as an aggressive *phallic* mother, about to attack the presumptuous and evil old decaying perverse male bureaucrat. The combination of protestations of innocence with self-righteous exhibitionism characterizes what Mack (1979:xvi–xvii) and I (Stein and Hill 1977a) have separately discussed as a narcissism or egoism of victimization.

Clearly a group's perception of its social status is portrayed in psychogeographic images. Finally, I wish to emphasize that since the bibliographic source of these data in contemporary societies consists of the public print, television, and radio media, it is accessible to all who know *how* to read for psychodynamic content.

Psychogeographically, each group has its repertory of "good" (positive social transference, that is, overestimated, overvalued, or idealized) and "bad" (negative social transference, underestimated, devalued, or demonized) groups outside its geopolitical and therefore conscious boundaries. Categories of allies and enemies, friends and adversaries are universals. For instance, each group has its historically indispensable bogeyman across the border (and/or polluting or menacing within) who enable them to focus their sense of paranoid endangerment and thereby to be focally rational in other parts of their lives. Such bogey groups and idealized groups alike both complete and stabilize one's own group (see Ebel 1983). This fact in turn compels us to differentiate between geopolitical and psychogeographic boundaries, since groups not only derive their internal stability through interaction with and perception of other groups but reciprocally have very parts of themselves located (unconsciously) within other groups. Out-groups' threats (even those that pose "internal" threat) are, in fact, dire necessities for group self-definition—historically, at least—lest the split-off, dissociated, and repressed ego-alien attributes return.

A common feature of the geotemporal landscape of culture is changelessness if not immutability at the core in the face of considerable change at the surface (cf. Hallowell 1955). Americans constantly seek to conquer some "new frontier"; Jews are liturgically admonished to act as though they had just been redeemed from slavery in pharaonic Egypt—this despite the fact that the historical liberation occurred over three millennia ago. The group mythology of historical memory exerts a profound influence upon the perception of group space.

The USSR is a *geopolitical-military* colossus reaching from Europe to the Pacific Basin. Yet *psychogeographically* and *geotemporally,* the Great Russians and those who have identified with the supraethnic Communist Revolution, feel themselves to be small and vulnerable and surrounded—an *island* in fact—and summon up vast contemporary military capabilities to deal with the present as though it were identical with the historically *remembered* past. The myth of the past is the filter, so to speak, through which we assess the present, although in fact each situation is quite new. Whatever be the American motivation, the Great Russians perceive the menacing ring of land- and sea-based missiles to "confirm" the continuity of Russian history, and therefore the necessity of responding to it by unyielding patience, efforts to break out from the encirclement, and building the capacity for massive retaliation. The "arms race," "missile race," and "space race" must be seen in the context of Russians' perceptions of space and time (as well as those of the West). One might even speculate that the special appeal for the Russians of Marxist-Leninist doctrine, together with Russians' own selection of aspects of that ideology that conform with their own culture (e.g., predominance of group over self), lay in turning passivity to zealous activity and in converting all the world to the same supraethnic, supranational, and suprareligious ideology so that the Russians would never again feel endangered.

Since the late 1960s, with the publication and popularity of such works as *African Genesis* (Ardrey 1961), *The Territorial Imperative* (Ardrey 1966), and *On Aggression* (Lorenz 1970), it has become intellectually fashionable to argue that human beings are "naturally" territorial, that we need and fight for our "turf" just as do all other animals. That this revelation culturally coincided in America with the escalation and peak of the Vietnam War might suggest a certain justification for the release of aggression. The more timeless issue, however, is that humankind fights and kills and dies not so much for *land* as for *meaning*. We inveterately confuse symbol with thing.

Economic needs are often wholly subordinate to and defined by psychological needs (or, more accurately, fantasies). Territory is symbolic. In ethnonationalist sentiment, ideology and political action, land, or geography are invariably central in symbolism. What, though, do they symbolize? How is such symbolism—and not some other—plausible? This is to ask: What do they symbolize, both as process and as structure? The answer seems to be: boundaries. Such elements as language, land, historic sites, music are conscripted to delineate more secure boundaries, to differentiate distinctly between us and them, between inside and outside, between good and evil, and so on. The boundaries must be closed, and anything which might threaten the perfection and greatness within must be excluded, e.g., through linguistic, cultural, demographic purging of that which might contaminate the purity.

Ethnonationalists particularly confuse realms, so to speak, as geographical boundaries assume psychological importance and characteristics. The land *is* the body, the mother, the father. Metaphoric thinking grades into delusional thinking, as the regressed self voraciously expands its boundary—to consume all that is possible. Thirst is now unquenchable, appetite is now insatiable, for the adult experiences the world as the once vulnerable-in-fact, indomitable-in-fantasy, infant.

The frightened nationalist addresses, because he/she must renegotiate, some of the most crucial issues of development: Where do I begin and end? How can I keep myself together? How can I avert annihilation? The adult now feels that he/she needs—for survival itself—increasingly more (see chap. 3 for a more detailed discussion of nationalism). Needs are bottomless; ambitions are unstoppable; resources are infinite. All one's wants are entitled to be fulfilled. But the threats are terrifying (annihilation, separation, loss, abandonment, castration). All obstacles must be removed. From local neighborhood to nation, the boundaries of the possible expand: imagination *is* reality. The world is my desire, distinguishable from desire only insofar as obstacles arise to thwart it (e.g., Slavic loanwords in late-nineteenth- and early-twentieth-century Hungary; Jews in National Socialist Germany; whites in the late-nineteenth-century Ghost Dance among Indians of the Great Plains, etc.). The world is there for me!

Nationalists' well-known territorialism—whether of the military expansionist variety, of the ideological pan-ismic variety, and so forth—is a function of regression. Such catchwords as "irredentism," "lebensraum," and the like *use space to express self-states.* To ask, from the point of view of, say, demographic reality, "How much land is enough?" is the wrong question until we understand the perspective from which those who claim to need—and deserve—so much perceive reality.

What members of the structuralist, symbolist, and interactionist schools of anthropology often have the data for, but seem to be unable to interpret, is the persistent need for the opposition, insistence on distinctness, and vigilant border patrol. What borders and boundaries are "about" is decidedly *not* the cultural camouflage frequently invoked to explain the need for difference and differentiation but the truly primitive basis of the need for difference and differentiation, that is, for radical us-them opposition. The "scarce resources" which many scholars purport ethnicity to be about trace ultimately to the fragile "economics" of infancy.

The more regressed or emotionally primitive the group-psychological organization, the more the territory will feel like a threatened infant-child symbiosis which is under threat or siege and must be protected and the assailant repelled. The more regressed or emotionally primitive the experience of the land, the more "territorial" is its defense—and offense—the greater the amount of splitting into all-good and all-bad pieces of land, the more expansive (omnipotent) the ego boundaries and therefore the increasingly voracious need for territorial expansion and protection from assault.

Over the history of nationalism one reads of increasing national need for "lebensraum" (living space), the wish to annex or absorb ("anschluss,") adjacent lands containing members of "our people" or "race," the ardent desire to redeem them ("irredenta," unredeemed) from the foreign "yoke," the wish to gather in dispersed members and restore them to their homeland (e.g., Diaspora versus Zionism). During periods of intense anxiety over one's group identity, precipitated in the historical world by narcissistic insults, pan-ismic ideologies and social movements are spawned. Here differences between groups are, temporarily at least, obliterated as the groups merge identities into a common identity: "We are all one." Suddenly one is no longer small, vulnerable, and in imminent danger of annihilation; one is immense, powerful, strong. In nineteenth-century Pan-Slavism, for instance, the Slavic nations of east-central Europe and the Balkans were no longer unimportant, inferior peoples endangered by Germany and other burgeoning nationalisms; rather, they all became the siblings under the protective muscular arm of Russia, their "elder brother" (see Kohn 1960). Now one was no longer a mere Bohemian or Croat; instead, one's identity and greatness stretched from the lower Balkans in the south to Moscow in the north and the Urals in the east.

Territorialism, then, is not a fixed given—as though the

convergence of the need for land and aggressiveness were an immutable phylogenetic fact everywhere the same. Territory is a psychogeographic representation of unconscious meaning: one fights for the symbol *as if* it were the thing symbolized.

The identity of every human group is bound up with how it imagines, symbolizes, constructs, and maintains its *boundaries*. For cultural content does not exist apart from, and without constant reference to, the shape, size, extent, and security of its boundaries. Group boundaries, whether "natural" (rivers, mountain ranges) or "man-made" (railroad tracks, clothing styles) are at once arbitrary and absolute; no room is left for ambiguity. Let me illustrate this paramount issue— Where do "we" begin and "you" end? What is "inside" and what is "outside"?—with reference to the Jews (See Stein 1975a, 1978, and chap. 4, below).

Walls have played an awesomely important role in Jewish history, both as realities and as metaphors. They symbolize a sense of permanent embattlement. In the two ancient Temples of Jerusalem, layer upon layer of walls separated an outer profane space from the most sacramental space of the Holy of Holies. In addition Jews have carried with them the psychological fortress separating the sacred from the profane. The inner space is sacred; the outer space is profane—and dangerously alluring (e.g., the tradition-alienating "shiksa" or Gentile female).

With the establishment of the Jewish State in 1948, and the Israeli conquest of Jerusalem in the 1967 War, the Western Wall, the last standing structure of the Temple destroyed by the Romans in 70 A.D., is perhaps the most sacred space to Jewish pilgrims. The Western Wall, also known as the "Wailing Wall," is the site for jubilation and lamentation, magical incantation and prayerful petition. It is more than a mere archaeological monument to the past. It is a defiant massif to the recurrent. Time is frozen. The wall is self-definition itself.

Now the presence of the wall is problematic: it is not simply "there" as a point of distinction where "we" end and "they" begin. Moreover, it is not altogether built by "them." The wall must be constantly reaffirmed, shored up, indeed, rebuilt. Ebel notes that in intrapsychic terms "the wall whose 'real' purpose is to exclude an imaginary enemy must have as its imaginary or real purpose the amputation of some portion of the self" (personal communication, 20 August 1979), yet to retain that disowned part of the self at a safe distance—embodied by one's most feared enemies (see chap. 3, below).

To my knowledge this component of what Devereux and Loeb (1943) have called "antagonistic acculturation" is rarely discussed in treatises on "ethnic boundaries," Jewish and otherwise. Structuralist anthropologists who attempt to account for ethnic persistence tend to draw upon Lévi-Strauss (1963), Barth (1969) and Leach (1964) and argue that, while "cultural distinctiveness may be a necessary condition for an ethnic identity. . . . for ethnic boundaries to persist there must be structural opposition between groups" (Hamilton 1981:953). By omitting affective issues, they miss what the "opposition" is about and resort to the tiresome shibboleth of competition for scarce resources.

Moreover, the wall is simultaneously a mirror: it gives us "the vantage point from which we can subject the rejected portion of ourselves to observation" (Ebel, personal communication, 20 August 1979).

Jews and Gentiles (a generic term denoting non-Jews, including Christians but not limited to them) have made a place for one another—each embodying the qualities of what Erikson calls the "negative identity" (1968). Each does not simply wall out what it cannot include: it retains it with fascination and revulsion at a distance. For each, what is consciously outside is unconsciously within the wall. The historical conflict between Jews and Gentiles represents the attempt to prevent the integration of the split-off and the return of repressed (see chap. 4, below). The "wall" is a shared fiction, and a dangerous one, for both sides are inextricably linked with one another.

It is important to consider not only the psychology of *place* but likewise the psychology of *movement* over space. The Great Russians experience their plains and steppe far differently from how Americans experience the Great Plains. The Russians huddled in their villages, later their cities, silent and motionless in fear of being overrun and conquered (see Gorer and Rickman 1962; Stein 1976). For Americans the Plains were less a danger than a challenge and an opportunity to engage in restless movement. Russians ever fear being fate's victim; Americans, aspiring to master fate itself, ever fear being slowed down or fenced in.

While in scholarly circles migration is predominantly regarded as primarily a political and economic matter and pilgrimage a religious one, I wish here to consider briefly psychologically overdetermining issues which influence the perception of the push-pull factors in migration and pilgrimage alike (see chap. 2, below). In migration one may leave a homeland permanently, temporarily, or in a cyclic (e.g., seasonal) pattern (see Stein 1980c). Perhaps needless to say, "return migrations" and the longing of refugees for the home from which they have been evicted must likewise be carefully examined for their motivations for movement. While migrations are often one way, pilgrimages are rarely so (except, for instance, for those who join religious orders and lead a monastic life within those orders). While in migration one seeks to find and establish a better life elsewhere, expecting permanent renewal there, in pilgrimage one seeks renewal at a considerable distance (and usually cost) from home but returns home "a better man." While pilgrimages have been associated since medieval times with journeys to religious shrines (e.g., Lourdes, Jerusalem, Mecca), the concept can profitably be extended to include travel within Europe to warm springs for mineral baths (activities which we might be tempted to call "mere" vacations), and long-distance journeys to medical-treatment centers for thorough work-ups (e.g., the Mayo Clinic in Minnesota) or highly specialized treatments (e.g., the Menninger clinic in Topeka, Kansas).

Both in migration and in pilgrimage there is the indispensable magic associated not only with place but also with the process of preparing and going to it. Great expectation and hope are held for what the destination will do for one's life. The process is a rite of passage embodying separation, often painful transition, and renewal within a new status (e.g., citizen, redemption, cure). One anticipates that life will be dramatically changed by outside circumstances. The place or site is invested with charisma or mana unlike anywhere within one's familiar round of activity. Its very outsidedness or remoteness confers upon it additional power.

The religious and medical shrine, like the new or adopted homeland in the emigrant's imagination, is usually the culmination of a long series of searches for betterment if not radical cures. Reality is clouded by wish; the true locus of the *charisma of place* is in the grandiosity of the pilgrim and immigrant. The act of faith is undertaken with the hope that it will offer—in a single magical sweep—rebirth, an undoing of painful losses and separations, and miraculous resolution of all psychosexual conflict. The impetus behind such psychogeographic representations is, unsurprisingly, idealization. And behind it lies the splitting of the inner world into all-good and all-bad compartments. The outer world simply follows suit.

A notable variation on migration is expulsion, persecution, or some less dire form of forced movement occasioned by political or economic conditions, that is, circumstances in which "push" factors tend—at least outwardly, initially, and consciously—to predominate over "pull" factors. Here one feels more the passive victim of circumstance than an active participant in choosing to leave. He not only may resent having to abandon what is loved and familiar—often abruptly—but may subsequently become "stuck" with an idealizing nostalgia toward what has been lost and wish if not plan for revenge against those whom he sees as having deprived him of his roots and past. Political refugees frequently exemplify this pattern. More strictly economic refugees and emigrants, on the other hand, may also be in search for greater personal freedom, enhanced status, and more rewarding employment in the temporarily and permanently adopted land. At the same time they may wish if not feel obligated to preserve affective as well as economic ties with their families and communities of origin.

"Absence," goes the cliché, "makes the heart grow fonder." Such nostalgia has become immortalized in an idealization of the homeland from afar. It has served as the taproot of much nativistic music, from regionalism through nationalism proper. The musical history of nineteenth- and early-twentieth-century romanticism demonstrates unequivocally that some of the most characteristically and passionately nationalistic music was written by the great expatriates. One thinks of the nineteenth-century Russian composer Mikhail Glinka in Warsaw, the Hungarian Franz Liszt in Weimar, the German Richard Wagner throughout Europe, the Polish Frédéric Chopin self-exiled in Paris, the Norwegian Edvard Grieg in Berlin, and the Russian Sergei Rachmaninoff in the United States. Each was more "native" when he was longing for home. One likewise thinks of the American composer Irving Berlin, who wrote his famous song "White Christmas" after having left the East for Los Angeles and Hollywood, and of the nineteenth-century American songwriter Stephen C. Foster, a southerner at heart, who wrote his "Old Folks at Home," a lament for the loss of the Suwannee River, while living in Pennsylvania. The latter two songs are, of course, strictly speaking regionalistic rather than nationalistic, but the distinction lies only in the symbolic geographic object of the nostalgia and heightened veneration.

The contemporary writer Alexander Solzhenitsyn, exiled from the Soviet Union, can be firmly located within the several-century-old Russophile, neo-Orthodox school of Russian intellectuals who despised secularization and modernization (since Peter the Great) and longed for the restoration of Holy Russia. As with Dostoevski and Tolstoi a century ago, Solzhenitsyn's religion serves as a medium for nationalist striving. The nativistic response is possible only in those who have left the tradition they now reverence from afar; it is an effort to overcome the painful separation they now feel. It is an affirmation of the link with what has been irrevocably lost. Stated differently, the link itself affirms the loss in the very attempt to deny, soften, or undo the loss (see chap. 3, below).

One finds the identical phenomenon at the political level: the wish to restore rather than painfully mourn what has been lost. Jews in the Babylonian captivity longed for the return to and restoration of Zion; under the leadership of the Persian king Cyrus, and the Jewish prophets Ezra and Nehemiah, the Jews did indeed return to their homeland. During and immediately following World War I, it was largely through the concerted political action of eastern and central European immigrants *within* the United States that the Austro-Hungarian Empire was dismembered and the successor nation-states Poland, Czechoslovakia, and sub-Carpathian Ruthenia were formed. These immigrants would make restitution for having abandoned the motherland by pressing from safely across the ocean for her autonomy, separation (from the "bad" parental empire), integrity, and ethnic purity. At present one finds a similar form of irredentism-at-a-distance in many American Jews, Armenians, and Irish.

As I discuss elsewhere (see chap. 2, below; see also Stein and Hill 1977a, 1979), physical or geographic separation rekindles and calls for reresolution of all earlier issues surrounding emotional separation, differentiation, and individuation. Immigrants may often feel "like fish out of water" or like "misplaced persons" and quickly attempt to replace lost links with the homeland by reconstructing it in the adopted community, rather than mourn the symbolic and real losses. They likewise may develop a host of physical complaints if not actual disease process and depression. Inner estrangement makes outer strangeness into a crisis. The experience of immigration may powerfully remind one of how much one exists within a widely cast libidinal field—and how much like an "island" one feels when deprived of it.

I hasten to add that this brief description subsumes not only the great peasant migrations, past and current, but also those of corporate executives and other professionals for whom the conscious advantages of career advancement and economic reward do not impugn the fact of psychogeographic disruption. Any sound program in assistance, support, and relocation must address the psychological as well as occupational process taking place—not, I might further add, to "help" workers simply to replace what has been lost, but to help them to work through the loss itself (see Volkan 1972, 1981).

Maps and the Emotional Topography of Groups

Just as it is only within the past two centuries that the geography of the earth and "space" have begun to be accurately mapped (e.g., radio astronomy versus mythical constellations), so too it is only recently—and in the West at that—that all human cultural and racial varieties have been subsumed under a single biological classification (psychologically, that is, a diminution of splitting and projection). In the fifth century, B.C., for instance, the widely traveled Herodotus described one-eyed, headless, long-eared, big-lipped, single-footed peoples and goat-footed types (later called satyrs) (Malefijt, 1968:112). In some pre-Linnaean systems of classification "the monsters [allegedly infrahuman types beyond one's own group] presented no problem: they were simply left out (together with man himself)" (Malefijt 1968:111). "In the 10th edition of Linnaeus (1758) man was given the name *Homo sapiens,* and the separate species *Homo monstrosus* was also listed" (Malefijt 1968:111).

Just as land and water beyond the boundaries of one's own group are invested with bizarre and exotic features, so are people outside one's group imagined to possess bizarre and exotic physical characteristics. Fanciful geography of geological features and fanciful geography of the distantly imagined human body are of a single piece. *Homo monstrosus* can take whatever form the psyche requires. Thus Hitler and the Nazi ideology depicted Jews variously as metastasizing cancer, as vermin, and as excrement. The erect, phallic Prussian soldier was counterpoised against the small, bent-over Jew. Likewise historically, Jews have been depicted as alien superegos or consciences (yet also as depraved ids). In the United States blacks (and, throughout Europe, Gypsies) have been depicted as unfettered ids, or as embodiments of untamed sexual and aggressive impulses. Groups likewise assign themselves and others specific sexual identities: thus the Germans as "masculine" and the French as "feminine"; the nomadic Masai in Kenya as "masculine" and the agricultural Kikuyu as "feminine." Northern Europeans and North Americans view southern Europeans and Latin (Central and South) Americans as "hot," excitable, moved by the passions rather than reason, and characterize themselves as the opposite and better. Those from the emotionally "warmer" and more effusive climes characterize their northern counterparts as "cool," aloof, arrogant. Clearly, emotional geography is as important as are the imagined shapes, sizes, and features of the body.

The very word "barbarian" derives from the Greek *barbaroi,* meaning "men who babble": in this manner classical Greeks referred to foreigners who did not speak Greek. Likewise, Slavic peoples call Germans *nemci,* "those who are mute," and so on. Stated differently, it is not that *we* cannot understand them or that we speak our language and they speak theirs, but they are defective, inferior, because their way of speaking differs from ours. Difference is experienced as narcissistic threat. Humiliation is inverted into superiority. What Freud referred to as the "narcissism of small differences: (1930:114) comes into play; difference is experienced as criticism, to which one responds by going on the offensive, as it were, and sharply criticizing others for *their* inadequacy (a projection of one's own).

Otherness and differentness are often perceived as assaults upon and seductions from traditionalism. A stalwart and unquestioning attitude toward the culturally sacred is necessary, for otherness and differentness remind us of our own inner splits and unresolved ambivalence—in a phrase, our imperfect love for a tradition to which we have sworn loyalty and reverence. Paranoia, then, sustains cultural identities and boundaries, for we perceive not our own wishes but others' supposed temptations and malevolence.

Erikson identifies the "pseudospecies" as "one of the more sinister aspects of all group identity" (1968:42):

Man as a species has survived by being divided into what I have called *pseudospecies.* First each horde or tribe, class and nation, but then also every religious association has become *the* human species, considering all the others a freakish and gratuitous invention of some irrelevant diety. To reinforce the illusion of being chosen, every tribe recognizes a creation of its own, a mythology and later a history: thus was loyalty to a particular ecology and morality secured. One never quite knew how all the other tribes came to be, but since they did exist, they were at least useful as a screen of projection for the negative identities which were the necessary, if most uncomfortable counterpart of the positive ones. This projection, in conjunction with their territoriality, gave men a reason to slaughter one another *in majorem gloriam*. [1968:41]

Psychosexually, one can conceive of "the other" across one's group boundary as even more primitive than barbarian, for barbarians, while certainly disparaged, are at least acknowledged to speak something, to be differentiated into male and female. A developmentally prior form which "the other" takes is the sexually *un*differentiated "it" that is wholly evil, one in which the "bad" parts of self-representation are merged with the "bad" parts of object representation and are entirely externalized. A definite article, usually *the*, prefixes the object, which in turn also takes the singular form, as though the evil were embodied by a single undifferentiated object (e.g., "the Hun," "the Jap," "the Infidel," "der ewige Jude").

Maps, in turn, are externalized representations of how we see the world, not the world itself. As semanticist Alfred Korzybski said (1941). "The map is not the territory." At best it is a flawed approximation, a guide which we can correct from more accurate input from reality. Yet who among us does not believe that at least *some* of our maps are not inerrant, that they must be right, that they must be immutable guides congruent with the territory? We invest many of our maps with the quality of necessity. Consider that only in 1983 did the Roman Catholic church acknowledge that in 1616 Galileo had been right about who revolves about whom (*Time* 1983a).

One Slovak-American in his sixties recalled with horror looking at a medieval map of Central Europe and not being able to find the Slovaks or Slovakia in the map. Long in search of a past he could be proud of, he remarked:

We Slovaks were already there by that period, but I couldn't find them. I kept seeing Magyar names. And I saw the word "Slaves" on the map, but our people weren't slaves. [On many early maps, "Slav" was spelled in Latin "Slave": what is important is his meaning that the Slavs were free, not slave.] I kept looking, hoping to come up with our people, but we weren't on the map.

One likewise thinks of the Hungarian word *nemzethalal* ("death of the nation"), that dread of disappearance by being engulfed in the "German and Slavic sea" during the late eighteenth and nineteenth centuries. The emotional climate is that of intense longing for the collectivity from an intense sense of isolation and loneliness that feels like disappearance, extinction, death, nonbeing. The map becomes a symbol of the self: non-"existence" in historical geography confirms what one fears about oneself at present.

A recent cartoon on the Op-Ed page of *The New York Times* (6 March 1983, E-19) depicts a map inside or superimposed upon a man's cranial vault. Guatemala and neighboring Honduras are depicted as bordered by nations named "El Cubador" and "Cubaragua." Moreover, these four nations appear as a single island which spans virtually the entire cranial hemisphere. Obviously this region is literally "on our mind" if not inside it. Furthermore, it is represented as altogether isolated from neighboring Central American countries, as well as from North and South America. It is greatly exaggerated in size, so as to become the "whole" picture. While Guatemala and Honduras are slightly darkened, El Cubador and Cubaragua are both lighter, suggesting some emotional contrast. In the minds of many Americans (USA, that is), the menacing image of Cuba has become literally fused with that of El Salvador and Nicaragua. By such linkage El Salvador and Nicaragua become available as hated targets. Finally, it will be noted that the "island" is literally split along the affective lines of good and bad, suggesting that it is here that the battle between the forces of good and evil are to be both isolated and played out.

It is well known that with Gerhardus (Gerhard Kremer) Mercator, the sixteenth-century Flemish geographer (1512–94), the representation of geography became less distorted by fantasy. With the European Renaissance many became increasingly *capable* of assessing reality more accurately, contaminating it less with anthropomorphic and ethnocentric exaggerations. As Ebel writes:

Medieval maps may have been deformed by the assumptions they tended to make about who was at the center of what—so that the world map bound into the *Muqaddimah* of the North African historian Ibn Khaldun portrayed North Africa as being approximately the size of China, and China as virtually nonexistent. But the victory over fantasy implied by the Renaissance achievement . . . appears to have substituted a compulsive *external* accuracy for a true inward purgation. [1980c]

In psychoanalytic terms one might say that the unmistakable psychogeographic achievement lay in a differentiation between self (or "us") representation and object (or "them") representation, and therefore the formation of "islands," so to speak, of reality testing. Perception of the other could still be contaminated with aspects of the self, but at least *some* demarcation, *some* diminution of projection, had been made:

. . . we define our identities by distinguishing ourselves from those who live on our "borders." That is to say, we tend to observe that "they are different because they live on the other side of the border" when it would be much more accurate to say that "the border is there because they are different." Or, with equal accuracy, that "the border is there because we perceive ourselves to be different from them."

Borders, in other words, are nothing to take for granted. Before they can exist in legal terms, they must be a living reality within the minds of those they divide. In turn, it is obvious that a border, once it has established itself as a psychological reality, is an important aspect of the sense of personal identity. For those who live on a nation's western border, for example, the eastern border is the furthest they can "stretch" while still retaining the sense of kinship and affiliation. The sense of certain shared qualities that keeps all the borders in place—north, south, east and west—can be said to "feed back" into the shape of individual personality. [Ebel 1980c]

An important psychogeographic characteristic of most maps, in addition to *what* is represented (and excluded), its *shape*, and the *relative size* allocated to it, is *where* it is located on the map. The centering of one's own group (national, ethnic, etc.) on the map is simply one expression of ethnocentrism. The sun may no longer orbit around the earth, but surely the gravitational field of meaning centers upon my group! This view of the world inevitably leads to a fear and feeling of being *surrounded* or *encircled* by hostile peoples, and in turn an offensive-defensive response to ethnocentrism's built-in paranoia (i.e., group = body; outside = threats to the body).

It is only in recent centuries, and among relatively small numbers of people, that people have become *capable* of looking at the world from several equally plausible and valid points of view—that is, using decentered frameworks. The view of "One Earth" by the astronauts from the moon (1969) is not only a novel aeronautical event but a psychogeographic one as well.

Islands have always fascinated the human imagination, for to be an island is to be detached and estranged. That is surely what John Donne had in mind when he wrote:

No man is an island, entire of itself; every man is a piece of the continent, a part of the main; if a clod be washed away by the sea, Europe is the less, as well as if a promontory were, as well as if a manor of thy friends or of thine own were; any man's death diminishes me, because I am involved in mankind; and therefore never send to know for whom the bell tolls; it tolls for thee. [1624]

What geography fails to provide, the human imagination fills in: as with Voltaire's deity, islands would be created by fantasy even when—and where—they do not exist. For surely to feel like an island, attracted to or menaced by one, does not require water. Islands are anomalies, alluring and terrifying.

My office was for a year in a reconditioned house a short walk from the administrative center ("mainland") of the department, situated then on the fifth floor of an office and medical-research building. The house was officially named the Family Development Center, subsequently renamed the Family Health Center. Unofficially, however, it immediately accrued such epithets as the Stress House, the Out House, and the Little House on the Prairie. Even on official departmental schedules it was referred to as the Stress House. One purpose of the house was indeed to conduct and study family interviews and family therapy with families. Moreover, one model that was influential in the interior design of the house was the Family Stress Clinic at the University of Virginia, Charlottesville.

There had always been uncertainty about where this aspect

of the department's program should fit, both structurally and emotionally, within the larger departmental whole; that is, it had been more outside than inside, symbolized by its spatial placement. Even though the department espoused a family-systems orientation, many department members remained uneasy dealing with family and psychological issues, especially those which they experienced as anxiety-evoking and less amenable to medical control. Therefore this portion of the group psyche, so to speak, was extruded and simultaneously relocated at a safe distance from the center, labeled a stressful place (projectively placing department members' and residents' anticipated stress within the house and its personnel), and occasionally humorously associated with an outdoors latrine, where frightening but fascinating excrement is both deposited and stored. Likewise, the distinction good = inside, bad = outside could be shored up psychogeographically through the division of labor *and* the strategic placement of faculty and other personnel. Although we occupants of the Stress House (a liaison psychiatrist, a family-studies researcher, and a psychoanalytic anthropologist) were officially "us" within the overall department, we were also unofficially—unconsciously—"them." Reality, at least in part, implements group-fantasy about reality.

After approximately a year in the "Stress House," I was moved into an office space on the newly acquired sixth floor of the main departmental office building. In part it represented an "ingathering"—for the first time in the department's history—of all faculty into a single facility, a realization of the chairman's oft-spoken dream to "bring the whole family together under one roof." My new office, situated at the end of a long hall behind double doors at the southern end of the building, became a kind of compromise formation—an "outside-inside," so to speak—expressing the greater inclusion of my psychoanalytic-cultural viewpoint *together with* its continued isolation (compartmentalization).

Over time, both geographically and functionally, the emotional distance of my "island" decreased, that is, was increasingly—if still tenuously and spasmodically—integrated into the emotional life and work of the departmental "mainland."

The island which had been originally cut off but kept available at an uneasy distance was still in many respects an island in the group fantasy of the department. But the island has been brought closer to "shore," and I have found that many faculty members have recently come to find temporary refuge and respite and safety (not just danger) on this "island"; for instance, many medical and nonmedical colleagues now come to my office to talk about personal and family issues, to seek my counsel about patients or families they are treating, and even to get away from political and administrative pressures and gain a perspective on them before returning to their own offices and psychogeographic region of the department. Recently moreover, the use of the name Stress House has diminished and no longer appears on official documents. The house is formally known as the Family Development Center. In summary, this small-scale, mundane example of an "island" illustrates the tenacity of boundaries, and the often inseparable difficulties involved in crossing or blurring them, because of the emotional burden they bear for those who erect and maintain them.

Another kind of island is that which represents bliss and paradise, or alluring excitement, separated from the prosaic and profane. One thinks of the Île de la Cite, in Paris, on which was erected the Cathedral de Notre Dame. During his Mediterranean voyages, Odysseus was tempted by the island of Circe. On a far more ordinary scale one likewise thinks of the countless vacation islands where people go "to get away from it all," that is, to make an explicit boundary between the mainland of busyness and the island of respite and renewal (e.g., Catalina Island, off southern California, "the island of romance").

Still another kind of island is that of all-bad. Prisoners have been condemned to such islands (e.g., Devil's Island, Alcatraz, fortress in San Francisco Bay); islands thus emotionally doomed are the sites of war games and nuclear testing (e.g., the South Pacific in the 1950s), for they can be destroyed with impunity (since they are already emotionally split off and therefore superfluous). Such islands are repositories for excrement.

The presentations of islands can also oscillate in their emotional valence. For instance, in the early and mid-1970s, New York City embodied the national image of decay, immorality, and the uninhabitable metropolis; from the late 1970s to the present it is seen as the "Big Apple," a kind of bountiful breast, a place of promise, hope, and vitality. In short, over the years the image of New York City has vacillated between a place that is all bad and one that is all good.

Islands serve likewise as testaments to incomplete emotional separation. They are an affront to boundaries of mainland or continental masses, for they are ambiguously neither here nor there. They are "transitional" between merger and individuation, and are the dangerous, hotly contested playthings of conflict over where one ends and another begins. One immediately thinks of Cyprus in relation to Turkey and Greece in the Mediterranean, of Cuba in relation to the United States and Latin-American nations, of Taiwan in relation to mainland China, and of the Falkland Islands during the brief war in the spring of 1982 between Argentina and Great Britain. One is loath to let go of claims to islands—or, conversely, island inhabitants are reluctant to sever their "ties" or "links" with the main ("mother") land altogether. One mistrusts the intentions of altogether independent islands, as though these islands represented one's own split-off and repressed "bad" parts. Indeed, these islands serve as virtually indispensable repositories of mainlanders' "bad parts."

Consider the grim mistrust held by the United States for rebellious and subversive Cuba—yet American policy not only aided the very success of the Castro revolution but currently, through the cut-off of direct diplomatic ties, not only does not officially recognize the regime but undermines it as well. Bearded revolutionaries and clean-shaven bureaucrats need and complete one another. Islands such as Cuba function as repositories of paranoid persecution fantasies, akin to earlier witchcraft accusations hurled against the tribe across the mountain or river: *they* could only be up to no good; *we* have no reason to feel guilty.

In figure 5 the island of Cuba zoomorphically becomes a menacing hungry communist shark heading toward the vulner-

Metamorphosis

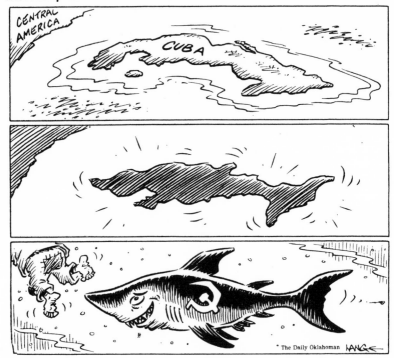

Fig. 5. From the December 6, 1981, issue of *The Sunday Okla-homan*. Drawing by Jim Lange. Copyright 1981, The Oklahoma Publishing Company.

able, exposed feet and underside of an anthropomorphized Central America. The fear of castration and oral aggression from others is typically also a projection onto others of one's own group's impulses and wishes. In figure 6, Castro, the bearded, radical, powerfully phallic communist castrator (note the size of the sickle and its handle), stands precariously close to Central American shores with their vegetation (wheat-penises?) which are vulnerably ready for his reaping (castration). Castro's Cuba has often been an American symbol of projected American adolescent impulsiveness and rebelliousness, at once admired and feared. Americans also fear punishment, if not also mutilation, for these motives in themselves.

Not only are islands felt to threaten the larger mainland, but inhabitants of islands also feel ambivalent about the land mass, vacillating between desires for union (e.g., Cyprus's enosis in pan-Hellenism with Greece) and defiant independence. Even where there is no physical ocean, a people nonetheless may feel that it is an embattled island in danger of ungulfment by its cultural adversaries; hence the seventeenth- and eighteenth-century Magyars' fear of drowning in a Slavic and

Harvest Time?

Fig. 6. From the August 9, 1981, issue of *The Sunday Oklahoman*. Drawing by Jim Lange. Copyright 1981, The Oklahoma Publishing Company.

German sea; the Israelis' fear of perishing in an Arab sea—coupled with the fear of being pushed westward into the Mediterranean (now increasingly Arabs' fear of perishing in Israeli-occupied territories); the white ethnics' fear of being annihilated by assimilation into mainstream American culture, of being destroyed in the "melting pot"; in Northern Ireland, Protestants' fear of being overwhelmed by the Roman Catholics.

A notable "island" in recent history was that of an embattled South Vietnam as envisioned by President Lyndon B. Johnson in the mid-1960s. Just as West Berlin and Israel are today spoken of in the West as "islands of freedom," likewise was South Vietnam from the mid-1960s. President Johnson made references to South Vietnam as a besieged Alamo—a reference to a fort in San Antonio, Texas, in which the valiant and outnumbered American defenders perished at the hands of the Mexican army during the Mexican-American War. (If we accept Beisel's [1985] analysis of American involvement in the Vietnam War, South Vietnam was the American island of punishment on which Johnson, and with him the United States, would be punished at their new Alamo for the fantasized crime of filicide and the elimination of the younger competitor-brother, namely, the assassination of President John F. Kennedy in 1963.) This specific island image is an especially exploitable one in American psychogeography, for it hearkens to the site of Fort McHenry (Baltimore, Maryland), to which the British laid siege during the War of 1812 and which inspired poet Francis Scott Key to write the words that later became the text for the American National Anthem. The fear of being annihilated by a sea of adversaries who threaten to engulf one's group—or, by displacement plus projective identification, who threaten to destroy one's ally—not only is a common one in history but rests on the universal fear of being absorbed in fusion with the mother.

Let me use a personal example to illustrate how the psychogeographic issues of island-sea-mainland influence the rational organization of the relationship between an academic department in an urban medical center and two community-based family medicine residency training programs that are subunits of the department 35 and 90 miles away respectively. In nearly a decade of teaching at all three sites, I have observed a constant emotional undertow that suggests separation-autonomy and other familial issues. The community-based programs are often referred to at the center as "satellite" programs and alternately as not separate units but parts of a unified, integrated teaching and administrative effort. Some members of the "satellite" program resent the centralizing tendencies and feel that not only is there competition ("sibling rivalry") between units, but also an effort to reduce local autonomy if not deprive them of their local identity and roots. Frequently in the perception of participants in the two smaller community-based training programs, there is an affect-based splitting of the image of local clinic leadership and leadership in "The City." Local clinic leadership tends to be seen as "good," benevolent, nurturant, while distant leadership is seen to be "bad," autocratic, depriving, punitive, and the like. Put simply, authority is split into the bipolar images of the "good father" and the "bad father." The program in "the City" is often called the "mother house" (i.e., as in the organization of the administrative and emotional center of a Roman Catholic order of nuns), and those in the rural programs resent the image that they practice in "the boonies." Those in the rural programs pride themselves on their affiliation with a major university and medical school (not to mention football team, the University of Oklahoma) and at the same time seek to preserve a distinct program and identity. One colleague jokingly suggested that the answer was to "secede from the Union"—a phrase that reveals the underlying separation-individuation issue.

While conflicts over allocation of resources and the division of labor between components of any enterprise are inevitable, there are here significant psychogeographic issues that are rarely addressed: Are we part of them, or are they part of us? Are we separate, autonomous, on our own, or dependent upon them? Are they free-standing, or are they dependent upon us? Can we hold our own, or will they try to absorb us? Are we satellites orbiting around some central planet, or do we have our own control and boundaries? Where do we begin and they end? Can an island ever be a mainland? Will this island be left to drown at sea? Will the satellites be loyal to the main planet, or will they try to break away from us? What will they do without us, or what will we do without them? In this psychogeographic system each sees itself threatened by the other (e.g., mother-infant and sibling rivalry). What we must not lose sight of, however, is precisely the systemic nature of the psychogeographic problem.

Perhaps we find islands so fascinating—indispensable—because they correspond so perfectly to the imagination; that is, they conform to and appear to "confirm" perceptually our inner splits into irreconcilable good and evil. We are not simply "mystically" drawn to think about aquatic environments—or worse, as some argue, possess a genetic or "racial" memory of the time our forebears lived in the water. For, individually, our earliest and perhaps most influential (see deMause 1982a) environment, prefiguring later geographic remembering, was uterine.

The Turkish Cypriot–born psychoanalyst Vamık D. Volkan, M.D., eloquently describes the psychogeography of his homeland:

. . . As a child I felt not only that Cyprus was altogether Turkish but that it was part of Anatolia, a literal translation of whose name, *Anadolu*, is "full of mother." Symbolically, Turkey was the motherland and Cyprus was its child.

Some of my own childhood memories may shed light on how Cypriot Turkish children symbolized a connection between the island of Cyprus and Turkey. Parents often spoke of Turkey and passed along to their children a sense of identity with the mainland country, which seemed a land of promise, much as America did to the immigrants to this country Niederland describes. The map of Cyprus made the connection concrete, since on maps the Karpasia peninsula of the island looks like an arm stretching toward Anatolia's (the mother's) Gulf of Alexandretta. I can still hear what we learned in elementary school on Cyprus: "Cyprus was once connected with Anatolia, but it sank into the sea. It rose, only to sink again. When it rose for the third time after its third submersion, it was, alas, no longer connected with Anatolia." This account reflects eons of geological change, and to this day I do not know how close it comes to the truth; but I do remember visualizing the island's being swallowed up by the sea, and the picture of this event, along with the fantasy of the island's rebirth, was very much before me up to my teens, especially when the island shook with the earthquakes we sometimes had.

In retrospect I can see that Cyprus represented myself in my own process of separation-individuation from my mother (Mahler 1963, 1968; Mahler and Furer 1963). The sequence of the island's submersion, reappearance, and ultimate separation from the motherland suggests a symbolic enactment of the trials and difficulties I underwent in the process of psychologically separating from my mother. As a small child I felt that another earthquake might reunite the two lands, and the yearning for reunion of what had been sundered persisted. I have no conscious memory of having made a symbolic connection out of the phallic pointing of the island's landmass into a Turkish gulf. [1979:12–13]

Most regrettably, few people have Volkan's hard-won retrospective understanding of their own psychogeographic investments. He also acknowledges that "the part-object relationship with the physical environment seems more and more evident, characterizing particularly responses to political stress" (1979:14): ". . . for Cypriots who regress under the stress of intercommunal conflict, the line between longing for the return of infantile omnipotence and actually experiencing it may be very thin indeed" (1979:14). Stated differently, to the person concretely experiencing the representation to be an inherent characteristic of the thing, there is simply no "psycho" necessary to prefix "geography." With respect to Cyprus, one must add that it is an island in search of a continent, whether by linkage or fusion. Greek Cypriots seek enosis with Greece, while Turkish Cypriots seek reunion with Turkey. In the identity conflict of Cypriots (Turk and Greek alike) lies the microcosm of the unfinished conflict between Levant and Europe (significantly, perhaps, from a psychogeographic viewpoint, the very term "Levant" traces to a word one of whose meanings is "to break away from" or "to run away from," the Eurocentric point of view).

Geologically, what are called straits, isthmuses, or canals are natural or man-made waterways between two larger bodies of water. One thinks, for instance, of the Bering Strait, the

Strait of Magellan, the Panama Canal, the Suez Canal, even the Saint Lawrence Seaway, in Canada. Associated with real hazards (narrowness, shallowness, collision with unseen obstacles, unpredictable weather, danger from enemies, etc.) are a host of *fantasied vulnerabilities*, which in turn engender defenses against these imagined perils, *together with* provocations that produce the wished or feared realization of the fantasies in reality. Thus canals, isthmuses, and straits "are" variously experienced as the alimentary canal (food intake, conduit, and elimination), the breathing apparatus, the birth canal, and the cardiovascular system. Interestingly, fantasy-laden geographic words are projected back onto the body and are internalized as its meaning (e.g., canals). Political speeches and news accounts are replete with fears of choking, suffocating, squeezing, becoming stuck in a passage, or being swallowed (see deMause 1982a). Reference to attack as sodomizing or rape is common, as is the fear that an enemy is "trying to shove something down our throats." Of course, none of these are "merely" fantasies, for we subsequently act as groups politically and militarily *as though* these dread bodily events were taking place. Political psychology builds much upon psychogeography.

Conclusions

This chapter has attempted to define and explore the scope of psychogeography: the attribution to and representation of space in the topography of the human mind. Unintegrated aspects of the self- and object representations and drive derivatives, unresolved psychosexual conflicts and body image are externalized onto people, places, and things which come to be the outer referents for psychogeographic perception and action. A theory of psychogeography as process and structure was suggested and was illustrated by case vignettes. I wish to reiterate that the purpose of this exercise has decidedly *not* been to create yet another "field" or "discipline" and further fragment (through splitting) inquiry in the very act of attempting a tentative integration. Psychogeography is simply a way of understanding how people construct the physical and social world based on fantasies about their bodies and their families.

The subject matter of this chapter extends into every area of life—how we feel and where we sit in professional conferences or union meetings, whether we prefer the cataclysm of the "big-bang" cosmology or the uniformitarianism of the "steady-state" theory of the universe, how Americans perceive the Soviets and how the Soviets perceive the United States, what we fantasize as we read maps—and the consequences of those feelings and fantasies. By making explicit those unconsciously motivated premises by which we understand and participate in the world, we are less given to act automatically or unself-critically upon them. This is far from a recondite academic exercise, for our survival as a species depends on the diminution of our endemic—and often pandemic—tendencies to use the world as a screen for our projections and externalizations and as an arena for the displacement of inner and familial hurts.

For both males and females the earth has long been a fantasy object, recipient of human beings' deepest longings and fears. From the earth mother we have expected nourishment; with the earth mother we have for millennia sought reunion and solace to overcome painful separations. As though the earth were a sexual object, "she" has been tenderly cultivated and violently raped. Lest "her" revenge turn against us, "she" has also been placated through sacrifice. Yet—the earth is not our mother. "She" neither hates nor loves us. Nor can "she" be mollified or defended against the ravages of incestuous sons, vile husbands, or vengeful daughters. Nor are we the earth's children, though we claim entitlement upon "her" as if "she" were our exclusive possession.

Outer space, too, has long captured the human imagination: one has only to think of the celestial constellations and of the mythological tales woven out of far less than thin air. Yet here, too, outer space is not a woman to be "penetrated," "exploited," and explored by oedipal males or masculine-identifying females. Nor is deep space the mysterious womb from which all living things emanated, a mystically maternal ground of our being which (or whom) we had better leave undisturbed, or an alternately benevolent mother who sends us neotenized aliens to perfect us (I am thinking here of the movie *E.T., the Extra-Terrestrial*, from the early 1980s). We needlessly fear punishment from other aliens or flying saucers who bear memory traces of the terrifying primal mothers and fathers whom we once feared might kill or maim us. Yet if earth, air, fire, and water are not persons, they are not quite disembodied "things" to which we have no relationship or bear no responsibility. That they are simply there for our exploitation and discard is itself an attitude that characterizes borderline and narcissistic disorders. The modern penchant to perceive if not make everything inert and dead is but the reverse side of the tendency to regard everything as alive (animism) if not also as assuming human form (anthropomorphism).

The perspective from psychogeography helps us understand what and who, as the human animal, we are. It instructs us about our limits and opportunities. The more we learn about ourselves and the world, the more, I believe, we come to realize that we are the mentors of one another's identities and maturity, that we are stewards of the earth, that we are deeply interrelated to one another and to the world, that the fate of each is bound up with the fate of all. By acknowledging people's tendencies to write their biographies on the face of the world, we can perhaps engage in more judicious and empathic social policy planning—and, in fostering greater personal integration and maturity, less inflame and exploit human vulnerabilities.

CHAPTER 2

"Misplaced Persons": The Crisis of Emotional Separation in Geographic Mobility and Uprootedness

Wir brauchen keinen Hurrikan,	We need no hurricaine,
wir brauchen keinen Taifun,	we need no typhoon.
denn was er an Schrecken tuen kann,	for the horrors it can bring,
das können wir selber tun.	that we ourselves can do.

—Bertolt Brecht and Kurt Weill, *Rise and Fall of the City of Mahagonny (1930)*, act 3

Human history is a long chronicle of movement over land and water. In this century human beings have taken to the air and most recently have gone to the moon as the beginning of the exploration of outer space. Like the "wayward wind" of the cowboy song, human populations have endlessly shifted as much as remained attached to the land. They often both leave and stay out of fears they scarcely can articulate. And those who leave, for some newfound land or some newly enticing identity, or for greater political freedom or for economic gain, rarely realize how much baggage they carry with them (see Stein and Hill 1977a, 1979).

Permanent settlement is more the product of a nostalgia for settledness and the restoration of lost continuity than historical fact. We have uprooted ourselves as often as we have sunk firm roots in some locale. Some have felt compelled to leave; others have been unable to budge from where they are—only to wish they could and resent those who left. Human movement has ranged from group migrations to mass invasions, from individual choices to "move on" to family and national expulsions, from travel to expand one's self to travel as the inability to "settle down." To the already considerable literature on the demography, psychosomatics, and human geography of movement across space, I shall now add in this chapter some observations on the psychology of this change. The study of the psychogeography of this physical movement is a study of its meanings and, in turn, of the developmental sources involved.

Based on five years (1978–83) of clinically based research in three family-medicine residency training sites in Oklahoma (Oklahoma City, Enid, and Shawnee), this chapter explores the vicissitudes of the largely white internal immigrant population to the oil-rich Sun Belt, and likewise that of Oklahomans who have recently relocated (rural to urban and vice versa) within the state. While the epidemiological literature linking somaticization, depression and migration is enormous, there remains a paucity of understanding of the individual and family dynamics involved. Moreover, there is likewise an overemphasis, I believe, on objectivist ("etic"), externally imposed criteria, leading to a minimization of the subjective ("emic") experience of the immigrant. We thus come to expect that the geographically foreign or culturally exotic immigrant would have a more difficult time in relocation and settlement than would a "merely regionally distinct individual."

Clinically based ethnographic data from Oklahoma families and individuals suggest that unresolved developmental issues of separation-individuation (Mahler, Pine, and Bergman 1975) in one's family of origin are far more predisposing to the sense of uprootedness and identity crisis than is the mere fact of (often superficial) cultural difference. The sense of being a "misplaced person," as many patients have called themselves, is more a matter of arrest in developmental time than one of dislocation in physical space—although it is in the latter frame of reference that time is displaced, symbolized, and enacted. Mobility is the occasion that precipitates, but does not cause, the separation issues.

Case examples are used to illustrate the discovery that separation-individuation issues often underlie the estranging and uncanny experience of "being like a fish out of water"; the examples also illustrate the function of mourning in working through the differentiation process, which leads to an attenuation of the use of one's erstwhile culture as defense against loss.

I further argue that the "culturally appropriate" therapy—
e.g., helping patients join groups akin to those back home,
recommending support or self-help networks, and prescrib-
ing antidepressant medication as primary interventions—are
often in fact antitherapeutic for the patient (or family) and
serve as an unconscious strategy of the clinician to avoid the
reviving in himself/herself of painful developmental separation issues.

Clinical strategies which appear to be adaptive can be in
fact antiadaptive, while genuine therapy consists of facilitating rather than inhibiting the process of grieving for what
has been lost.

Migration and Emotional Separation

The relationship between migration, uprooting, relocation,
and resettlement and the epidemiology of physical and mental
illness alike has long occupied the interest of clinicians and re-
searchers (Fador 1950; Murphy 1965; Mezey 1960; Seguin
1956; Hurst 1951; Weinberg 1961; Fabrega 1969; Zwingmann
1973; Nann 1982). While urbanization, development, secularization, modernization, and the like are neither invariably
nor necessarily associated with or causative of stress-related
pathologies (De Vos 1974:557–60; Inkeles 1966; Srole 1980;
Stein and Hill 1979), a certain tacit romanticization of the
allegedly simpler and better past has tended to dominate
clinical and scholarly thinking (see De Vos 1974; Hippler 1974;
Stein 1980c, d).

Much social science has incorporated an implicit ideology
about human attachments into the very fabric of its arguments
and assumptions about health and disease. The promotional
summary of Raoul Naroll's volume *The Moral Order: An Introduction to the Human Situation* (1983), for instance, includes the statement that the author "proposes that people
with strong social networks (traditionally the tribe or extended family) are less likely to stray from accepted norms,
while those with weak moral nets are more susceptible to social and psychological problems." I cannot fail but to note the

cultural climate, so to speak, which has nurtured and lent wishful credence to John Bowlby's allegedly biologistic "attachment theory."

Rural life is often characterized as based on long-term relationships, natural helping and support networks, visibility, lack of anonymity, a limited circle of interpersonal contacts, kinship control of behavior, and limited geographical range (see Youmans 1977; Bachrach 1981). These are highly valued—as much by the investigator as by the native—and contrasted with city life. Yet this rural-urban dichotomy is a false, "ideal type" that omits the fact that city and countryside are as much states of mind as they are places and that the "urban village" (Gans 1962) may perpetuate the above "rural" characteristics in an urban setting (see Sklare 1972). Studies of Italian-Americans in Rosalia (Bruhn 1965) and Japanese-Americans in California (Marmot 1975) are repeatedly cited as tendentious cultural documents to assert the position that cultural traditionalism is healthy and stress-free while acculturation and urbanization are stressful, if not evil (see, however, Banfield 1958; De Vos 1973; Hippler 1979, 1981). However, the dynamics of traditionalism are underexamined, while those of modernism are overexamined, making for not only a false opposition but superficial discontinuity. Anyone familiar with Italian opera from the mid-nineteenth through early twentieth centuries is well aware that life in Italy—or in "Little Italy"—was anything but idyllic.

Migrations and relocations, expulsions and uprootings are part of the fabric of human history. Religious or cultural origin myths commonly relate the loss of some primeval paradise as a result of some human misdeed. The infant upon first sensing that its care giver is separate from its own deep cravings; the toddler cast out of specialness by the arrival of new siblings with whom imperfect love must be shared; the oedipal child who can no more completely (or seemingly so) possess the parent of the opposite sex; the adolescent who must emotionally leave home to found his or her new home in the succession of the generations; the middle-aged parents who must begin to let go of their offspring; the aged who must make peace with letting go of life itself—these are but a few of developmental phase-specific prisms which refract the experience of emotional withdrawals, real separations, and unprepared-for losses of the life cycle. These inner "prisms" not only influence how physical separation will be experienced, but may likewise affect the choice to emigrate and relocate. Outer events never simply "cause" inner experiences, for they are always mediated by a "representational world."

Volkan writes: "Throughout our lives we are influenced not only by interaction with important living people but also by the representations of the dead that reside within us, in the form of identifications or of separate 'presences' (introjects) either in ourselves or in those with whom we interface" (1981:37). Moreover, "when one comes to a milestone in life such as marriage, promotion, or a move from one place to another, one typically activates the images of dead others who have been realistically or symbolically significant in one's life" (Volkan 1981:35). Thus migration can serve as a powerful external referent for the reactivation of unfinished emotional business. In the context of health care, it is precisely how this return of the repressed is met by healers that determines whether the material rising from the unconscious is lifted from repression or is rerepressed through the manipulation of cultural symbolism and ritual. In migration as with all other environmental influences, at issue is not *whether* reality affects subsequent adaptation but *how* it does so, mediated as it always is by developmental issues and elaboration by fantasy.

The Oklahoma Context

From the middle 1970s a major internal migration occurred within the United States toward the Sun Belt states in the Mid- and Southwest. Its effect was tantamount to a massive relocation of millions of Americans in the early 1980s from the supposedly decaying and economically declining urban centers of the North, the Northeast, and the Far West. In Oklahoma, for instance, unemployment was 5 percent, one-half the national rate. This geographic mobility led to widespread rekindling of delayed emotional separation issues in the patient population (Stein 1982b, 1985a, 1987). This identical process is concurrently taking place on a local scale, as persons from smaller rural Oklahoma towns and individual farmsteads marry and move to larger towns and cities, whether prompted by employment opportunities and setbacks, marriage and new residence sites, or the wish for greater freedom from familial interdependence. While the town or city may spatially lie only a few hours' drive (at most) from one's home of origin, the distance in cultural time often seems to span as much as a century.

On both the national and the local scale, the *experience* of emigration and resettlement is often no less unsettling, uprooting, and disillusioning for the present internal migrants than it was for the generations who migrated to North America from Europe and for those worldwide who today seek to begin life anew in the United States. We need to inquire more closely into those differences which make a difference (see Korzybski 1941; Bateson 1972b) in determining health and mental health outcomes from migration, and which need to be taken into account in health-care planning.

From its opening to white settlement in the great land "runs" of 1889 and 1893 to its celebration of 75 years of statehood in 1982, Oklahoma has long prided itself on being a haven for the restless, the adventuresome, and the disgruntled within the United States. In their official cowboy lore Oklahomans refuse to acknowledge that the frontier is closed or is but a memory of the past. The tenacity of Oklahoman (and regional) religious conservatism must be understood as an institutionalization of social control in relation to this persistent ethos. The attractiveness of Oklahoma has changed but little over its first century of white habitation. The state is simultaneously a place to settle—often with a vengeance—and to remain protestingly unsettled. The lure of unclaimed land redeemed from the Indians has, a century later, been succeeded by the attractiveness of jobs and "wide-open spaces."

While oil rigs and antlike oil pumps have dotted the land for several decades, it is only within half a decade that Oklahoma, like the rest of the mythically defined Sun Belt, has been discovered or invented as the Land of Opportunity (and plenty of opportunism). State and region serve as something of an island within America, a land of unbridled expectation (and therefore vulnerability to rapid disillusionment), one which it is hoped will reverse all setbacks and losses of one's past life. With both the immense wheat crop and the oil industry tied to the vagaries of the national and international economy, riches and rags fluctuate widely and wildly. Soaring hope and plummeting despair intertwine the economic and the emotional in more than simple cause-and-effect relationship.

Unfinished developmental business from the families, occupations, and regions of origin influence how Sun Belt economics is perceived and therefore experienced. One invests life with meanings that encompass jobs and dollars. Jobs and mobility are symbols as well as facts. One must carefully discern those meanings the internal migrant brings and imposes on the new land. One must painstakingly inquire what all the migrant is leaving behind if not fleeing, and what all the migrant is seeking and expecting to find. That is, emigration and resettlement must be seen as part of an intensely personal process giving expression to the relationship among the past, the present, and the future which influence the perception of the here and now. The immigrant's dream of "streets paved with gold" (or dotted with oil wells) obviously colors his or her encounter with reality.

Even reality cannot be taken exclusively at face value, for one makes of it what he or she needs to see in it. Thus possession of a job may represent the autonomy one has not yet inwardly achieved and serve as a bulwark of self-reliance. Unemployment may abruptly disarm the defenses of individualism by thrusting the individual back on old unresolved dependency issues. Many "drifters" attracted to Oklahoma may use a series of "bad jobs" to externalize and perpetuate difficulties with authority originating in the family. Bosses, layoffs, doctors, emergency rooms, clinics, and social agencies are perceived as conspiring to deprive internal migrants of those advantages which they have come to expect from the environment (often as a "right").

One's sense of identity often encompasses a sense of place—where one "belongs," to whom and to what one is "linked."

The boundaries of the self are defined by a psychogeography of place. Uprooted from these, one may well have a lucrative, even stable, job but feel as though he or she has gained the world but lost the soul. The land of opportunity—fulfilled and failed alike—becomes the land of unfinished mourning. For most, the very fact that emotional separation and mourning are at issue remains unacknowledged. This is usually discovered only during the course of therapy. New symbols are sought to replace the void left by the absence of the old. For some, becoming a patient is one way of regaining one's caretakers—and their wide network as well. Here "secondary gain" is but a euphemism for how much the patient has to lose should therapy "succeed." One somaticizes or otherwise displaces onto outer new symbols rather than become painfully conscious of developmental issues one did not even know he or she had, ones heretofore kept in abeyance in a tight network of relationships—familial, occupational, neighborhood, religious, recreational, etc. The emotional economics of migration and resettlement are as important to explore as are those economics, narrowly defined, which influence the likelihood of receiving one's paycheck.

Patient Profile

Patients in this group of newly relocated persons often present with a wide variety of initial complaints, anxiety, depression, marital discord, somatic complaints: delinquent behavior among children, to name but the most common. Likewise, women ranging from their late teens upward, who were recent arrivals, will come to the Family Medicine Clinic for their prenatal care. Relocation is as much on their mind as the pregnancy itself. Early in treatment these patients, male and female alike, will begin describing themselves and their life situation with terms and themes that become recurrent if not redundant intraindividually and interindividually: "misplaced persons," "displaced persons," "isolated," "stranded," "like a fish out of water," "alone."

These people not only feel out of their element but are painfully aware that something is missing. It is as though the "element" from which they are parted is felt to be a part of themselves that they no longer have or was torn from them. The environment which had completed the very boundaries of their selves is no longer present. Their sense of "alienation" follows from a nagging feeling of uncanniness, if not an over-whelming feeling of depersonalization, for they truly do not know any longer who they are. Their external frame of ref-erence—one which is in fact a complex allocation or exten-sion (Hall 1977) of self-functions to others—is absent. What remains are the fragments in search of wholeness. "Place" is felt to be part of "person"; whereness is experienced as in-separable from the whoness. Thus the image of the "fish out of water" is especially apt dynamically: it portrays the link-age between inside and outside, the permeability of self and context.

Often their occupational and residential choices, church memberships, social and recreational group choices, physi-cian(s), and clinic(s), even the selections of homes and auto-mobiles, take on the character of replacement or substitute objects. They attempt to restructure the new and strange in terms of an "identity of perceptions" (Freud 1900) with the old and familiar. The new environment takes on the character of a home away from home, or a distant outpost of the original home itself. In the midst of dramatic change they seek to create the illusion that little or nothing has changed. Directly or subtly, they ask of their physician(s) to help them find a place and network of relationships to call "home," often adopt-ing their family doctor, clinic, and medical center as a person and place to visit and experiencing the outing itself as a social occasion.

These activities and relationships represent an attempt to fill a void in their lives. They become symbols that are in-vested with the quality of "transitional objects" (Winnicott 1953)—the first not-mother and not mother-me objects of childhood such as the ubiquitous blanket or cuddly doll. However, while transitional objects originally served *progres-sively* as a developmental bridge between symbiosis and dif-ferentiation of self, they now serve *regressively* as a way of symbolically reaching out and clutching for a past now gone. It is the psychic task or function of these new objects to restore an emotional surrounding like the imagined original one, to deny separateness, to reverse or undo loss, to patch up one's incompleteness, indeed to complete the self by external props. Taken as a whole, "tradition" or "culture" is used to erect a bulwark against separation, loss, and death. The process of geographic detachment triggers a restitutional process of reattachment.

The specific form which the compulsion to repeat takes among immigrants—distant and local alike—is the formation of an "identity of perceptions" (Freud 1900) between past and present based upon the investment of the host environment with the burden of transitional object-relatedness (Winnicott 1953; Modell 1963). This can be a pervasive process or a focal one, part conscious or entirely unconscious in motivation. The goals include restaging the past with the hope of doing better this time around, denying and making restitution for separations in the very act of separation, annihilating or reversing linear time by recreating the past in the present (even when one is overtly fleeing the past, as in political revolutions), shoring up one's painful sense of incompleteness by erecting buttresses of the self in social-symbolic reality, and splitting off or repressing aggression which one fears has harmed if not caused the loss of the original objects and their symbolic world. In a phrase, the immigrant's quest, often with medical complicity, is to reestablish the broken or severed tie with the original object and symbolic object world.

While physical separation often acutely precipitates the onset of symptoms and the search for health care, the experience of emotional separation is the *chronic* underlying factor. Just as Lesse (1974) has argued that chronic functional somatic disturbances successfully mask depression, likewise I suggest that a preoccupation by physician and patient alike with external conditions of migration, settlement, occupation, and support networks can mask separation difficulties. By investing one's "whoness" with "whereness," and deriving one's sense of identity from a sense of place, one's new identity, like the old, becomes virtually context-dependent.

Context loss is experienced as though it were object loss.

One aborts the process of grieving for the old by frantically trying to replace it with the new. Dynamically, the "new" becomes what Volkan calls a "linking object" an externalized representation of the lost or dead as though it were still available (1972). Like the familiar "replacement child," the *replacement object world* preserves the original ambivalent tie in the present. The loss of context is experienced as a deprivation to be overcome by maintaining ties with the old and familiar and by recapitulating a familial environment out of the material of the strange. One can on an individual basis as much as on a group basis establish what might be called a permanent diaspora or refugee identity (see Loizos 1982), in which a perpetual commemoration of the lost identity becomes the basis for the current one.

Resettlement, then, both draws upon ego strengths and revives erstwhile vulnerabilities. It is a literally unsettling experience which prompts a reresolution of *all* developmental issues. Just as Blos (1962) defines adolescence as a "second individuation crisis," we may likewise, and with psychodynamic aptness, refer to the emigration-immigration experience as yet a third individuation crisis, in which the boundaries of the self must once again be renegotiated.

Cultural Therapy

Patients coming to the Family Medicine Clinic with symptoms and sequelae related to migration, separation, and loss tend to receive from their physicians a matrix of what might be called "culturally appropriate" or "culturally expectable" treatment. This includes some combination of the following modalities: (1) supportive counseling; (2) antidepressive medication therapy, often in combination with antianxiety medication; (3) medication specific to functional organ disturbances; (4) consultation with or referral to a wide spectrum of community social agencies, self-help groups, voluntary associations (churches, fraternal lodges, etc.); (5) counseling strategies to help the patient develop a personal "support system" in the host community; (6) return visits to reassess psychosomatic-family-social-occupational status and the effectiveness of medication regimens. One might call this therapy a form of replacement therapy: one replaces in the patient an idiosyncratic and disturbing symptom with a conventional and reassuring one (see Devereux 1980:17–18).

Initially I not only supported this seemingly holistic or comprehensive approach in Family Medicine residency training clinics at which I taught but supervised the process as well. Over time, however, I came to discover from the patients themselves—who are always our best teachers, if but we listen—that prescriptions of support, medication, and a multitude of community "linkages" and "networks" (two of the current buzz words) were more palliatives than bona fide solutions to the problem.

As the two case studies that follow suggest, this "cultural" therapy was not only shallow and simplistic but deceptively misleading, for it failed to address the ambivalence which these patients held toward the old and the new alike, expressed in the very urgency of getting one's "support system" in order. Clinically, although I did not begin this venture in applied anthropology to vindicate psychoanalytic theory, such confirmation was soon forthcoming. As Volkan summarizes: "The most widely accepted psychoanalytic view of the grief process takes into consideration drive investment in the representation of the dead, and an unconscious and eventually successful struggle to loosen the ties to this representation in piecemeal fashion" (1981:18). To recognize this, however, one first had to inquire into the *meaning* to patients of "support," "family," "linkages," and the like, not simply to prescribe them. "Support," etc. came to be seen as less the solution than a patching up of old hurts by new idealizations that only postponed the feelings of emotional separateness.

Lamentably, the official biomedical model is often congruent if not identical with the depressed internal immigrant's "folk" model of disease etiology and treatment. As a result, hypochondriasis, somaticization, and depression proper are treated by both as an "it" rather than as a disturbed aspect of the self. The "it" is either organic or external, a defective factor of the body or of the environment. In a cultural *folie à deux*, clinician and patient collude in depersonalizing the disorder, making it exclusively into an object of organic concern and/or social support *in order* to avert painful subjective meanings for doctor and patient alike. In a sense, doctor and patient (together with surrounding culture) share a somatic and environmentalist delusion about the nature and thereby the treatment for the spectrum of symptoms associated with uprooting, relocation, and resettlement. Therapeutically, clinicians appear overeager to "prescribe" reattachments for the distress of separation and loss rather than explore with their patients the inner representations of their attachments (intrapsychic and interpersonal) that had led to the yearning for a sense of community. During the course of therapy, the surfacing of aggression toward the objects of one's devotion—past and present—provided the initial and sustained cue that all was not well with this cultural therapy. It was at this point that I came to realize that resocialization and social control—universal components of therapy—were not the solution but a defense against grief and therefore a new problem superimposed on the original. Two case studies illustrate the process of discovery and therapy.

Case 1

Amanda Mooring is a 26-year-old married white female with an 18-month-old male child. She came to the Family Medicine Clinic on her first visit complaining of depression of approximately two years' duration. She complained of frequent crying spells, loss of appetite for regular meals, the desire for binge eating of sweets, difficulty in sleeping, and loss of interest in sexual intercourse. Physically she was an "obese" white female (221 lb, 5'4") who was neatly dressed in jeans and a cotton blouse. She sat with her shoulders slumped, and when the family physician asked what he could do for her she began to cry. She cried through most of her subsequent interview.

She dates the onset of her illness to approximately two years previously, when she moved from a large city to a small town in Oklahoma following her marriage. Although she had previously had several friends, after her move she felt "stranded" in a town without friends. At the time of her clinic visit, she was adjusting to another move to a new town after her husband's transfer in his job. She had been living in the second new town for eight months. Despite her hopes for relief, she had still found no outside friends. She had become more depressed when she was unable to change her lifestyle significantly.

In subsequent clinic visits, Amanda reported that her depression was not alleviated by medications such as Elavil. She stated that it was only when she had moved that she had begun to notice her feelings of insecurity and rejection. She described the new community as one composed of "clicks" that were unwilling to accept her and her husband as friends. She experienced initial difficulties in finding employment as rejections. Amanda also felt that her mother-in-law's attitude of bitterness was in part due to the fact that she had been taken by her father-in-law to a different region in Oklahoma where she had been isolated from her friends and family. Amanda feared the same pattern would happen to her as well. The more she sought acceptance by people other than her husband, the more she experienced herself as rejected.

Some of Amanda's early crying episodes during conversations at the clinic occurred as she related situations that had made her feel angry. She resented some of the burden of her household obligations that she wished her husband would share with her. Over a period of six months, however, Amanda made remarkable progress by using a combination of medication that better regulated her sleep, and by consultation. The clinic personnel who were consulting with her attempted to improve Amanda's self-confidence, esteem, and sense of self-worth. Over time she was crying less frequently than before and was beginning to draw boundaries in coping with her families. She became more firm in delegating certain chores to her husband, yet was more accepting of the fact that he is "not perfect." The couple seemed to communicate better with each other over time. She stated that she would be glad to have her mother-in-law come to their home for a visit, but would not permit herself to be bothered by the older woman's eccentricities. Amanda sought the advice of her parents regarding the purchase of a car, but was considering an option different from the ones her parents had proposed.

On her own initiative, Amanda became a member of Overeaters Anonymous in the town in which she now lived. She began to be satisfied that she was building adequate friendships from this group. She also managed a paper route by herself, thereby providing more income for the family. In her last consultation at the clinic she no longer complained of depression and actually expressed a feeling of confidence in herself. Her husband had also told her that he noticed she is "coping" much better and is no longer "losing control and crying all the time." She reports that her acquaintances in Overeaters Anonymous now call her on the phone about organizational matters as well as "things that friends would talk about." She seems quite pleased with her progress.

Comment

In its *outer* form this case differs from the more expected pattern of moving from rural to urban (although in terms of sheer numbers and prevalence, many of the in-migrants to and within Oklahoma in search of work in the oilfields come to small-town settings from cities in or out of state). Yet for Amanda the consequences were the same, for she had lived within the city as though it were a closed, intimate, "rural" network that had given her the security of home.

Work with Amanda initially concentrated on the relationship between her depression and her many changed social circumstances. Only gradually did we come to "take into account the repercussion in the mind of happenings in the external world rather than the happenings *per se*" (Volkan 1981:19). That is, we came to explore with her how her representational world mediated her experience of those circumstances. Her "stresses" lay not so much in the events themselves as in their emotional significance for her.

A very giving, generous person who feared that the expression of anger would lead to the alienation of affection and thereby the loss of her protective social cocoon, Amanda first came to resent others for depriving her of the self she could not have. In her discovery and "owning" of her anger toward them, she began to feel that she possessed and had a right to possess a distinct self that would not be destroyed by others' anger. For her, harmony, consensus, and being the "good wife" had all been maneuvers to deny and undo the aggression which would bring harm to them and thereby incur their wrath and in turn make her *feel* separate from others. Aggression became a force of differentiation, leading to a period of grieving for her lost erstwhile "perfection" and an openness to new types of relationships. Her sense of isolation needed no longer to be overcome by filling it with friends—and food.

Only at the end of treatment did she seriously begin dieting; by then she no longer needed to overfeed herself for what others might withhold or deprive her in love. Early in treatment she dejectedly protested her husband's taunts about her size: "I need to begin to like myself before I start thinking about what I'm going to do with my body." I commented, "There must be a lot about yourself that you dislike," whereupon she wept and subsequently began to link words, feelings, and memories whose connection she had heretofore resisted. This marked a turning point in her treatment, for she began to mourn her own imperfectibility, for the lost perfection of others, and for her loss of unity with them. Her nonverbal anger began to be verbalized as she consciously could feel herself to be separate from others, their ministrations and deprivations. Approval from others—her husband, mother-in-law, church groups—no longer served as the measure of her own self-approval. Having achieved a differentiation of self- from object representations, she proceeded to integrate a sense of self and a sense of environment which no longer needed to allocate to the environment reparative functions of the self. She no longer had need of the "water" to sustain the "fish."

Case 2

Chuck Jones is a 25-year-old white male who was originally seen at the Family Medicine Clinic for complaints of restlessness, insomnia, and low back pain of three weeks duration. The initial physical examination by the family physician revealed a mildly obese, anxious-appearing white male whose general examination was within normal limits. He was treated with a prescription of Librium. Three months later he was advised that he would need to be seen at the clinic again before his medication would continue to be refilled.

During his second visit the patient complained of feeling very agitated and uptight. He reported no problems at home and seemed most agitated by his job as a traveling salesman, though he had no desire to quit his job and stated that he enjoyed it. During his discussion with the family physician Mr. Jones was sweating profusely from his forehead, constantly readjusting his tie, and consistently shook his legs, occasionally kicking the exam table. The clinician talked at length about the need to find other avenues aside from use of medication to relax and control his anxiety. An attempt was made to minimize his use of medications, and arrangements were made for him to enter a biofeedback and relaxation program at the local hospital.

Four days later Mr. Jones returned to the clinic for a follow-up visit. He reported that the biofeedback was helpful but that his medication, Vistaril, was ineffectual. He related past episodes in which he had experienced derealization and depersonalization (e.g., appearing as an outsider looking at himself) and expressed fear that without the aid of Valium or Librium these feelings would return. Yet he expressed fear that he would become dependent on medications and desired psychological help. It was at this point that the clinic consultant was asked to join the physician in seeing this patient for psychosocial consultation.

Chuck's history revealed that he was from Chicago, Illinois, and had moved to Oklahoma approximately one year before. He was the second of five siblings and the oldest son. Since Chuck was the first male child, he felt as if his father regarded him as "a model son who would follow in his father's footsteps and also become an electrical-supply salesman like his father." He was expected to be his father's model for the other siblings. Chuck had been married to Kathy just over a year before, and they had no children at this time.

Chuck seemed very disturbed over guilt feelings about use

of drugs such as acid, psilocybin, and marijuana primarily during the time that he was in high school. He felt that he had let his father down and raised the specter of losing his father's love, by "experimenting with drugs in the past." His eyes became tearful while discussing his feelings of guilt. He seemed obsessed with control of his feelings now, and with his fear of losing control of his feelings. An obsessional, any threat of experiencing anger heightened his anxiety.

As the consultations progressed, it became apparent that Chuck could maintain himself without the use of Librium or Valium as long as he made frequent appointments for consultations. He seemed to progress even further when his wife, Kathy, began to join the consultations. With time he developed a trust and confidence in Kathy which allowed him to discuss his feelings with her, rather than at the clinic as often. Their relationship as a couple seemed to grow considerably.

It became apparent that Chuck and Kathy came to Oklahoma to start a life of their own without the added pressures of strong family expectations and "domineering" fathers. However, moving from Chicago to Oklahoma presented a cultural shock to both Chuck and Kathy. They had difficulty making friends in their new hometown. Chuck's father remains a national figure among electrical suppliers, a reputation which accompanied the son to Oklahoma. Coming to the Sun Belt to advance on his merit, he found himself constantly greeted and complimented as "Jones's son," which made him feel even more entrapped as "daddy's boy"—a term he used with derision.

When Chuck and Kathy turned their feelings back to their homes of origin, their unresolved sense of ambiguity was reignited as in Chuck's experience of love and resentment toward his father and his troubled recollections of his early experience with drug dependency. As the couple attempted to make Oklahoma their own home, and Kathy became pregnant with their first child, Chuck had difficulty "maintaining control" over his feelings about drug need and abuse, his father, and the fact that they felt like "misplaced persons" in a small Oklahoma town. He "kicked himself" for allowing his father to persuade them to purchase a small, dilapidated house in need of much repair (which Chuck engaged in singlehandedly) over a larger, newer house they had preferred. He proceeded to explore how he was able to succumb repeatedly to his father's intimidations and became angry both with himself and with his father for doing so. With some difficulty his idealization of his father began to diminish as his anger toward his father increased. As he allowed himself to clarify these feelings, he was also better able to differentiate his need to please his father from his need to be free of comparison with his father.

Chuck and Kathy last visited the clinic before a move to another state. Chuck had accepted a new job helping two other associates open their own electrical-supply company. He felt that this step was based on his own merits and achievements and had been gained through his own hard work. The couple felt much less "misplaced" in their chosen home and tended to feel more "misplaced" in their homes of origin. They expressed confidence in their ability to build their own business and family for the future without fears of loss of control or drug dependency. Chuck embarked on his new destination with the feeling of being more a man and less his father's boy. Infrequently haunted by his internalized past—and capable of examining such visitations when they do occur—he was better capable of choosing his future.

Comment

Chuck set out with his wife westward from Chicago to strike out on his (and their) own, only to follow so closely in his father's footsteps that he was haunted by his omnipresent shadow. Struggling desperately to be his own man, he found himself confirmed at every turn as his father's boy. For him, "drugs"—that widespread vehicle of the late 1960s and early 1970s for instantly vanquishing vexatious reality—marked his first break with his father, for which rebellious wish he subsequently atoned and against which atoning he rebelled. In Oklahoma he rebuilt piecemeal his emotional environment of origin. He was kept in check by his dread of loss of control and by flashbacks which reactivated his father's now-internalized disapproval.

Rather than further blunt his affects with officially sanctioned medication, therapy attempted to help him examine those frightening affects and their underlying object cathexes. Behind the cultural idolatry lay an assortment of frightening introjects of the Primal Father that oscillated with an identification with the aggressor and the hallucination of his Stern Judgment. Able consciously only to love—and obey—his father, he was able to learn that he also hated him and that the hate murdered neither himself nor his father. The more he was able to achieve a differentiation from the father imago and gradually to accept the ambivalence of oedipal sonhood, the more he was able to take leave of those symbolic objects that had expressed and confirmed his inner status as "misplaced person." Stated differently, once these outer trappings no longer symbolized his inner self, they were relinquished in favor of symbols that now represented a more integrated and differentiated self. Treatment avoided the temptations of "occupation counseling" or advising on "how to choose a home" and explored with Chuck the meanings of work and home, etc., so that, less driven by unconscious conflict, he could more freely choose his future. That private and shared "culture"—from occupational to residential choice—served as symbolic "linking objects" (Volkan 1972, 1981) was a mutual discovery over the course of two years' work together.

In certain features, these two cases could not be more divergent. Chuck is clearly an obsessional character organization, while Amanda is a depressive. Chuck's migration was from a leading North American metropolis to a mid-western city which retains many rural features; Amanda, on the other hand, moved from a mid-western city to a small, provincial town. Yet the intrapsychic function of both their symptom complexes was identical: to preserve a tie with the past, to deny and reverse the losses that had taken place, to set up outside the self a cultural world of "linking objects" (Volkan 1972, 1981) that would shore up the inner denial, repression, and splitting system. The course of therapy for both helped them examine what was represented in the "cultural" material, to examine the ties and affects that underlay their "transference" to these symbolic objects, and finally to *loosen* (the exact opposite of cultural "support" and "replacement" therapy) those symbolic ties and internal representations that had kept them in emotional bondage. (For additional case material see Stein 1983a, 1985c.)

The Contemporary Nostalgia Ethos

There is considerable cultural legitimacy in short-circuiting the painful work of mourning and the emotional separation to which it leads. What might be called the contemporary nostalgia ethos (Stein 1974b, 1979; Stein and Hill 1977a) acts as a powerful countervailing—and I might add, countertherapeutic—force in its sentimentalizing of the past as a way of compartmentalizing ambivalence. One thinks, for instance, of the popularity of the television serials "The Waltons" and "Little House on the Prairie," both of which celebrate the putative togetherness, warmth, and harmony of bygone days. Since the late 1970s the publication and television serialization of Alex Haley's *Roots* has spawned widespread interest and activity in genealogical search into one's presumably more noble and conflict-free ancestral past. And in the summer of 1982, Stephen Spielberg's film *E.T., The Extra-Terrestrial*, became a box-office triumph, as audiences accompanied the lovable creature, mistakenly abandoned by his spaceship, in his (and our) search for "Home."

American culture now teems with alternative, often competing, attempts to revitalize if not replace the family. In the early 1980s legislation appeared before the U.S. Congress to strengthen the traditional patriarchal family. The family-therapy and family-medicine movements have the family as their unit and focus of treatment. The Unification Church promotes itself as "the one true family." One recalls that the People's Temple, which culminated with the mass suicide of 911 persons in November 1978, saw itself as a family in which, quite literally, death was the preferable alternative to a disruption in familial togetherness. "The family," then, is not merely a sociological unit; it has become an ideology *about* identity and affiliation. Contemporary ideology about roots and ties makes the task of separation all the more difficult to achieve, since it represents what many are powerfully defending themselves against.

One of the little-examined dangers of the nostalgia ethos, with its illusion of one-big-happy-reunited-family, is that all aggression which might threaten to disrupt the unbroken harmony and unity is displaced and projected onto convenient target individuals or groups which come to embody all one's own disavowed "badness." As with witchcraft beliefs universally (see Kluckhohn 1944), the intactness of the self or group is attained and preserved by accusing those outside one's self- or group boundaries of one's unconscionable wishes. The sense of imminent danger from without is essential to the preservation of security from within. The two case studies discussed above abundantly illustrate that the achievement of emotional separation among two "internal migrants" was facilitated by their acknowledgment of previously disavowed anger toward current and past persons from whom they had previously split off all hostility and which split had led to the search for a perfection in new environments.

This chapter would lead to the conclusion that any radical distinction between voluntary and involuntary uprooting must be questioned as spurious, for it attends exclusively to outer circumstances. Nor does this distinction take into account the interdependence between, say, invaders and invaded, conquerors and conquered, one which may come to last for centuries. Nor, moreover, does it consider the dynamics of the invaders or usurpers, who for their own psychohistoric reasons may be reversing defeat into victory (see Freud 1920) by turning others out rather than being turned out at the mercy of others. Often, too, outer invaders or colonizers come to bear the conscious brunt of the displaced familial symbolization of those invaded or colonized. For those who flee in search of a new homeland or neighborhood, what is left behind comes to symbolize the "perfect" mother-infant symbiosis, hotly defended even—or especially—at a remote distance lest reality interfere with idealization. In the wake of individual and collective expulsions and relocations alike spring up cults which would reclaim or revitalize the past by destroying time (see La Barre 1971, 1972). Like individual "linking objects," perpetual collective memorials to historical hurt and disaster have the shared psychological purpose of "sealing over" deeper issues that *must not* be remembered. In many respects "public" is a massive defense against "private" (see deMause 1982a; Stein 1983b).

The implications for health planning or political planning are stern for would-be uprooters of others and self-uprooters alike: to ignore the unconscious dynamics of the process is to sow the wind and reap the whirlwind. Or, in the stinging words of Shakespeare's Shylock in *The Merchant of Venice*, "The villainy you teach me I will execute; and it shall go hard but I will better the instruction" (act 3, scene 1). One thinks immediately of the vengeance of the counteroedipal superego within conquerors and revolutionaries and the revenge-ethos of displaced, disinherited refugees who now vow to usurp the usurpers by asserting their "natural," "national," or "human" rights.

Metapsychological Reflections on Migration and Culture

This chapter, which began with an inquiry into meanings attached to *migrations in space*, concludes with the dawning awareness that the subject matter has all along been *migrations in time*. It is into geographic, hence cultural, "space" that the burden of generational and intrapsychic "space" is displaced, projected, and played out. Put another way, space is the stage on which the dramas of time are enacted.

For many—even for whole groups—culture is a bulwark of the inability to mourn. It enshrines the denial of linear, biologic time. Through culture we give form to our dread. In culture we give our anxiety over death, loss and separation an abundance of objects, animate and inanimate. We distract ourselves by fashioning symbolic containers for that anxiety, by affixing wished-for time in space. Time, we command, *must* be cyclic, reversible, condensible—in a word, *manipulable*—if wish is to prevail. Even the colossal triumph of the acceptance of linear time is not exempt from distortion if not domination by wish. For the reality of biological inexorability can readily be overshadowed by the fantasy of continuous, inevitable progress. The dreamtime of the eternal past and the anticipated perfection of utopian futurism are alike great refusals to acknowledge the Reality Principle. Either way, death is swallowed up in victory, as the nostalgic past comes closely to resemble the future millennium. The universe may well oscillate, be in steady state, or be the product of a "big bang" long ago—such are our currently competing cosmologies,—but all metazoan life requires death. Our cosmologies merely bargain away what we already know. In culture one not only acquires personal immortality but purchases the immortality of those from whom he cannot separate. "Group" as an entity in and of itself transcends as it links the living, the dead, and yet unborn. Culture thus conceived is the collective magical extortion of time: "Let there be," proclaims the oral omnipotence of words, "And there was. . . ."

In large measure culture everywhere is a living cemetery that binds the living to those whose memories must not be allowed to wane. Symbols of projective and displacive culture are monuments to failed separation. The very language of "culture" is often intended—by natives, nativists, and anthropologists alike—to override the language of "biology." Cultural ideology writes its own "human biology." Through culture one externalizes in others and in physical nature those functions and *parts of the self* and *representations of early relationships* which, because of ambivalence and primitive splitting, one could not fully integrate and internalize. Much of what we speak facilely and approvingly as "cultural continuity" is heir to the incompleteness of internalization and representational differentiation. Likewise, in socialization or child rearing, one transmits through projective identification to the next generation as tasks, values and loyalties those questions which one is forbidden to pose, and the answers which one is forbidden to question. These become "the sacred." One psychic purpose or function of Durkheimian "collective representations" is to prevent the consciousness of individual differentiation. In social consensus we think like others to avoid the aloneness of thinking for oneself. Dare we, however, speculate even further that the very structure of society may be *over*determined by unresolved mourning and separation? Here I am thinking specifically of unilineality, extended families, multiple mothering, ancestor worship, closed corporate communities, and other forms by which sentiment is institutionalized into social form.

In this chapter "culture" not so much denotes an independent variable or context to which people adapt as it constitutes a symbolic or representational system that is heir to the inner "representational world." Stolorow and Atwood define the latter as "a kind of pre-reflective background into which the events of the person's life are continuously assimilated on the dimensions of which his experiences continuously take form" (1979:43). The representational world is the inner template from which outer meanings are formed (see Stein 1983e). "Culture," or, more generically, "group," here comes to be the cognitive-affective derivative of the inner representational world. The social construction of reality (the framework of two decades of symbolic interactionist writing) lives out these inner premises. Since culture is used to represent and to replay the vicissitudes of early object relations, any threat of "culture loss" is experienced as renewed separation and object loss.

In the microcosm of psychoanalysis and psychoanalytic psychotherapy one commonly finds resistance to insight to be rooted in a fear of loss of one's identifications; the analyst or therapist comes projectively to be accused of trying to deprive the patient of his or her values, family, and culture. Writing of psychotherapy with Irish-Americans, Spiegel writes illuminatingly:

While it is perfectly true that one aspect of the Irish-American patient's resistance is associated with the Subjugation-to-nature value position, this is by no means the whole story. The value orientation accounts for the patient's resignation, his inability to conceive of the possibility of change, in the cognitive area. A real change within the personality has not been in his experience, and he just doesn't see that it is possible. However, there is an emotional as well as a cognitive side to this kind of resistance. On the emotional side it is associated with the identification with the angry, critical parents. The attachment to the internalized parental images is intensely ambivalent and masochistically satisfying. The treasuring of the sense of sin is, from one point of view, a conscious derivative of the highly libidinal, unconscious cathexis of the internalized, scolding parents. In addition, the scolding parent within becomes a tender forgiving parent whenever a confession takes place. The alternation between sinning and confessing is necessary to the maintenance of the internal, libidinal dynamics. Furthermore, sinning or the alerting of the sense of sin in the external object is the primary way of getting the object's attention.

These considerations are directly pertinent to the transference problem in the management of such a patient. It is not only that the patient remains cognitively unaware of the possibility of change. In addition he has no wish to change in the direction which the therapist expects him to. Giving up the crushing sense of sin means, essentially, renouncing the relation with the internalized parents. [1971:333]

Culture, one might say, is the final bastion of immortality's protest. Does not culture transcend the self? Is it not superorganic? Is not the whole greater than the sum of its parts— *must* it not be so? Since one of the principal, if not the dominant, purposes of culture is to rectify (make restitution for) the vulnerabilities and pains of childhood, to be deprived of one's culture through migration or otherwise is to be exposed to those ineffable dangers all over again. As a defense against the revival of painful associations, one constructs social and symbolic networks of "associations" which once again gloss over the past. Myth triumphs over memory: or, myth is the only acceptable form of remembering.

Just as uncompleted mourning places a "seal over" (Volkan 1981:6) the underlying pathology, likewise does culture place yet another seal over the process of mourning. A paramount, yet little discussed, function of culture as a representational system becomes that of serving as a "living memorial" (Volkan 1981:6) to the relationship with the dead or lost object from whom separation has taken place. In culture, symbolic ties are institutionalized and ritualized not to loosen them—as would be the case in the work of mourning (Freud 1915)—but to preserve them, indeed, to create and sustain the illusion and conviction that no loss has taken place, or in the least to diminish the pain and reality of the loss. This further illustrates the metapsychological point that, in the wake of separation, loss, and death we not only seek to preserve our relationship by identifying with an internalized representation; we also create *externalized representations,* idiosyncratic or shared, that serve the same purpose but in a different domain of life. Ritual and symbol tend to "confirm" unconscious wish, since they take place in the "reality" of sensate experience and action (see La Barre 1972, 1975). Ritual and symbol are to consciousness what the manifest content is to dreaming, and both are followed and further "sealed over" by secondary elaboration. Becoming the measure of reality, culture thereby substitutes illusion for reality, since "it" is more compelling.

We are loath to "harrow the house of the dead" (W. H. Auden), but would enshrine it as a tradition and enshroud it in mystery. As *process,* culture is symbolic remembering (and forgetting); as *structure,* culture is the prescription of what shall be remembered (and forgotten). The burden of preserving representations of the dead and lost cannot be assumed by a single generation alone but becomes that of each new generation: in view of the weight of this process, to speak of it as "child rearing" or "socialization" is virtually euphemism. Culture-appropriate child rearing, like culture-appropriate healing or curing rites, guarantees that problems will be perpetuated *through* the next generation; through projective identification they guarantee loyalty and ensure that the problems will not be solved. How could they, since to solve them is to "kill"—at least in fantasy—the inner and exteriorized representations of those who are deemed necessary to life, survival itself.

Migration undermines those fragile private and collective certainties to which we adhere about the human condition. It is for many a crisis that precipitates an ardent quest to reaffirm old inner representations in new contexts. Therapy worthy of the name does not collude with the patient's wish to fashion new lies for old but assists him or her in the conscious acceptance of a reality that must have already intimated itself to him or her.

Let there be no mistake about it: in therapy, too, one undertakes yet another migration with its own threat of deracination. But the common accusation that the therapist "deprives" the patient of his beliefs or culture is a projection of the accuser's own ambivalence toward sacred tradition. In the painful odyssey of therapy the therapist lends his or her allegiance to help the patient understand those allegiances of his or her own. Through the transference the patient recapitulates history and is thereby released from further recapitulating history. The very premise of nativism is spurious cure through historical falsification; the very premise of authentic therapy is cure through the uncovering of the past. Viewed in terms of the latter, migration becomes more a matter of opened alternatives and less a matter of compulsive reenactment of the past.

CHAPTER 3

Russian Nationalism and the Divided Soul of the Westernizers and Slavophiles

It is the fate of rebels to found new orthodoxies.
    —Bertrand Russell, "The Psychoanalyst's Nightmare" (1934)

Generally it is infinitely better to have no history than to keep up in the people the inclination to falsehood. It is a wrong piety to wish to cover up the error of our forefathers; the only means of honoring the memory of our fathers consists of abandoning their mistakes.
    —Ernest Denis, *La Bohème depuis la Montagne-Blanche* (1931)

Our age abounds in nationalist sentiments and movements. The United States under the leadership of President Ronald Reagan vows to get tough and restore its pride at home and its muscle around the world. Iranian nationalism under its Shi'a Islamic leader the Ayatollah Ruhollah Khomeini has demonstrated to the world the extent to which the eruption of rage and the mobilization of violence can serve to coalesce a frightened and threatened group identity. Such dynamics were seen earlier this century in German national socialism and in the multiple nationalisms that collided in World War I.

Nationalism plays out the psychogeography of the integrity and security of boundaries: linguistic, literary, musical, political. All may see where "we" end and where "they" begin, what is included inside "our" identity and what is excluded if not expelled outside into "their" identity. The historically earlier "watch on the Rhine" has given way to national strife over what is to be Greek or Turkish on Cyprus; what territory and which people are to be included in the state of Israel and how far that state should extend; whether Israelis, Palestinian Arabs, and Arab states will acknowledge the existence of

Israel and whether Israel will recognize the Palestinians; and whether the United States and the Soviet Union will take their quest for secure national boundaries into outer space. In this chapter I explore the chronic problem of the identity boundary of historic Russia—one that our modern world has both inherited and intensified.

In his review of Boyd Shafer's *Faces of Nationalism*, Louis L. Snyder notes that nationalism is "essentially a historical force based on psychological motivations" (1974:287). My analysis of Russian nationalism accepts this premise, and it is the point of departure. Through the application of the comparative-historical method and cross-cultural comparison, this formulation can be further tested. Expanding Snyder's phrase, the questions to be posed are: How does nationalism develop as a historical force? What are the conditions under which the psychological motivations that underlie nationalism develop? And how does nationalism as an identity and an ideology congeal into a "persistent cultural system"? (see Spicer 1971). These questions direct our inquiry not only to chronologically antecedent but to necessary and sufficient conditions that precipitate nationalism as a response.

Russian nationalism is discussed at several interrelated levels of analysis. The ideology and polity of the Slavophiles and Westernizers are explored in terms of the relation between Russia and Western Europe. On this scale the system of reference for Russian nationalism is the European community, with Russia constituting one *culture* within the wider *social-structural* system. Russia has always dwelt on the excluded and self-isolated periphery of European society and culture, if not "beyond the pale," yet playing a vital role in European history. The nature of this alienation is further explored through the eyes of the Slavophiles and Westernizers who were symptomatic of the chronic cultural stress, and whose solutions attempted to overcome this alienation (see Anderson 1971; Blum 1961; Gorer and Rickman 1962; Kohn 1960; Lampert 1965; Malia 1961; Muller 1957; Ruud 1974; Shafer 1954; Stein 1976).

If the dialectical relationship (in the generic sense of a struggle between opposing ideologies rather than in the narrower, Marxist sense of class conflict) between the Slavophiles and the Westernizers can be viewed as a microcosm of the wider international conflict, then an exploration of individual lives within these two movements should, at the level of analysis of the person, also be a microcosm of this same condition. I suggest that the lives and works of Alexander Herzen, Alexei Homyakov, and Fëdor Dostoevski (see Freud 1928: 177–94)—the three individuals to be discussed briefly here— articulate and refract the struggle between the Slavophiles and Westernizers, between "fathers and sons," between the Russian East and the European West, and so forth. Perspectives drawn from structural anthropology, social psychology, sociology, and psychoanalysis will delineate the relationships between these levels, not "reducing" history (and historiography) to something else but translating the flow of events into a *structured process*. Here I stress, with reference to both individuals and groups, what Erik Erikson (1968:309) has called the *complementarity of identity and ideology*, and the *complementarity of history and life history*, as they codefine one another. The Slavophiles and Westernizers, including Herzen, Homyakov, and Dostoevski, are seen as *prototypic* of their era—and, with hindsight, we can also say "prophetic" as well—and can be approached as culture-historic texts whose analysis illumines the context in which they are embedded.

"Barbarous" Russia and "Civilized" Europe: A Brief Family History and the Roots of Identity Conflict

Let me state axiomatically what I have to demonstrate: that posteighteenth-century Russian nationalism is unthinkable apart from the ambivalent relationship between Russia and the West and is in fact an attempt to resolve that ambivalence by radically restructuring the perceptual, cognitive, affective, and behavioral "set" or pattern. In a review essay on prerevolutionary Russian nationalism, Charles Ruud notes that there is "substantial agreement [among scholars] that a general sense of lagging behind the West was the principal stimulus and shaper of nationalism in the late eighteenth and nineteenth centuries" (1974:276) and that the Russian nationalist response "still contained an unacknowledged feeling of Russia's backwardness" (1974:278). A substratum of inferiority underlay the overcompensatory protest of superiority. In 1829 the philosopher Chaadayev lamented Russia's alienation from Europe in a statement that reflects—from the viewpoint of a "Westernizer"—that deep tension between the conspiratorial autocracy of what Lenin later called "our Asiatic and barbarous land" (quoted in Muller 1957:303) and the progress and civilization of a Europe from which Russia had been isolated both out of *fate* (the Byzantine legacy, the invading hordes from the East, the centuries of attack from the West) and *choice* (in defiant reaction to the judgment of the West that Russia was indeed Asiatic and barbarous):

We have lived, as it were, outside of history, and have remained untouched by the universal education of the human race. . . . Isolated from the world, we have given or taught nothing to the world; we have added no thoughts to the sum of human ideas; we have in no way collaborated in the progress of reason and we have disfigured everything that penetrated to us from this progress [Chaadayev, quoted in Muller 1957:292]

Against this profound self-hate, self-doubt, and shame the "Slavophile" nationalists from Plavilshchikov to Karamzin, from Dostoevski to Solzhenitzyn, counterposed Russian self-aggrandizement, mission, and pride as virtues—though in the form of passive-aggressive Russian piety and humility (which in turn held in check but were frequently overcome by monumental ventings of fury).

In this chapter, rather than emphasize the ideological differences between the Westernizers and Russian Slavophiles, I explore the circumstances that produced these two opposing ideologies and the dialectical relationship between groups traditionally thought to be opposites. Stated differently, I explore the *deep structural* process of *opposition* that has generated the *surface structural* field of antinomies (cf. Lévi-Strauss 1963, 1968; Porshnev 1973; Spicer 1971; Stein 1975b). I also suggest that this dialectic lies at the heart of nationalistic movements in general and that the nationalist *resolution* of this conflict consists of a *systematic* set of *reversals* or *inversions*—for example, from doubt to absolute certainty, from ambivalence to a radical separation of categories of loved and hated objects, from shame to pride. Nothing can remain blurred; everything is subsumed under the rule of "either-or." Here my emphasis is not exclusively on the internal dynamics of the "conversion" experience but on the relationship between the resolution and the conflict (both within and without) which requires resolution.

Bogdan Raditsa writes:

The tormented efforts of the Russians and Slavs to find and express themselves stemmed basically from their encounters with the West . . . under the influence of German romantic thought, the Russian and Slav intelligentsia tried passionately to participate in the great events of the nineteenth century. The multiform crisis of that century spurred the rise of nationalism throughout the Slavic world. To this same period we can date the origin of a profound, and still unresolved, conflict or spiritual dilemma between Slavophiles and the West. . . . Which way, then, was the intelligentsia to turn? Toward the West or back to Russia? Both ways seemed beset with contradiction and complexity. [1967:1082–83]

The resolution consisted of a tortuous vacillation between "total rejection of the West" and "a nostalgia for the West" (Raditsa 1967:1083). So long as the dialectic persists between Russia—or the Soviet Union—and the West, all efforts at resolution will be abortive, no matter how "decisive" or "permanent" their appearance.

Throughout the eighteenth and nineteenth centuries Russia symbolized and personified the atavistic, autocratic, conservative, and repressive reactionary giant to the East. Western Europe defined itself according to a set of binary opposites in which Russia represented what the West was not. Within the European stratification system of social-status hierarchy, the West was on top, and the East was on the bottom (the internal *Western* stratification system later became the basis for nationalist differentiation within the West). So long as both "sides" accepted this ordering, Russia's self-image was negative, and could be changed by the repudiation of Russian culture or by the repudiation of the Western European system of valuation.

At first glance the former led to the lineage from Decembrism through Herzen to Lenin, that is, the Westernizers; the latter led to the lineage from "official nationalism" through Dostoevski to Stalinist Soviet Russification, that is, the Slavophiles. That this division into ideological lineages oversimplifies reality is discussed below. Here note, however, that the Slavophile ideology that repudiated the West as the basis or measure of self-evaluation nevertheless utilized the same criteria for mutual comparison: only now the valence or sign was changed, and what was formerly positive was now negative, and conversely. The following list of contrast pairs thus summarizes an image mutually shared by West and East, and in the East by both Westernizers and Slavophiles.

West European Self-Image	*Russian Self-Image*
Civilized	Uncivilized
Advanced	Backward
Progressive	Reactionary
Enlightened	Fanatically religious
Mannered, polite	Course, uncouth
Democratic, egalitarian	Autocratic, despotic
Rational	Mystical
Stable	Unstable, uncontrollable
Peaceful	Violent
Urban	Rural
Bourgeois, urbane, aristocratic	Rustic, peasantry
Westernized (Rome etc.)	Easternized (Byzantium, Tatars, etc.)

"Mutually shared," however, can be a deceptive notion, since we are talking about not a static reality, but a dynamic one (see Campbell 1967; LeVine 1965; Campbell and LeVine 1968, 1972). On the one hand, the Russian nationalists defined themselves in opposition to what the West represented: against the French, German, and Polish urbane and aristocratic manners the Slavophiles counterposed peasant earthiness and naturalness (which, however, was influenced by the philosophy of Rousseau—a Frenchman). On the other hand, the Slavophiles co-opted Western European categories of virtue but filled them with Russian characteristics; thus Russia became more "civilized" than the decadent West; Russian Byzantine-Tatar "backwardness" was in fact more "advanced" and "progressive" than the voracious, militaristic West; Russian Orthodox mysticism was a higher form of "reason" than the legalistic, Roman "rationalism" of the West, and so forth.

A fixed and constricting identity was *confirmed* from without and *affirmed* from within Russia, creating a vicious circle of mutually validated stereotypes. The Western powers, fearing contamination from the angry big brother to the East, habitually block Russia—and presently, the Soviet Union—from synthesizing her past with a long-sought membership of equal status within the Western community. Being put and kept in her place, Russia is condemned to perpetuate her past—a past that, beginning with the eighteenth-century nationalist revival, became *actively chosen* rather than *passively endured* (Freud 1920:16). The enhancement of positive self-esteem and the recapturing of initiative were both underlying motivations for and functional consequences of the development and elaboration of Russian nationalist ideology. A further consequence, however, was the greater isolation and estrangement of Russia from the West—though this time the Slavophiles were, so to speak, playing by their own rules, not those dictated by the West.

What we in the West often take to be distinctively Russian, that is, a specific form of culture alien to ourselves, is not something sui generis, the product of a kind of local spontaneous generation, but is a cumulative synthesis and continuously synthesizing process of action and meaning that has evolved in a specific culture-historic environment. What we see as cultural *differences* are the result of an ongoing process of *differentiation* (cf. Porshnev 1973; Lévi-Strauss 1968; Stein 1975b) in a dynamic field. Although the *fact* of cultural differences is a legitimate subject of inquiry, I am here most concerned with the *act* or process of differentiation that becomes "time-frozen" between cultural boundaries and identified as differences.

The unity of Russian culture and history is predicated, inter alia, on its structure and function within the European system of social stratification, namely, power and prestige. It follows that the precariousness and marginality of Russian culture with respect to European social structure—with Western Europe from Versailles to Weimar setting the standard and constituting the "reference group"—would make an *internal* Russian identity conflict a Russian expression and attempted resolution of an *intercultural* conflict (see also Campbell 1967; LeVine 1965; Campbell and LeVine 1968, 1972; Porshnev 1973; Lévi Strauss 1968; Stein 1975b). Russian "history" and "tradition" are not mere givens from the East; they were constantly reinvented, confirmed, redefined, and synthesized out of relation with the West. Defensive isolation and Slavophilism cannot be understood in an exclusively national context. Irrespective of how hard the Russian gentry and intelligentsia tried to "civilize" themselves, they and their nation were scorned as barbaric and unenlightened—and unenlightenable. The anguish of the Westernizers and Slavophiles alike was that both had crossed the boundaries, found life on either side of the boundary untenable, and spent their lives attempting to give meaning and definition to their own boundaries and identities—and, in the process, to the boundaries and identities of Russia, Europe, and the East. Their own conflicts over boundary and identity are *isomorphic* with the conflicts experienced by Russian culture as a whole and as a part within the international system.

To name but three, there were isomorphisms between the sense of personal shame and national shame, between personal inferiority and national inferiority, and between the conviction of personal backwardness and national backwardness. Here I refer not to such specifics as industry, literature, or music but to the totality, the pervading cultural *ethos* that abstracts from the "specifics" and subsumes them all. The ethos synthesizes meaning and in turn generates it so that the "specifics" become embedded in it. Thus "industry" or "art" comes to symbolize and relate to much more. The nationalist achievement is to transform a sense of shame about one's origins into a sense of pride, inferiority into superiority, backwardness into the vanguard of time's arrow (recall that

Herder prophesied that the Slavic peoples would become the next great European civilization, succeeding the Germanic peoples, who had already reached their peak). Russia, the *object* of comparison, became the *measure* by which all other peoples would be compared. The Russian Slavophile origin myth that sought Great Russian beginnings long antedating Peter the Great attempted to reverse a sense of lowly origin—of which they were constantly reminded by the presence of Westernizers and Westernization—into one of *noble birth*. The Russians became not the cursed but the messianically chosen.

The concept "transformation" is significant for the analysis of Russian nationalism, and of nationalistic movements in general. Claude Lévi-Strauss, the French structural anthropologist, defines the principle of transformation as *the insistence on difference* (1968). It denotes a process involving the redefinition, segregation, inversion, or reversal of cultural elements on either side of a cultural boundary. As such, it describes a distinctive cognitive and affective (emotional) feature of nationalism. The cognitive reorientation symbolizes, and the new behavioral regimen ritualizes, a decisive conscious reorganization of an unconscious emotional or affective conflict. Here contradiction, ambiguity, and ambivalence are seen as giving rise to heightened chronic stress that is resolved through a thorough cognitive, affective, and behavioral reorganization.

The emotions expressed by nationalist sentiment are diagnostic of their opposite: they celebrate the inversion of deeply felt feelings that must be lived down and denied. Hence the insistence on the maintenance of inviolable boundaries. Nationalism could not exist, its boundaries could not be secure, unless it had an opposing out-group with which to define itself by contrast. It is deeply bound up with what it must exclude to maintain its own integrity. The "enemy" is internal as well as external, and hence must be both retained and kept at a distance (cf. Erikson 1968, 1974). I discuss more fully the implications of "the enemy within" when I discuss the relationship between the Slavophiles and Westernizers.

I have found Erving Goffman's discussion of "stigma" (1963)

especially helpful in this effort to understand the relationship between Russia and the West. Ordinarily we think of stigma in terms of two discrete groups within a single society, the "normals" and those "stigmatized" by the normals, or the "mainstream" and the "minorities" and the like. But, as Goffman shows, stigma encompasses "a pervasive two-role social process in which every individual participates in both roles. . . . The normal and the stigmatized are not persons but rather perspectives" (Goffman 1963). The very rigidity of the cognitive and emotional and often spatial segregation of the stigmatized by the normal attests, however, to the depth of connection. Each, through fear of a split-off (or ego-alien) part of itself, becomes afraid of the other. The normals are able to maintain their illusion and conviction of normalcy and superiority by dissociating the abhorred aspects of themselves and locating them in their outcastes, and must guard against contamination by what they have repudiated and magically "discovered" in the out-group. The stigmatized, in turn, must deal with their discreditation.

How does one live with stigma? Simplistically, through a combination of depression (self-hate, self-deprecation, self-blame) and overcompensation in fantasy and/or reality (escapist religion, new ideology, activism). The "combination," however, is in fact an ambitendent pendulation between feelings of worthlessness and grandiosity. Two decisive factors in the resolution of stigma are the intensity of stress and the constraints of the environment. Those stigmatized can try to escape their condition by attempting to assimilate and "pass" as members of the "normal" or "dominant" group; that is, they can deny their past—a past that, incidentally, they may wish to escape quite apart from the effect of stigmatization. Conversely, they can deny their wish to participate in the "normal" or "dominant" sector of society, deny that this sector of society is the measure of their self-esteem, and reverse the condemnation of ascribed status so that their condition is rationalized as chosen and superior.

Transpose this model to the relation between Russia and Western Europe, and to the emergence of the Westernizers and Slavophiles. The West was indeed the "norm," the model for emulation, the basis for comparing oneself (see Ruud 1974; Anderson 1971). Russia both lived out and lived down the invidious stereotypes held by the West. Russia both internalized and repudiated the stereotypes, pendulating between the glorification of Russian antiquity (Czar, *mir, Narod*, Orthodoxy, the "natural" peasantry) and the quest for acceptance as a sibling in good standing in Western "civilization" (implemented through Westernization), which quest often included the repudiation of all things Russian. In the attempt to rid themselves of stigma, the Slavophiles rejected the West, and the Westernizers rejected Russia. Behind both, however, lay a pervasive self-hate and a magically omnipotent concern for the purity of their categories—and of the danger of their defilement by the other side (Douglas 1970). The glorification of Russia (the reversal of the erstwhile negative and positive) and the repudiation of Russia ("identification with the aggressor") were two ways of managing the conflict.

Both the Slavophiles and Westernizers were *self-conscious* about their past in ways that a "native" would (and could) never be. The Slavophiles had to imagine and reinvent a romanticized past from which they were experientially far removed. The Slavophile had to idealize what he or she could not be and venerate an innocence he or she no longer possessed but yearned for. Moreover, romanticization and idealization serve as defenses against ambivalence and rage; hence the degree of the elaboration of the former is in direct proportion to the extent of the latter.

One must be an alien from a tradition before one can be conscious of its existence as a "tradition"; while immersed in it, one cannot call it even "culture," because it is simply coexistent with the way one goes about living life. A native is not conscious that he or she is a native. It requires distance, in fact, *alienation*, to produce the type of heightened self-consciousness that characterizes a *nativist*. Only one who is already an *outsider* to one's own tradition, painfully conscious of the discrepancy between one's present status and that of a native—even if one has chosen to forsake one's nativity— could have the wish to *return* to the *inside*, to reassert (and reinvent) one's nativity.

Having lost their traditional history, Slavophile nativists had to remythologize the past to invent an acceptable history, a past that restored both initiative and self-esteem so that from this past they could imagine and work toward a tolerable future. Yet, try as they did, even the mightiest Slavophile minds, from Homyakov to Dostoevski, could neither write nor reason themselves to the naïve faith they sought. No effort was final, and the goal was elusive, because the *method* could not meet the task, and because their secret longing for the West haunted and subverted their single-minded effort. They mistrusted reason even as they reasoned and had therefore to reason all the harder. The very insistence on superiority attests to the depth of the conviction of inferiority; thus the necessity for such massive denial and overcompensation—which in turn could never be sufficient but required continued assertion. Herein lies the motivation and meaning behind the proliferation of literature, from the writing of history to the creation of lyric poetry, by the Slavophiles. Suffice it to say, for the moment, that those who became Westernizers were equally alienated and marginally Russian, and they too utilized romanticization, idealization, and relentless polemic in the service of their ideology and cause. The underlying conflict was the same for both; only the resolution differed—and the tenuousness of that very fragile resolution is attested to by the frequent vacillation and conversion of the Russian intelligentsia from one ideology to the other.

I turn now to the writings of the psychoanalyst Heinz Kohut (1966, 1971, 1972), whose formulation of the dynamics of narcissism and narcissistic rage provides a key to the psychodynamic underpinnings of Russian nationalism in particular and the group psychology of nationalism in general (see also Zonis 1984 for the application of Kohutian object-relations theory to the understanding of contemporary national revolutions). The problem of the epigenesis of narcissism from infancy through adulthood focuses on the development, differentiation, transformation, and cohesion of the *self*. Each phase of human development involves a task of synthesizing new demands, opportunities, or constraints, with the reawakened conflicts specific to prior stages. Each stage is not reducible to earlier ones but must integrate them: one must deal simultaneously with the past and present and anticipated future at once. Pathology results when early failure and later traumatization combine forces to overwhelm a culturally sanctioned system of defenses—and in periods of social change when expectations are not fulfilled, when norms and values are in conflict. Nationalism, I hold, is a monumental group psychological effort to cope with environmental failure and inner trauma that is simultaneously a regression to pathology, an adaptation to the prevailing (and chronic) condition of international relationships and imagery, and an attempt to prevent further regression.

Let me briefly present Kohut's model. The failure of environmental compliance with expectation for fulfillment of *self-esteem* and *initiative-mastery* needs threatens to fragment the cohesion of the self by undermining one's idealizations, re-awakening "feelings of inferiority" and challenging the "omnipotence of the [infantile] self." Shame and rage combine forces, producing a narcissistic rage whose predominant features include an attempt to recapture omnipotence through the exercise of absolute control and the exhibitionistic insistence on being admired. At the group level group regression produces chronic group narcissistic rage that is resolved through the attempt to "re-establish control over a narcissistically experienced world" (Kohut 1972).

Kohut speaks of "the readiness of the shame-prone individual to respond to a potentially shame-provoking situation by the employment of a simple remedy: the active (often anticipatory) inflicting on others of those narcissistic injuries he is most afraid of suffering himself" (Kohut 1972:381). Moreover:

The existence of heightened sadism, the adoption of a policy of preventive attack, the need for revenge, and the desire to turn a passive experience into an active one, do not, however, fully account for some of the most characteristic features of narcissistic rage. In its typical forms there is utter disregard for reasonable limitation and a boundless wish to redress an injury and to obtain revenge. The irrationality of the vengeful attitude becomes even more frightening in

view of the fact that—in narcissistic personalities as in the para-
noiac—the reasoning capacity, while totally under the domination
and in the service of the emotion, is often not only intact but even
sharpened. [Kohut 1972:382].

Discussing the relationship between narcissistic rage and
aggression, Kohut writes:

The enemy . . . who calls forth the archaic rage of the narcissistically vulnerable is seen by him not as an autonomous source of im-
pulsions, but as *a flaw in a narcissistically perceived reality.* He is a
recalcitrant part of an expanded self over which he expects to exercise full control and whose mere independence or other-ness is an
offense. [Kohut 1972:385–86]

Finally, in the consolidation of chronic (implying both time
and pathology, though I would insist on the adaptive point of
view) narcissistic rage;

Conscious and preconscious ideation, in particular as it concerns
the aims and goals of the personality, becomes more and more sub-
servient to the pervasive rage. The ego, furthermore, increasingly
surrenders its reasoning capacity to the power of the grandiose self:
it does not acknowledge the inherent limitations of the power of the
self, but attributes its failures and weaknesses to the malevolence
and corruption of the uncooperative archaic object" [i.e., those who
personify presently the early parent; the reexperiencing in new circumstances archaic injury to the self]. [Kohut 1972:396]

The consequences of stigma and ostracism for Russia should
be clear from this framework, for it relates simultaneously to
early environmental failure and unfulfilled current expectations both of the individual Russian and of Russian culture
psychohistorically. Here life history, culture history, and international relations are symbiotically linked. Both the individual and the nation must cope with present circumstances
that include the conflicts of earlier stages of personal or group
history. If we can speak of the Slavophile ideology as delusional, we should also keep in mind Freud's observation (1911)
that behind every paranoid delusion is a kernel of historical
truth, that it is not all imagination, that there are (defensive)
reasons for a delusion.

Let us return to Russian history. The elite, the nobility, the gentry, and the intelligentsia *sought* membership in Western civilization—one cannot simply say, for instance, that Westernization, from industrialization to the military, was forced on the Russian people by Peter the Great (it was, indeed, resisted). It was sought far more than it was imposed from above. Upon rejection and disillusionment with the possibility of rapprochement and integration with the West, there developed a grandiose, megalomanic glorification of the very Eastern tradition of isolation, alienation, and enclosure that was a haven of safety even as it was a curse and prison. The sense of inferiority and shame were denied by an inversion of values and identifications—and identity.

Peter the Great, that ambivalent hero of Russian history, had moved his capital west from Moscow, symbol of the East, to what became Saint Petersburg, the "window on the West," and sought "warm water ports" to end Russian isolation—as much symbolic as commercially practical. Two centuries later, the Russian Revolution that in ideology embraced and tried to consummate the Westernization and internationalization of Russia (though in turn stripped of the "capitalistic" ethos), returned the capital to Moscow, and was followed by Stalin's ruthless Russification program—in the name of Soviet progress. The revolution and its inheritors were as sensitive to comparison with the West as had been their czarist precursors. How else, for instance, could we understand the "Lysenko affair" that began in the 1930s with the struggle between "Western" genetics and "Soviet" ("Russian") environmental biology and culminated in Stalin's embracing of Lysenko?

The *passivity* of isolation, encirclement, insulation, exclusion, and cultural difference were reversed into an *active* process of cultural differentiation. The new configuration was characterized by aloofness, exclusiveness, messianic superiority, and heightened defense and offense. Mother Russia was elevated in status to assume the historic mission of Rome and Byzantium; Moscow became the Third Rome and, later, home of the Third International. Mother Russia became the Chosen of God, guardian and evangelist of the Truth of the Orthodox and Marxist Pentecost (cf. Muller 1957). Chronic individual and group narcissistic rage underlay the *systematization* of a culturally sanctioned delusional system that defined self-esteem and provided power and initiative. What could not be achieved in "reality"—that is, through integration with western European civilization—was sought and achieved "magically," with *a new reality magically defined.*

Through stigmatization Russia has been prevented from pursuing what we might call "mature" national goals and has adapted to its chronic condition regressively through a "narcissistically experienced world based on rage" (Kohut 1972), the Slavophiles functioning as articulators and rationalizers of the new identity and ideology. Where *wholeness,* the integration of parts, cannot be achieved, a rigidly *totalistic* (Erikson 1968:74ff.) personal and group configuration based on the radical exclusion of what is repudiated as alien is chosen. Certainly Slavophilism is totalistic—and, like other nationalisms, politically totalitarian—as are and were the radical Westernizers. But by focusing too narrowly on the conflict between the nativists and the assimilationists, we lose sight of a crucial fact: without including in itself what it had repressed, made alien to itself, and projected onto Russia, *Western Europe* (with all of its diversity) *was prevented from becoming whole also,* and became equally totalistic. The very civilization that regarded itself as the measure of humanity could not be fully human because it had cut off from itself those qualities it then proceeded to accuse Russia of "possessing." We have here an elementary fact of social psychology. As Donald Campbell writes:

The naïve ingrouper [in this case, Western Europe; but equally applicable to Slavophile Russia] perceives the different characteristics of the outgroup as causing his hostility. He feels that were it not for these despicable traits, the outgroup would be loved. The outgroup's opprobrious characteristics seem to him to fully justify the hostility and rejection he shows toward it. The social scientist sees the opposite causal direction: Causally, first is the hostility toward the outgrouper, generated perhaps by real threat, perhaps by ethnocentrism, perhaps by displacement. In the service of this hostility, all possible differences are opportunistically interpreted as despicable, and the most despicable traits are given most attention. [1967:825]

Just as the Slavophiles and Westernizers were locked into symbiosis, needing one another to sustain themselves, so were Western Europe and Russia. Hence the paradox of Slavophiles' insistence on independence and difference from the West and their relentless effort to restore the Russian past and obliterate Western influence. Cyril Bryner writes:

Though Slavophilism preached national exclusiveness, it was so involved in the culture, aspirations and habits of Europe, it found difficulty in extricating itself from the spirit of the times, which it allegedly considered to be un-Russian and undesirable. Slavophilism was a Slavic-coated Romanticism founded on the humanitarian ideals of Herder. Herder's dream of a universal brotherhood of man was embraced by the Slavophils who as they grew more nationalistic, endowed the ideal Slav with more and more of the qualities of the ideal man, and the ideal man with the qualities which were supposed to be typically Slavic. [1939:1]

What the Slavophiles were to call the "historical mission" of the Slavic peoples—the defeat of the decadent and decaying West by piety or by force—was an ideological consequence of Russian contact with the West and did not antedate it, despite the rewriting of Russian history to demonstrate otherwise. There would have been no need for group narcissistic assertions of omnipotence and for exhibitionistic displays had it not been for the shame and rage induced by relations with the West. In Kohut's model the specific "transformations" of narcissism which lead to abhorrent group psychological consequences are the result of the traumatization of inherent "narcissistic structures" that strive for initiative and self-esteem. Like Kohut, Erikson sees the radical resolution of identity confusion in "'totalistic' rearrangement of images . . . an inner regrouping of imagery, almost a *negative conversion*, by which erstwhile negative identity elements become totally dominant, while erstwhile positive elements come to be excluded totally" (1963a:313). Moreover, he speaks of "the *specific rage* which is aroused wherever identity development loses the promise of a traditionally assured wholeness" (p. 313). At the cultural level Edmund Leach (1964) has noted that the insistence on *cultural* difference is the product of *so-*

cial relations, cultural differences that in turn lead to the reification and stabilization of social relations.

Slavophile Russian history was written to fulfill the identity and ideological needs of the present, to clarify a literally confusional state, one of "identity confusion" (see also Erikson 1968:131ff., 212ff., 214–15, 165ff.), by (paradoxically) confusing historical fact with the need for a justifying myth, selecting from history to redeem and justify oneself historically. Herder's timely philosophy of the nation-Geist, with its belief in the Slavic peoples as the wave of the future (and, in the Russian Slavophile version, the Russians serving as the vanguard of the new wave), provided profound external ideological rationalization, support, and verification for a belief already well developed. On the one hand, the Slavophile nativism was a manifestation not of national-ethnic continuity but of *discontinuity* with the immediate past. It was an effort selectively to resurrect and venerate the distant past, a past seen as free from ambivalence and contradiction. On the other hand, the all-or-nothing quality of the discontinuity— the *eradication* of the immediate historical past by the withdrawal of identification with it and with those who personify it, together with the subsequent search for and invention of a usable past—suggests that the former was part of a regressive, restitutional attempt to establish an equally radical *continuity* with a preambivalent past. The Motherland and Fatherland symbolized this new historical identification. One's newly chosen ancestors were mythic and idealized, archetypal of those imagined contemporaries (the noble peasant, the mystical czar, the Slavic man as *the* "human being") who would in turn be the founders of the eschatalogically imagined future.

With the Slavophile, a narcissistically conceived self and world became, as a further consequence of regression, fused with the idealized maternal object, and, to avoid oedipal conflict, equally with the idealized paternal object. The oedipal father became the external enemy, for example, Western Europe; and representatives of the enemy within Russia, for example, the Westernizers, the secularized clergy, the liberal gentry, and the bureaucracy that mediated between the people and the czar and rendered him (or Him) unreachable. The Slavophile became the champion of Mother Russia and of its protector the czar, defending the Mother against *violation* attempting to restore her purity (virginity?) by the systematic attempt to eradicate foreign influences.

What we observe here is yet another variation on the conflict between East and West, Slavophile and Westernizer— namely, to borrow from Turgenev: Fathers and Sons and, as Sidney Monas (1965) suggests, Mothers and Sons as well. I deal with this specific conflict in the last section of the chapter, but let me here briefly outline its shape. The ambivalence and contradiction of the *liberal fathers* of the 1820s and 1830s induced the *rage* and *radicalism* of the *sons,* sons who came to embrace the absolutisms either of Westernizer or of Slavophile. But in a sense the dynamic is timeless and not limited to one generational dyad. The conflict resided within, as well as between, generations. The Czar Alexander II who freed the serfs in 1861 became a reactionary. Dostoevski began as a Socialist and ended as a fanatic Slavophile and hater of all things Western. And, as J. L. Black (1973) has shown, the Russian historian Pogodin first courted the Poles as fellow Slavs and later condemned them as defectors to the West and a threat to the Russian Empire.

Charles Ruud writes that "the autocratic tradition continued and gave its form to Bolshevism" and that "the Leninists proved to be the beneficiaries of the liberals' failure" (1974: 283). Leninist Bolshevism is rooted equally in the liberal Decembrists and in the radical liberal socialism of Herzen, to whom Lenin traces his ancestry. The revolution, and the Soviet Union, succeeded in perpetuating the autocracy, though clothed in an ideology that denied and masked the continuity. The liberals were fated to failure because, for the most part, they did not believe in themselves, but were establishmentarian conservatives playing with liberalism. Robert Langbaum writes that the liberal aristocrats "profess revolutionary ideas but live in the old upper-class style—playing along with conventions they no longer believe in, while subverting the rules by which the upper class disciplines itself" (1973:244). Similarly, "Aging liberals . . . take up the new radical ideas in order to be in the swing and feel young again. Also bored upper-class people find the new radical ideas exciting and play with them . . . the revolutionary, become fashionable, moves in the highest circle of the establishment" (Langbaum 1973: 245). If reactionaries were crypto-liberals or radicals, the liberals were crypto-reactionaries. Likewise, Slavophiles were crypto-Westernizers, and Westernizers were crypto-Slavophiles. The liberals betrayed a cause they did not really believe in; their tacit loyalties lay elsewhere.

The demoralized sons of the liberal gentry felt betrayed by perfidious parents. The "sons" act out what were ideals meant only to be spoken, not fulfilled; when the sons demand the realization of these ideals, the parents are beside themselves to explain what produced such rebelliousness—even as the "sons" act out *for* the parents what the parents cannot themselves do. The Nietzschean transvaluation of all values, in its Russian expression, is an effort decisively to break out of parental value contradictions and ambivalences—and to resolve the contradictions and ambivalences now within themselves. Only a new order, with its eradication of oppressive tradition and fraudulent liberalism, could produce unity of mind and society. Against inauthenticity is counterposed a superauthenticity, whether Slavophile or Westernizer, to defend against ambivalence—and not infrequently to wreak havoc on the objects of that ambivalence, under the sway of what was discussed earlier as narcissistic rage that knows no bounds. As Erik Erikson writes, "Intolerance [serves] as a defense against identity confusion" (1963a:262), reversing confusion into absolute conviction.

From the Decembrists and the Society of United Slavs (1820s) through the Russian Revolution nearly a century later, the Russian intelligentsia, isolated and alienated from monarchy, peasantry, and Europe, played a decisive and prophetic role. Sons of a largely and compromisingly Westernized gentry, they attended Russian universities or prestigious Western centers of learning, only to emerge without past or future. Westernization, "enlightenment," accorded not integration but alienation both in Europe and in Russia. From this fundamental rootlessness, from the inability of either society to "assimilate" them, emerged the *opposing* and *subtly complementary* dogmas of Slavophilism and Westernization.

The Westernizers repudiated the passivity, humility, and Orthodoxy of Russia, phrasing their radical idealism in Western "language." The Slavophiles, with their nativist slogan "Autocracy, Orthodoxy, and Nationalism" *(Narodnost),* elevated the czar to a mystic religious symbol, rendering the throne virtually apolitical, while they venerated the romanticized peasant as the pure and uncorrupted human being. Cyril Bryner writes: "While the Slavophils tried to model themselves on the Russian peasant, they did not succeed in making their imitations of the peasantry more than a masquerade" (1939:2). The lineage from Aksakov to Tolstoi idealized, and virtually caricatured in their personal style, those whom they could in good faith neither wholly liberate nor oppress. Tolstoi wore his *mujiik* garb while maintaining his estate. The Slavophiles could not be Russian enough, and the Westernizers could not be sufficiently Western. Slavophilism was a desperate quest to *put down roots;* Westernization was a radical attempt to *uproot.*

In one sense Slavophile and Westernizer were reciprocals of one another in their rivalry, disputation, and invective; at a deeper level they were complements—they needed one another to oppose and do combat with (intellectual, political, ideological, and military) and to "complete" themselves even as they waged war on that dissociated part of themselves. Each defined its identity out of opposition to the other, but in the wholeness of the two parts we can see the identity crisis of Russian culture. One should not make an absolute distinction between putting down roots and uprooting, because in fact both factions were great uprooters and seekers of a defensive identity. Both began as idealistic *reformers;* in their rage over demoralization they became *uprooters.* The parental generation who could not trust themselves could not inspire trust or be entrusted in the next generation, a generation that in turn sought to be uncompromisingly trustworthy either as absolute radicals or absolute reactionaries. As with Goffman's (1963) analysis of "stigma," the Slavophiles and Westernizers, and all dialectical opposites, are not persons—though they would insist on being understood as very distinct groups of persons—but perspectives; the relationship between Slavophile and Westernizer is a pervasive two-role set in which each participates in both roles. Ideological difference is precisely the mechanism by which the illusion of separateness is maintained. So we are talking about "siblings" in the same "family," not unrelated clans disputing over territory.

One can early see this family quarrel in the opposing ideologies within the Decembrist revolt of 1825, for example, those who sought a federalist constitutional government modeled on the United States versus those who insisted on the primacy of czarist centralism; those who demanded the abolition of autocracy, bureaucracy, and serfdom versus those who sought greater centralization and were unsure what to do with the serfs. Uniting both factions was a revitalization of Russian history, a glorification of Russian antiquity, and a rejection of foreign influence—even as the rationale for nativism lay in the French and German Enlightenment and Romanticism and was catalyzed, as were the other emergent nationalisms in Europe, by what was perceived as the monumental arrogance of the Napoleonic conquest. Beneath the fervent patriotism lay "a devouring feeling of social inferiority," "a feeling of social insignificance" (Lukasevich 1968:121). Similarly, "The feeling of national shame—the prime motive for the founding of the secret societies—would subsequently be replaced by a sentiment of pride in the glorious history of the Fatherland, implying an intensive idealization of the past and a patriotic historical pragmatism" (Kostka 1966:366).

Significantly, one means suggested to reclaim the Russian past—meaning for some, before Peter the Great, and for others before the invitation of the Norseman Rurik for "protection"—through the destruction of the profaned present lay precisely through an act that pervades Russian history, from the legendary Vadim of Novgorod to the Soviet Kremlin intrigues and purges: regicide. One abrogates the past through the grand gesture of tyrannicide, whose very enactment encapsulates and reaffirms continuity with the past. One breaks with the past with the means (and unconscious ends) of the past.

What Lenin and the Bolsheviks were to enact with the slaughter of Nicholas II and his family recapitulated the same scenario. The fraternal order of egalitarian comrades rapidly assumed the traditional authoritarian structure as the revolutionary and postrevolutionary brotherhood struggled for primus inter pares, with the followership not quite as equal as the leadership. Leon Trotsky was expelled and later assassinated for seeing this all too clearly. As the czar was the idealized "Little Father," so the mythological Stalin of the 1930s became a worthy successor to the sacred *autokrator* Ivan the Severe (crowned 1547), "Our Own Dear Father Stalin," still mediating between heaven and earth, orthodox Communist atheism notwithstanding. What the Decembrists considered—"murdering the tsar for the purpose of abolishing autocracy" (Kostka 1966:366)—the Bolsheviks carried out and then reversed.

While Lenin once insisted that the path to socialism lay through "political democracy" (i. e. Western), he later denounced as reactionary and counter-revolutionary any self-determination for the workers, repeatedly attacked "democratism" and "freedom of criticism," and emerged the iron-willed of Russian vintage (Muller 1957:303). What he condemned and liquidated he and the Soviet Union became. Hand in hand with the new "realism" and utopian idealism there continued the ancient tyranny and sentimentality against which the revolution was waged. Ivan the Severe became a national hero (and, with Stalin's blessing, a score by Prokofiev), and Tolstoi became a Russo-Soviet saint.

If revolutionary ideology stressed a final break with the oppressive past, from both the ruthless autocracy and the servile peasantry, the revolution, its charismatic leaders, and its routinized bureaucratic successors nevertheless insisted that Soviet art be of the people, while the men of steel enshrined and recapitulated the atrocities and depressions of their czarist progenitors. Like the Slavophiles they romanticized the virtuous peasantry while perpetuating the "culture screen" (Dunn and Dunn 1963, 1967; Whyte 1970) and cultural distance between themselves and the "free" peasantry, who were bound not to the *mir* but to the *kolkhoz*. From the advent of freedom in 1861 under Alexander II through the variable agrarian policies of the Soviet Union, the peasant became a further-entrenched servant of the state, now tied to the soil by a dictatorship of the *urban* "proletariat" elite that remained dependent on a conservative peasant base. A theme that cannot be too highly stressed is the ambivalence toward authority and dependency and the need to perpetuate archaic relationships—personal, cultural, and political—from which a monumental break was made through revolution (Stein 1974a, 1975b, 1976; Stein and Hill 1973; Erikson 1974). The dialectic between the Westernizers and the Slavophiles persists in contemporary Soviet society, with conflicts largely the same as those that troubled the Decembrists and their descendants; and as with the earlier Slavophiles and Westernizers of the czarist era, the core conflict remains; only their resolutions differ.

Let me turn now from an exploration of Russian nationalism at the macrolevel, that of international relations and cultural differentiation, to the microlevel of individuals, first Herzen and Homyakov and then Dostoevski, to discern how such literary and intellectual leaders of the nineteenth century were—and remain—prototypic of the conflict of the Slavophiles and the Westernizers. In changing instruments from a wide-angle telescope to a microscope, I hope to illumine the wider process by exploring its microcosm, just as the first portion of this chapter should provide the context for the analysis of a narrower field of vision.

The Dialectic of Herzen and Homyakov

The interlocked fate and conflict between the Westernizers and the Slavophiles, whose "dual unity" (Mahler and Furer 1968) or symbiosis constitutes the Russian identity, is nowhere better exemplified than in the friendly but earnest disputation between Alexander Herzen and Alexei Homyakov in the mid-nineteenth century (Kohn 1960; Bryner 1939). Although both the Westernizers and the Slavophiles shared the same "love for

the Russian people, for Russian life, and for the Russian character" (Alexander Herzen, in Bryner 1939:3), they

> like Janus or like the two-headed eagle looked in different directions,
> and at the same time our hearts beat as one. . . . They [Slavophiles]
> turned all their love, all their tenderness, toward their oppressed
> mother; while among us [Westernizers], a foreign bringing up weak-
> ened that tie. We were in the hands of French governesses; too late
> we learned that not she, but the dismissed peasant woman was our
> mother—this we guessed ourselves thru [sic] the similarity of our
> features, and because her songs were dearer to us than French farces.
> We came to love her greatly, but her life was too narrow. Her room
> stifled us with its smoke-dimmed faces peeping out of the silver
> frames of icons; the priest with his regalia frightened this woman,
> subdued by soldier and government clerk. Even her everlasting
> weeping over her lost happiness grated on our hearts—we knew she
> had no happy memories—we knew her happiness lay before her;
> that beneath her heart was the seed which was to be our younger
> brother, whom we would acknowledge as the elder. [Herzen, in
> Bryner 1939:3–4]

Herzen's profound sense of inferiority, marginality, and outsidedness (in the family—where the eldest son was a junior
father—in Russia, and in Europe) reflects deep conflicts in
separation and individuation, exaggerated by the fantasy of an
unborn, younger brother being the true elder. Herzen vacil-
lates between a melancholy over his peasant mother's narrowness and ignorance and the cosmopolitan widening of his
world through the French governess. Though he can neither
wholly accept nor reject either, he is more inclined toward the
latter. Yet in that very choice he must pay with the sense
of uprooting and abandonment of the mother. If both Westernizers and Slavophiles were Russian Socialists at heart,
Herzen and his successors found their Socialist ideology in
French and German writers. The Slavophile ideology of socialism traced its roots to the peasant *mir;* the collective in
agriculture, family, and Orthodoxy; a mystic czar; and the
"oppressed mother."

An ontogenetic perspective on the Slavophile ideology can
be gleaned from significant aspects of Homyakov's life. Bryner
writes:

Alexei Homyakov came of a family in which the tradition of old patriarchial Russia was strong. Though his improvident father did his best to ruin the family by losing a million rubles at cards, the household was dominated by Alexei's mother, a woman of solid virtues and great strength of character. Alexei was entirely his mother's boy. His surroundings had none of the atmosphere of the decaying gentry. . . . Homyakov's estate was a healthy, going concern, whose master combined patriarchal benevolence with Western sanitation and machinery without the benefit of Western manners which had proved to be so disastrous for many a Russian squire who found himself torn between two worlds. . . . The piety of his home helped him keep aloof of the radical movements. The religiousness of his mother was transmitted to him without any disturbing interlude. [Bryner 1939:6–7]

It is doubtful, however, that his frequent contact with revolutionists and his attendance at the University of Moscow merely confirmed his contempt for radicalism or Enlightenment skepticism. Following his graduation he entered the army, fulfilling an ambition burning since age eleven to fight for the liberation of the Slavs, his singular love: "Except for his early military poems, there are no dreams of individualism, but only a longing for an Orthodox, Slavic collective" (Bryner 1939:8). Fighting for the "oppressed mother" became the theme of his literary life. Unlike Herzen, self-alienated from his own home, Homyakov was "the chosen" and transferred this chosenness to the Russian mission, to save mother Russia and Slavdom from foreign violation. The ancient oedipal triangle took on a distinctive cultural flavor: the valiant son in defense of the Russian mother, protecting her from and avenging himself on the "improvident" gambler and partly Westernized father. The "mother's boy" became in adulthood the mother's champion.

Yet his very weapon against everything the West stood for (rationalism, legalism, Protestant individualism, warlikeness, arrogance, pride, ambition, materialism) was a piercing rationalism. He embodied precisely what he combated. In his philosophy and theology he was a Hegelian anti-Hegelian: "This man who pretended to scorn reason was one of the most talented dialectitians of his time" (Bryner 1939:5). As much as he spurned *legalism* and individualism, he was a formidable debater and arrogated to his own personality and wisdom what he argued should be absorbed in the mystical body of Mother Russia. He venerated and championed the peasant only at a distance. If Homyakov used Western dialectical rationalism as a weapon against itself (and a split-off part of himself), he likewise utilized his own individualism to combat individualism. In a sense he became his own reductio ad absurdum. Having spent a lifetime using *Western* tools to try to prove the superiority of intuition and mysticism, he jettisoned rationalism and sought faith. His Westernism was far more profound than is usually assumed. He had to spend a lifetime of *virtuoso polemic* to try to prove what he could not *experientially* assume. Thus Bryner's insight that "his mysticism was one of longing rather than fact" (1939:9)—hence his romanticism.

Other "causes" in Homyakov's life likewise reveal the character of his inner split. Though disdaining the decadence of the West, he was a popular frequenter of the Moscow literary salons and enjoyed his prosperous estate, both modeled on the "enemy." The arrogance, ambition, and pride of the West was inverted into a scarcely obscured trinity of national superiority, the messianic destiny of the mystical body of Russian Orthodoxy, and the peasant commune humbly elevated to become Russia writ large. Disdaining physical force and Russian militarism, whose introduction he blamed on Peter the Great, he preached spiritual strength through meekness and pacifism. Yet his youth was filled with romantic dreams and adventures of fighting wars of liberation against the Turks: "Give me a horse and give me a sword, and to that distant land I shall fly like an arrow, and rush into the bloody fray'" (quoted in Bryner 1939:8). Although he disdained Peter's conversion of Russia into a militarist state and rejoiced at Russia's defeat in the Crimean War, he believed that Russia should militarily aid her Slavic brethren when necessary. When the spiritual force of passivity and meekness will not capitulate or win over the enemy, then a monumentally destructive force (and rage) lies ready to enter into "the bloody fray."

Note the similarity to Tolstoi's *War and Peace*. In the latter

Mother Russia would meekly wait, endure, and outlive the decadence and arrogance of those who would violate her. General Kutuzov knew that winter and fate (and disease) were on the side of Russia. But after the strategic retreat that allowed Napoleon to burn and plunder Moscow and be hemmed in by the winter, the savagery of the Russian counterattack was fathomless. Tolstoi, the Christlike figure, the wavering convert from and between gentry and peasant, wrote *War and Peace* as a plea for peace but equally, and contradictorily, as an indulgence in the horrors and ferocity of war.

In terms of character structure and philosophy Herzen and Homyakov were very different Russians: but in their "composite" lies a microcosm of the conflicts and ideologies that underlay the nineteenth-century Russian nationalism, the revolution, and the emergence of the Soviet Union. This "composite" is the "real" Russia. The decisive early Westernizing cosmopolitan influence for Herzen was the French governess, who, to recall Herzen's text, weakened the tie with his oppressed peasant mother. Conversely, the oppressed mother was the experiential core of Homyakov's life, and the very nature of the attachment ensured his "narrowness." Herzen sought reuniting with the mother he felt he had abandoned (his bitterness adumbrates Maksim Gorki by half a century); yet he could not fully return, because the peasant mother was "foreign" to him. He was an alien in his own land and elsewhere. Homyakov was never able to break out of the earliest symbiosis, and guilt for the wish found restitution in the idealization of land, *mir*, Orthodoxy, and Narod. Herzen struggled against what he sought; Homyakov struggled against what he was engulfed by. Herzen struggled against the enveloping seductiveness of peasant meekness; Homyakov struggled against the seduction of separation from peasant meekness. Herzen lay on the frontier of the revolutionary; Homyakov lay on the frontier of the reactionary.

In finding each other, they enjoyed exhilarating and monumental debates, seeing in the adversary the rejected self, which—and who—was cleaved to as he was fought. Herzen and Homyakov were the two-headed eagle with a common (divided) heart. This common heart was the symbiosis, the "dual unity" (Mahler and Furer 1968) with the peasant mother. Herzen had abandoned her and was haunted by her persistent presence; Homyakov idealized her and fought in vain the symbiotic tie. Herzen could not "return"; Homyakov could not "leave." In having each other as an alter, they could preserve what they could not relinguish. For Herzen, Homyakov personified ancestral fusion with mother, land, and nation; for Homyakov, Herzen personified the break from the devouring symbiosis. Each fulfilled for the other what the other had wished, repressed, and denied—and, in disputation, projected and displaced. In doing combat with Homyakov, Herzen struggled with his guilt by labeling Pan-Slavism backwardness and darkness. In struggling with Herzen, Homyakov fought his own wish to break away. He resolved his guilt over the wish by identifying with and idealizing Mother Russia and by splitting off repudiated aspects of himself and projecting them onto Herzen and Westernization. This resolution became the basis of his Pan-Slavic ideology.

What of the male, the father, the "active"? His presence for both Herzen and Homyakov is at best shadowy. Herzen was willing to retain a *liberal, active* czar; Homyakov wanted a *mystical, religious, romantic, passive* czar. In becoming Westernized, Herzen had become the *activist* and in doing so had "violated" the mother. In his Pan-Slavism, Homyakov preached *pacifism* but struggled to break out of it by going to war, by writing often fierce war poetry, and by alternating in his Pan-Slavic ideology between awaiting the ultimate Slavic victory and assenting to military aims to achieve it—all in the defense of the Holy Mother. If in Russian culture history masculine activism is a countervailing wresting from the condition of female passivity, then there can be no separation or individuation that is not in some way directed *against* the mother. Stated differently, any affirmation of autonomy must involve a repudiation of absolute dependency upon which the mother is absolutely dependent: any "for oneself" is simultaneously "against the mother."

For Homyakov, the proselytizing traditionalist, "active" and "passive" were reconciled through the idealization of the Motherland and the Little Father, the former whom he could defend, and the latter whom he could obediently serve. The "masculine" side of Orthodoxy, Autocracy, and *Narodnost* provided simultaneously a defense against the feminine side and its idealization. For Herzen, the apostate, both the father and the mother were violated, and neither filial piety nor idealization of the mother could be accepted without compromising his vulnerable selfhood. Suggestive of the ambivalence within Homyakov's resolution is his "affair" with the Westernizers. If his *patriotic* zealotry can be understood as a defense both of and against the mother, by being a better man, and his *nation*alist Orthodoxy can be understood as an idealization of the "good mother" image, then his fascination with the Westernizers can be understood as an attempt to wrest himself out of maternal Russian engulfment and from paternal contradiction, from which process he recoiled and consolidated a defensive identification (and identity). Homyakov's mystification and mythos of Russia can be understood as a "religious conversion" whose roots lie in a massive denial and inversion of the threatening wish to break out of the "Russian Winter" and all it connotes.

For Herzen the process was the opposite—a mirror image. His "foreign" upbringing, together with his long exposure to "foreign" influences, produced a "weakened" internalization of and attachment to Russian culture. He combined a keen intelligence, alienation, bitterness, futility, radicalism, guilt, and longing. A reformist imagery of a new society alternated with an empty and rageful nihilism. As he welcomed the enlightenment and liberalization of Russia, he lamented the influence of Western un-Christian rationalism and depersonalization. He had to repudiate the past or be overwhelmed by it. The all-or-nothing became a new social order versus oblivion, between which he constantly vacillated. Herzen was prototypic of the widespread condition of nineteenth-century Russian intellectuals, rootless, cut off from their past and an active place in the Russian future by the coconspiracy of themselves and a society ambivalent and contradictory toward autocracy and liberalism, unsure of its own values. Herbert Muller nicely summarizes the resolution: "Militant atheism,

nihilism, anarchism—all amounting to an inverted Orthodoxy" (1957:299). Stated differently, the profane is sacralized,
and the formerly sacred is desecrated.

Dostoevski: Absolute Freedom and Absolute Despotism

Some observations on the life and work of Feodor Dostoevski
may further illumine the dialectic between Herzen and Homyakov, the Westernizers and the Russian Slavophiles, and the
oscillation between nihilism and moralism. For in a sense
Dostoevski combined Herzen and Homyakov in himself. He
began with "inverted Orthodoxy" and later converted to Orthodoxy. From a century preceeding Peter the Great, French
culture, and later Voltaire and "Reason" were not merely
French *exports;* they were eagerly *imported* ("diffused") by
the nobility and gentry as elements of a widening identity and
equally used as a wedge against tradition. It is not coinciden-
tal that the preoccupation among the great European writers
with suicide, death, and will emerged in the aftermath of the
Napoleonic Wars. In addition to stimulating a resistant and resurgent nationalism, the Napoleonic era also offered the vision of an alternative to the oppression and ignorance of tradition. In a sense the cosmopolitan Napoleonic superidentity of
a united Europe, though in its later stage suffused with (and
undermined by) French nationalism and imperialism, burst
the walls of every eagerly awaiting ghetto it encountered. The
breath of freedom was both welcome and unwelcome.

Dostoevski, son of Orthodoxy and Russian soil, was Westernized and later repudiated his Westernization. In a thought-
ful essay on literary works dealing with the ambivalent liberalism of "the fathers" and the violent nihilism of "the sons,"
Robert Langbaum writes of Dostoevski:

Dostoevsky belonged in the 1840's to a socialist group; when the
group was dissolved by the government, he had laid upon him a sentence of death that at the last minute was commuted to imprison-
ment in Siberia. In prison he came to see the error, not of his generous impulses, but of the materialistic principles on which they were

based. He came to believe . . . that social compassion would bear terrible fruits unless rooted in Christian principles [1973:244]

In discussing Dostoevski's "moral awakening" (Freud 1928), it is not enough to speak of a "conversion" from error to rectitude, because even at his most penitent and proselytizing, he must combat whatever persistently threatens to undo his strongest convictions. Thus, as he puts in the mouth of one of his conspiratorial revolutionaries, Shigalov: "I started out with the idea of unrestricted freedom and I have arrived at unrestricted despotism," we must wonder about the dialectic between the two.

His writings are the battleground of his struggle and document his ultimate solution as the return of the prodigal son. Dostoevski is as much an accomplice in the radical individualism of his characters as he was the heralded prophet of Russia and Orthodoxy. He needed both to *commit his crimes* and to *receive his punishment:* for example, in *Crime and Punishment* his murder of the old woman (pawnbroker) as the apotheosis of nihilistic individualism; his punishment by the male custodians of society; and his reinitiation into the Russian community and communion. Raskolnikov arrogated to himself the right to take the old woman's life because he was above the law, above everything, a Russian *Übermensch*, transvaluating all of civilized value. Raskolnikov repented and was reborn—likewise Dostoevski. Devoting volumes to patricide, matricide, deicide, and suicide, he ever returns as a new man to the community of repentants, enjoying a moral awakening following upon sordid sin.

Dostoevski desperately needed a God and spent the whole of *The Brothers Karamazov* trying to prove God's existence to himself. As a convert and proselyte in the latter half of the nineteenth century, he cursed apostates and heretics like Herzen. In *The Possessed,* Kirillov discovered absolute freedom—proclaiming it by fiat—when he decreed that if God did not exist all things were possible. Before, when God existed, everything was his will; now that he is dead, all is *my* will. The highest embodiment of this newfound self-will is suicide, because in doing so he becomes God himself. To prove his freedom, he must destroy himself. The rootless, self-uprooted, Westernized, self-willed man overflowing with hubris could not endure the freedom he had wrested by his own radical self-uprooting. *The Possessed* contains a further inexorable need for crime and punishment: Stavrogin raping the helpless and virtuous Matryosha, which forced her to suicide, was followed by his suicide, "a grim, naked need for a cross, for a public execution." Again, his moral awakening is contingent upon the commission of sin.

For Dostoevski, historical awareness—his projections of his life history and his insight into the fraudulence of upper-class liberal fathers—was the demon that possessed the intellectuals, the radicals, and the terrorists of Russian society and led them to revolutionary politics. Their social conscience was only a masquerade, a façade for their sociopathy. Revolutionary values were undermining the true and lasting values of Russia. Like Oedipus, who saw and understood too much, he cursed his eyes and "blinded" himself. Ideas and knowledge, because self-uprooting, become a curse that is repudiated for the blessings of simple piety. Although the peasant and the *mir* were equally idealized by the Westernizers and the Slavophiles, Dostoevski sees in the Westernizers (i.e., "Socialists") a direct line from liberal anarchism to nihilist terrorism:

Dostoevsky, who was writing about the Russia of the 1860's, asks what happens to the children of a liberal generation that has called into question all received values. Dostoevsky . . . connects the gentle nihilism of the fathers with the murderous nihilism of the sons. [Langbaum 1973:230]

Out of disillusionment with the halfhearted liberalism of the fathers emerges the radical revolutionary order of the sons. Stated differently, parental confusion over their own ideals and values (e.g. liberalism versus autocracy)—expressed in contradiction between word and deed, between different acts, between what is said and how it is said—generates identity confusion in the children, because the parents have subverted both the new and the traditional values: the *perfidy* of the parents generates the *rage* in the children. The hollow compassion and murderousness that Dostoevski condemns in the revolutionaries (Nechayev, Bakunin), are not merely external enemies but internal ones as well, with which he must constantly struggle: "Dostoevsky . . . blames the radicalism of the sons upon the liberalism of the fathers. In destructive and violent nihilism, Dostoevsky sees the logical consequences of that subversion of traditional values, especially religious values, which has always been inherent in the liberal tradition of free thinking" (Langbaum 1973:243). The problem, though, was not "liberalism" per se but what it represented: an *ideology* associated with an erstwhile *identity* that was based on conflict-ridden *identification* with parental and surrogate figures.

In the nihilistic revolutionaries and intellectuals he locates the enemy he once was (and remains); he struggles against the *adolescent* solution he once embraced (Erikson 1965). For early Dostoevski the flirtation with socialism and anarchism succeeded only in further alienating him from Russian family and tradition: it heightened his conflicts even as it temporarily resolved them. His subsequent "conversion" to Orthodoxy and Russian Slavophilism had constantly to struggle with earlier abortive resolutions and remained a goal rather than an achievement. He repeatedly drove his characters to murder and suicide to illustrate the "empty relativism" (Erikson 1965) of the intellect and historical awareness, while constructing scenarios of "moral awakening" to offer Russian pietism as the only salvation.

Beneath the "repetition compulsion" to portray and reenact the *cycle* of crime, punishment, absurdity, remorse, guilt and divine illumination lay a profound accusation of the ethical untrustworthiness of the whole of contemporary Russian culture—and his own. To cope with this moralistic outrage of hate and self-hate, Dostoevski became the ideologue of "reactionary" Russian Orthodox messianism, whose doctrine later was to infuse the militant atheism of the Russian *Revolution* in its manifesto of salvation from the contradictions of Russian and Western history in one monumental housecleaning. What Dostoevski would most vehemently have condemned he prepared for, and, in a sense, was apologist for. Holy Russia was to conquer the world, if not with "humble charity," then with messianic zeal; if not in God's name, then at least in Russia's; if not by truth, then by force. Dostoevski saved himself by atoning, by "selling" his soul to Mother Russia; yet, through his novels, he killed part of himself. Alexander Herzen had found his "cause" in Westernization, only to have his daughter commit suicide, a sign of the cul de ·sac toward which such radicalism leads. Dostoevski left it to his "protagonists" to act out *their* murderous obsessions, while he could condemn it all "from above" as a man who had been saved. Dostoevski, like Homyakov and other Slavophile converts, spared himself the reductio ad absurdum that Herzen's family *lived out*, choosing Orthodox Slavophilism as an alternate form of "self-annihilation."

In his morbidly dogged effort to test and question—and break—the limits of family, morality, society, and meaning, he had become his own existential absurdity. He had killed and questioned mothers, fathers, gods, and societies and in his guilt rediscovered salvation in the selfsame idols he had smashed.

Whatever the ideological persuasion of these varied writers and activists of nineteenth-century Russia, what unites them is a profound ambivalence toward paternal and maternal figures both of childhood and of the present, exacerbated—often fatally—by the self-uprooting of Westernization. They lived under regimes—and parents—that were alternately and even simultaneously liberal and repressive, reformative and obscurantist, open and reactionary, progressive and intractable. The image of the spectrum of fathers—from parental to priest to czar—was inconstant, vacillating between the idealized "Little Father" and the distant brooding and wrathful despot. The czar himself became increasingly remote and unreachable as the mediating bureaucracy densely proliferated.

Sidney Monas has suggested that in addition to the archetypal Russian theme of sons versus fathers (patricide, filicide, regicide, etc.) is an obscured theme of "Sons against Mothers" and "Mothers against Sons," from which opposition he posits much of Russian history to flow (Monas 1965, cf. Erikson 1963a; chap. 10). This is not to reduce Russian nationalism to childhood but to inquire into the "coconspiracy" of Childhood *and* Society (Erikson 1963a) in the transmission and recapitulation of parental conflicts. Often the children seemingly can resolve parental conflicts only through some form of radicalism in an effort to preserve any self-esteem and initiative and manage the pervasive guilt and shame that would undo their fondest efforts. The ideology of Russian nationalism, as of nationalistic movements generally, was an attempt to provide a future by way of the romanticized distant past, where the present and the immediate past offered no tolerable future. Conversely, the ideology of Russian radical Westernism (culminating in the revolution) was an attempt to provide a future through making a holocaust of the past, since its oppressive presence in the present equally offered no tolerable future. Yet, as I have discussed, each ideology was closely bound up with its opposite, just as were the Westernizers and the Slavophiles, who were members of a conflict that extended to an even wider "family" even when the extent of its membership was hardly recognized.

Conclusion

In this chapter I have suggested that radical Westernization and radical Slavophilism were opposing ideologies and identities that arose from a common conflict and situation and represented alternative means of resolving that conflict. The two "extremes" provide insight into the gnawing and chronic discontent of the "mean," no less real because less spectacular—until it erupted in the revolutionary period of 1905–22. The "mean" to which I have referred is the "place" and "sense of place" of Russia in the European family of nations (which anxiety over status and power reverberates from the infant's earliest experience to his or her position in the sibling order, and so on). I have suggested that the hidden and repressed side of Russian Slavophilism was Westernization and that the hidden and repressed side of Westernization was Slavophilism, each subverting, opposing, and needing the other for completeness.

Some discussion of the lives and work of Herzen, Homyakov, and Dostoevski was offered to support this hypothesis. The *cognitive* contradictions, *affective* ambivalence, and *behavioral* inconsistencies of these three historical figures mirror in extremis the dynamics of Russian history, latent since at least the sixteenth century, made increasingly manifest by subsequent sociocultural and socioeconomic change. These three figures were among the most sensitive "victims" and articulators of these conditions. As a triad to which many names could be added (including, currently, Sakharov the Westernizer and Solzhenitzyn the Slavophile), they personify the necessary relationship between internationalism or supranationalism and nationalism, between universalism and particularism, between cosmopolitanism and parochialism, with the failure of the former member of each pair as a precondition for the development of the latter.

Much research in psychobiography beyond the scope of this chapter is needed to investigate the parent-child relations and developmental precursors that underlay the cognitive and emotional capacity of Russian and earlier Western European nationalists for imagining, creating, and investing in something so hitherto encompassing and integrative as a nation. Writing of early-nineteenth-century German nationalists, for instance, Beisel argues:

The kind of mothering earlier generations received—or rather, did *not* receive—meant that they viewed their bodies, because of the intra-psychic fragmentation caused by excessive rage, almost entirely as part objects. The kind of intrusive mothering the nationalists received [one based on the mother's meting out of love as she is able to exert full control over her infant's body] meant that they were more capable of experiencing their bodies as a totality, and, like other Romantics who projected the same sense onto an organic Mother Nature, projected it onto the transcendent nation with which they sought to merge. [1980b:12]

Later he argues that, while fantasies of "belonging" are universal, not all such fantasies can be adduced as evidence of specifically nationalist sentiment, the latter of which he defines as "the regression of an intrusively-mothered psychoclass to a collective fantasy of preoedipal fusion defensively labeled a 'nation'" (Beisel 1982b:351). This is a challenging hypothesis that deserves to be tested insofar as possible by a careful reconstruction of the early lives of Herzen, Homyakov, Dostoevski, and others.

Ruud writes:

The Slavophils' view of the West was entirely an emotional reaction, rooted deeply in the personalities of the Slavophils themselves. . . . The fervour of the Slavophils and their personalized nationalism opened the way for later Russians to express their conflicts in terms that depended upon hostility between Russia and the West. [1974:280–81]

While the Slavophiles projected "in universal terms their own private experiences" (Ruud 1974:281) and thereby created and rationalized a self-fulfilling prophecy in the relations between Russia and the West, their very "private experiences" and "emotional reaction" are nevertheless rooted simultaneously in personal and culture history. The Slavophiles who waged their personal struggles on the historical stage did not develop in a historical vacuum. The personalities of the Slavophiles are historically rooted in the bedrock conflict between Russia and the West and are inseparable from it. The very personal conflict they projected is prototypic of a wider cultural conflict that they had introjected or internalized (precisely the dynamics of the shaman) and then reprojected onto "history"— re-creating, perpetuating, and necessitating the very hostility toward the West that originally derived *from* the West.

This analysis should also clarify somewhat the relation of the Bolshevik revolution to Russian nationalism and Socialist internationalism. Although Russian nationalism was officially rejected by the Revolution, the Soviet and "Western" choice quickly became subverted by its hidden face—and by renewed pressures and threats from the West and East. Though couched in new ideological garb, the dialectic between the Slavophiles and the Westernizers persists to the present. It remains an intense problem of the Russian/Soviet identity— and of the identity of the West. See also chapter 5, which brings this very conflict to our doorstep.

CHAPTER 4

The Binding of the Son: Psychoanalytic Reflections on the Symbiosis of Jews and Christians

The reader about to begin a chapter about psychological themes which pervade millennia of the Judeo-Christian relationship might well wonder what the history of religion (or interreligious strife) has to do with psychogeography—that is, with spatial representation. In a more traditional psychoanalytic and anthropology-of-religion vein, I could reply that the image and character of supernatural beings are formed by one's experience as a child within a family and are subsequently projected onto or into space, where the spirits or deities dwell and do their work. For instance, I might talk about how God is perceived to inhabit the world "above" and Satan is perceived to reign from the netherworld "below," and how these in turn are often related to the sacred head and the profane bowels and genital region, respectively. I could compare the beliefs in spiritual beings within the two traditions, e.g., the tendency within Judaism to locate God outside, and the tendency within Christianity to locate God both outside and inside (the doctrine of immanence). Likewise, I could explore the unconscious meanings of various sacred places (houses of worship, shrines) within Judaism and Christianity. For example, although both Jews and Christians of all denominations venerate the Holy Land and regard a variety of places as holy, Judaism is far more bound to particular geographic space than is Christianity.

This more traditional and familiar approach to the study of religion and interreligious conflict I shall not pursue. Instead, in this chapter I concentrate on how Jews and Christians as *groups* perceive themselves and one another and the consequences of that unconsciously influenced perception on inter-group relations. Religions, we have long been taught, are matters of individuals' "ultimate concerns." Similarly, the referent or object of those ultimate concerns is usually regarded as the theological doctrine, the belief system, or the spiritual beings themselves. In this chapter I shall argue that participation in a group, and the distinction of one's own group from another's, is *itself* an inextricable part of those ultimate concerns that occupy the core of a person's identity. The question, "What are Jews and Christians?" may also be phrased, "*Where* are Jews and Christians?" or, stated differently, "What exactly is the historic boundary between them?" I discover, much to my surprise, that while the official boundary between them is unmistakably marked—as much as any mighty river or massive mountain range that separates two adjacent territories—at the level of deeper meaning disowned parts of Christians have continued to wend their way to becoming "intrinsic" characteristics of Jews, and exactly the reverse as well.

This chapter, however, should be read as an instance of a far broader course in Jewish history than that wended by Judeo-Christian relations alone. The latter should be construed as a variation on a theme that has far deeper and wider roots. For, while to Jews Christians are Gentiles (Yiddish: *goyim*, a term for all "others" that simultaneously acknowledges differences and is contemptuous of those who are different), not all Gentiles are Christians. Contemporary Israeli-Arab-Diaspora Jewish relations, too, could be seen to play out the unconscious drama identified here. To say that this chapter is about the Jewish role in history—one not limited to a single, long episode in that history—one taken and assigned by numerous historical partners, only attests to the power of repetition in *all* of human history.

Contemporary social reemphasis on ethnic identity (see Stein 1975b; Stein and Hill 1973, 1977a, 1977b) suggests that an important underlying factor in the persistence of cultural difference is the insistence on such difference, which is expressed in boundary-maintaining symbols, emblems, totems, and rituals. In this study of the continued reassertion of Jewish identity, which now combines the ethnonational and the ethnoreligious emphasis (Stein 1975a), I suggest that to focus exclusively on Jews would be a major methodological error— that what must be scrutinized is the often fatal symbiosis between Jews and Gentiles (that is, non-Jews) in the reciprocal, simultaneous preservation of each group's "own" identity and that of the repudiated "other." Not despite traditional enmity but because of it, each group utilizes and needs the other against which to define itself; the two are interdependent (see Stein 1984).

As Loewenstein (1951) observed in his classic psychoanalytic study *Christians and Jews,* antipathy toward Jews is rooted in the shared history of Judaism and Christianity, "a cultural pair." The phrase is felicitous, for it goes to the heart of the dynamic inseparability of two traditions that insist on the inviolability of their sacred boundaries and their separate integrity yet are unable to live either with or without one another. Loewenstein argues that, while the Christian stereotype of the Jews has undergone numerous accretions of cultural content since early Christian times, the underlying core of the conflict lies in Christian ambivalence toward the heavy conscience derived from Judaism, exacerbated by ambivalence toward the dogged survival of Jews through nearly two millennia of Christian persecution.

While I am in agreement with this oedipal interpretation, I wish to expand it by inquiring into those Jewish cultural psychodynamics that perpetuate Jewish stereotypes of Christians. What is in fact repressed within each tradition is magically discovered and struggled against in the tradition of its opposite. Just as Christians recoil against their debt to the Jews (superego), Jews in turn recoil against a similarly unspoken debt to Christianity: the successful Christian revolt against that repressive moral burden—the Law and its suffocating strictures—that Jews dare not admit to be *their* wish (id). For beneath the compulsive Jewish loyalty to "the intellectual tyranny of authoritarian tribalism" (La Barre 1972:591) lies a simmering recalcitrance and an occasional open volcano of revolt against an obsessive Sabbatarianism that encompasses every moment of every day of the week.

Because of the constant danger of the uncanny recognition

of the dissociated as part of oneself, Jew and Christian alike must reaffirm "what I am" by emphasizing "what I am not," the ritual confirming the myth of difference through the representation of sense data. Boundaries of personal ego and cultural ethos are thereby (temporarily) shored up, and what is inside is clearly distinguishable from what is outside (ego-syntonic and ego-dystonic, respectively). Nevertheless, the degree of recognition of underlying likeness and attraction is attested to by the extent of insistence on difference and revulsion. While what is perceived to be culturally alien is dynamically ego-alien (that is, split off), the affective valence of secret attraction is reflected by the energy invested in the countercathexis of repudiation.

The relationship of "antagonistic acculturation" (Loeb and Devereux 1943) has interlinked two traditions for nearly two millennia. The officially stigmatized group (e.g., the Jews, in the context of dominant Christendom) must deal with its discreditation. But since stigma is a systemic pathology of relationship, both groups are alternately ingroup *and* outgroup and hence are *mutually* discredited irrespective of the institutionalized status, relative power, and rationalized myths of superiority held by the dominant group (see Goffman 1963). Clearly, what must be vigilantly kept outside the boundary of ego and ethos is something externalized yet unconsciously internalized. The incompleteness of the externalization (paralleling the incompleteness of the introjection of one's parent tradition) is what has caused the persistence of Judeo-Christian symbiosis. Each needs the other outside to do its dirty work, but not so distant as to be unavailable for fascination and contempt. The wider systemic boundary of projective identification *subsumes both groups.*

Perpetuation of the "oppositional process" (Spicer 1971) and intergroup "dissociation" (Devereux 1975) are essential to the intragroup stability and solidarity of each group and to the intrapsychic stability of each group member. These cultural defense mechanisms sustain each group. The systematic relationship between Jews and Christians implies that one cannot be adequately discussed without at least *implying* the other; I hope to make the implications explicit.

Jewish Group Identity and the Theology
of Oedipal Sacrifice

Among the "dissociative" characteristics and consequences of dysfunctional ethnic identity, Devereux (1975) includes (1) the reduction of an individual to "one-dimensionality" (p. 66); (2) the highly ritualized, "insistent, and even obsessive clinging to one's ethnic (or any other 'class' [in the mathematical sense]) identity" (p. 67); (3) hypercathexis of ethnic identity, with the subordination or exclusion of other components of identity, as a means of shoring up a flawed self (p. 68); (4) the creation of a closed-system identity; and (5) the "obliteration of individual distinctiveness" (p. 65). ". . . a hypercathecting of one's ethnic identity leads . . . to the annihilation of the individual's real identity. . . . Yet, man's functionally relevant dissimilarity from all others is what makes him human: similar to others precisely through his high degree of differentiation. It is this which permits him to claim a human identity" (p. 66).

From a psychodynamic point of view, the basis of Jewish-Christian opposition lies in a reciprocal dissociation, which can be approached through an exploration of the oedipal paradigm of each tradition. The analysis of Jewish-Christian symbiosis can begin with a discussion of the significance Jewish tradition places on the father-son relation. Some recent comments by Rabbi Benjamin Z. Kreitman will serve as a "text" and a point of departure for a comparison of the Jewish identification with the Father, the Christian identification with the Son, and the relationship of this difference to intergroup stereotyping. Note that in this passage the reaffirmation of ethnic Jewishness is synonymous with a reaffirmation of an identification with the austere father and the patristic deity. This rebinding to the tradition transparently expresses the Jewish oedipal paradigm. In 1975, Rabbi Kreitman wrote:

Many have let their ardors of Jewish loyalty be cooled by indifference and unconcern. Others, more sensitive, have begun to give expression to their doubts and fears; doubts about the reasons for Jewish survival and fears over what perils may be imposed on their children, bearing a Jewish identity.

The issue over which the American Jew agonizes now is not alone whether he should continue to be a Jew but over the question whether he has the right to impose this frightful choice on his descendants.

In Biblical terms the question is: Must we respond affirmatively to the command of destiny: "Take your son, your favored one, Isaac, whom you love and go to the land of Moriah and offer him there as a burnt offering" (Genesis 22:2).

. . . We are the precipitates of centuries of suffering, of pain and heroism. Unlike other areas and other centuries, the American Jew living in an open society has a choice and an option. His position is akin to that of the first Jew, Abraham, whose decision to be a Jew was free from the coercion of fate, birth and the shame of betrayal. Our response at this juncture bears an extraordinary historic character.

To remain silent to the demand of "Take your son" in this hour is to surrender to the demonic in life. Not only will the Jew be diminished but humanity will be diminished as well. Even to the most secular-minded, the stubbornness of the Jew in continuing to exist and be a creative force gives faith for tomorrow.

Emil Fackenheim, who has given much thought to the theology after the Holocaust, writes: "To be a Jew after Auschwitz [is] to bear witness against [those who hate Jews] in all their guises. It is to believe that they will not prevail and to stake on that belief one's life and that of one's children."

Given the nature of human evil, the choice of not being a Jew for the sake of the future security of one's children becomes an even more frightening decision. Fackenheim uncovers the dreadful possibilities of such a choice: *"By choosing for our children not to be victims* (read *Akedah*. BZK) [we] may be exposing them to the possibility, or the likelihood, that they will be murderers."* [Quoted in Geffen 1975:6–7]

(For broader discussion of the theology of Fackenheim, see "The Ingathering," in Stein and Hill 1977a. The *Akedah* refers literally to Abraham's tying of Isaac's limbs in preparation for sacrificing him on the altar [Genesis 22:9]. Traditional rabbinical interpretation emphasizes Abraham's willingness to obey God's command, that is, God's test of faith. The focus is thereby shifted away from Abraham's own intention or plan to his readiness to comply with God, who had no intention of requiring Isaac's sacrifice.)

It is the readiness to bind over the next generation that is troubling. To be a Jew after the Holocaust—not merely Auschwitz, but the cumulative Holocaust of Jewish history—is not only to defy "them" but to fear that future generations of "us" will become "them," the demonic adversary. Jews must bind over their children as potential victims or sacrifices to ensure that they will not join the enemy. This reflects not a faith either in tomorrow or in one's children but the dread of both. To save oneself and one's children, one must sacrifice them; without this, so goes the unerring logic, both Jews and the remainder of humanity will be diminished. The future security of one's children lies in their maximum vulnerability, which is subsequently transformed into an identification with the father (aggressor) who so graciously spared his son (and children). Vulnerability becomes security, as son becomes father, and all become the children of the God of Israel. Such is the substrate of the creative force that gives faith for tomorrow, that makes for stubborn persistence, that makes Jews so valuable to humanity.

This "rewriting" of Rabbi Kreitman's passage—a passage representative of much modern Jewish thinking—is intended not to be cynical but to make explicit the grave doubts that underlie the prescription for security. I would argue that to succumb to this prescription is to surrender to the demonic in life through a historic "acting out," rather than to transcend it by working the conflicts through. In the act of protecting one's children and safeguarding their future, one condemns them to the very fate one would consciously (and conscientiously) avert. One constantly dares and gambles with fate, and when Holocaust comes, one is able to protest one's innocence. It is "they" who are persecuting "us." What we fail to recognize is that "they" are playing the father-persecutor role for us; we are then the innocent son, awaiting a totemic ram in the brush and rescue from above. In choosing to bind over our sons, we place them in peril: survival becomes a way of inviting self-destruction; placing in jeopardy is a means or preparation for coping with danger.

Although I shall be discussing the traditional father-son Jewish paradigm, I suggest that much of the mother-daughter relation in Jewish tradition has the same emotional valence.

In her unpublished short story "A Sign From G-d," Florence Hamlish Levinsohn has a passage that supports this hypothesis. Her protagonist says:

. . . having been the firstborn though not a male, I have often felt a certain kinship with Isaac. I have wondered many times if God did not appear to my mother and instruct her, Take now thy daughter, thine only daughter, whom thou lovest, and get thee into the land of Moriah, and offer her there for a burnt offering upon one of the mountains which I will tell thee of. Sacrilege? A woman offering a sacrifice of her daughter? Perhaps. To an atheist what is sacrilege? I felt I had been saved from the sacrifice. Perhaps it was only the martyrdom my mother practiced that led me to that belief, but . . . I carried about for many years the belief that, there, but for the grace of God, would I have been sacrificed on the altar. Having been saved, I must now withstand a thousand tests to prove the felicity of that earliest judgment. I had been chosen among many who had been so chosen, one of the many firstborn who were chosen. . . . The great test of faith and love, that had been given to the father first, then to the mother was now to be given to the firstborn, as it should be. If we are to inherit the kingdom, or the hearth, depending on our sex, surely a test of faith and love is in order. [1977:2–3; quoted with permission]

Martyrdom, victimization, and reparation—and the perpetuation of "tradition"—are shared both by males and females. What this passage makes so abundantly clear, even as fiction, is how the secular dramas of everyday Jewish life closely follow and give meaning to, even as they are given meaning by, the larger-than-life dramas of sacred text.

The ritualized sacrifice of Isaac does not compel God's indebtedness to Abraham's descendants, although this was his promise, a price for protection (cf. Schlossman 1969:88). Beneath the official promise of chosenness for fruitfulness and conquest lies the unconsciously censored promise of chosenness for perpetual sacrifice and victimization. Israel was the "suffering servant" long before the Suffering Servant figure of sixth-century (B.C.) Deutero-Isaiah. The coeval existence of moral masochism (martyrdom-sacrifice) and identification with the aggressor (acceptance of the overwhelmingly demanding and repressive Covenant) has its Judeo-Christian mythic archetype in the persons of Abraham and Isaac. According to tradition, God's promise of fertility to the aged Abraham and Sarah was contingent on the acceptance of the Covenant that required circumcision. But what was *explicitly* a token sacrifice to the Father was *implicitly* an insufficient offering. Neither the displaced sacrifice of the totemic ram (from Abraham through the Temples) nor the "token" ritual offering of the foreskin in circumcision served as adequate substitute for the continually valent repressed wish that would be satisfied with nothing less than full elimination of the son—either through the father's envy of the son's threat or through the son's need for punishment owing to guilt over envy of the father.

Each accretion of ritual following ritual, new defense replacing old defense—from human sacrifice of the firstborn male to animal sacrifice, to the abolition of animal sacrifice and the institution of personal pietism, to the self-sacrifice of Jesus on the Cross—was less a "theological advance" than symptomatic of the fact that the conflict underlying the Akedah had never been sufficiently countercathected by myth or ritual. The more intense the wish and the more inadequate current defenses against it, the more elaborately it had to be defended against and disguised through the proliferation of stronger rituals that regulated volatile father-son and God-human relationships. The lineage of Mosaic, Priestly, Talmudic, and Orthodox Jewish Halachah (Law)—"behavior modification" in increasingly more paralyzing dosages of external regulation toward instinctual extinction—attests to the need for overbearing constraints to keep in check an overbearing wish. This in turn generated the very opposite of its intent, namely a recalcitrance and latent rebellion toward the very authority it had set up to combat the unacceptable wish. The original intent (sacrifice of the son), though officially repudiated, is unavoidably "smuggled" back into the very tradition that has manifestly transcended it. Unwittingly, or, rather, unconsciously, the Jewish people themselves came to be the perennial sacrificial victim (masochistic identification with the vulnerable and guilty son) *and* those who demand of others increasingly numerous and severe sacrifices and renunciations (sadistic identification with the omnipotent father).

To overemphasize the overt differences between Orthodox Judaism and Pauline Christianity over the subject of sacrifice is to fail to discern the persistence of sacrifice in Judaism even in its absence. La Barre notes that the faith of Pauline Christianity lay in "the mystery of [Jesus'] sacrificial death, a faith invented and promulgated by Paul" (1972:608). La Barre continues:

In a curiously masochistic identification with his Messiah, Paul proclaimed that Christ was a human sacrifice that God had commanded to mollify God's wrath (Romans 3:25). If Abraham had abolished human sacrifice of the Firstborn, and later Jews had abolished even animal sacrifice, Paul restored human sacrifice—but now with a jumble of symbolisms of the archaic scapegoat, Paschal lamb, the murdered son-god of the Great Mother, and the Orphic Dying God who was eaten to confer immortality! [1972:608–609]

While in the literal sense it is true that Judaism abolished human and animal sacrifice and that, through Paul, Christianity reinstated the former, in the psychodynamic sense Judaism *never* abolished the *original* sacrifice. The nature of the sacrifice transformed the sacrificial dyad of literal father-son, Abraham-Isaac, God-father (son), into the relationship between God and the entire people of Israel. Jews, in sadomasochistic identification with both father (and Father) and son, became the Jewish Paschal lamb who, as scapegoat, takes away the sins of the world. Christianity continued the displacement and dissociation of the sacrifice; Judaism became the religion of a people who *remain the sacrifice itself.* For Pauline Christianity, no longer was the terrible, transcendent Father unapproachable. Human helplessness and sinfulness in the face of divine wrath was alleviated and the chasm bridged by a Son whom the Father himself had sent to redeem an otherwise unredeemable mankind through His death and resurrection. Through the crucified and resurrected Christ (resurrected by God himself), mankind had a chance at salvation. Judaism has no such vicarious sacrifice and magical victory. The Jewish people are their own offering, their lives their own expiation, to the Father whose agents they remain and whose conscience (Law) they have internalized.

In his paper "Circumcision as Defense," Schlossman argues that the Covenant of Divine Mercy toward God's chosen people was contingent on the "acceptance of the foreskin as a token sacrifice in lieu of the son" (1966:351). The totemic ram becomes the substitute *full* sacrifice; circumcision becomes the *token* sacrifice. Earlier pagan instinctual indulgence was supplanted by the austerity of instinctual renunciation before the demands of Yahweh. Schlossman cogently asks:

Did Abraham on the occasion of becoming a father remember his childhood envy and wishes to destroy his father? It seems plausible that he made peace with his father's spirit by offering a sacrifice, the foreskin of himself and his sons. The young father propitiates the envy of the God representing his father by sacrificing a piece of his son's penis, in fantasy an extension of his own. Instead of taking, he gives; and since he gives a part, God will not take all. [1966:351–52]

Elsewhere Schlossman summarizes Shalom Spiegel's reconstruction of the Akedah as follows:

1) Abraham did sacrifice Isaac on Mount Moriah, 2) God resurrected him, 3) Abraham in his zeal proceeded to sacrifice him again. This was stopped by the Angel of the Lord, 4) the reason for the sacrifice was a transaction—an exchange of Isaac for His indebtedness to the descendants of Abraham in the future; when in trouble, the Jews could call on God's compassion and mercy by reminding him of the Akedah. [Schlossman 1969:88]

On archaeological and manuscript-textual evidence, La Barre (1972:593) suggests that there were likely many Abrahams, in fact eight centuries of them, from 2100 to 1300 B.C. This would seem to support the Spiegel-Schlossman argument of multiple sacrifices of Isaac, though not necessarily by the "same" man.

I question Schlossman's suggestion that "circumcision appears to be the last phase of a particular evolutionary process of sacrifice to the gods" (1966:351). Human sacrifice was replaced by displaced offerings, to be sure, but the next stage became self-sacrifice—from austere instinctual renunciation to the Christian self-offering of Jesus the Son to God the Father. I suggest that the ancient "cruel rites" never disappeared; rather their form changed. Among the Jews such sacrifice ultimately took the form of self-victimization as the eternally suffering servant who was punished from without. With early Christianity, Jesus became the "lamb of God" (Agnus Dei) who came to "die for us" to take away the sins of the world ("qui tollis peccata mundi"). The dangers of bisexual and oedipal reinstinctualization and reprimitivization were never fully bound by a tradition of shared myth and ritual. Primeval conflicts underlying ego and cultural *structure* led to the need for subsequent *restructuring*.

La Barre asks: ". . . can a society never modify the cultural superego, the Sacred Past? Not so long as it insists that salvation comes only through allegiance to the sacred past! Cultural compulsions constrain societies as firmly as compulsive systems bind the individual neurotic" (1969:170). Each successive mythico-religious re-solution becomes a new defense (countercathexis) elaborated to replace those currently inadequate to cope with the "Ur-anxieties" (castration, parricide, destruction) that remain repressed. The new solution, as a compromise, becomes part of the problem, further compounding it, generating secondary anxiety and the need for more rigid defense to cope with the pseudo-problems posed by new myths, taboos, prescriptions, and proscriptions. Personal history and cultural history become homologous examples of vicious cycles that proliferate into spirals of pathology. Essentially, the psychohistoric and ethnohistoric paradox is that, precisely because they are inadequate compromises, no amount of sacrificial tokenism, no abundance of rams, no once-and-for-all redemptive son is sufficient. The disguised return of the repressed makes of any "mystery on the mountain" a perennial mystique that substitutes reality distortion for reality testing.

Here the superordinate place of the shamanistic, rabbi-prototypical Moses in Jewish tradition might well be reexamined (cf. Reid 1972). He has been the central patriarchal figure in the mythic revelation and consolidation of the Covenant and the Law and in the social transformation of scattered Semitic pastoral tribes into the "nation" and "peoplehood" of Israel. He is respectfully (never affectionately) known as "Moshe rabenu," Moses our Teacher, a son-become-father lawgiver of his people through the transmission of the Law of God. (He is in no way an intermediary in the manner of Jesus, who interceded as the son in behalf of God's children; rather, Moses is the mediator between God and Israel, the medium who conveys the will of God to his people, a father rather than a son figure.) With a refocusing on the sacrifice and Akedah of Abraham and Isaac (through its later expressions in Halachic Judaism and Christianity), Moses and the Law do not so much recede in importance within Jewish tradition as become historically subsequent psychodynamic and cultural secondary elaborations on the oedipal theme of sacrifice. Symbolically and ritually they represent efforts to cope with the nuclear conflict at the core of Jewish history.

Tradition and Scotomatization

It makes perfect sense that Jewish tradition should focus on Moses and litigious-pietistic adherence as a culturally elaborated *defense* against its deeper conflicts—except, of course, that such adherence perpetuates the very conflicts it would cure by repression, creating the very opposite effect of the desired defense. The defense process psychodynamically, culturally, and historically seems akin to Hans Selye's "disease of adaptation," bringing further harm as it offers compromised (and decompensated) protection. Protection (defense) by adherence to the Law makes for short-term safety and long-term self-induced vulnerability, since the most strenuous adherence is never enough. And when calamity befalls the Jewish people, it is not to the tyranny of the Abrahamic Akedah that one looks but to the need for stricter law, observances, and penances because, as the Prophets long ago exhorted, Israel has fallen into error—away from the Law. The Law as solution becomes a barrier to the uncovering and transcending of the real, as opposed to the pseudo (though experienced as real), problems.

La Barre states that

in folkloristic terms the past *explains* the present, not the reverse; to suppose past tradition *sustains* present folklore requires retrospective falsification of revelation. We believe what we believe about the Unknown partly for historical reasons, and partly for projective psychological, not cognitive reasons. Cognitive science is essentially anti-historical; it seeks ahistorical validities on grounds of *present* testing, not of traditional authority or of sacred *past* revelation. More than any other, this epistemological shibboleth of *ground for belief* critically distinguishes the adult mind from the infantile authoritarian personality. [1972:598, n. 33]

Later La Barre continues: "The sacred culture of any society is the storehouse of its emotional and intellectual defeats in the forgotten past. Sacred culture is the autistic side of history" (1972:634–35). The "past" becomes an excuse that, through projection, removes responsibility for choices in the present; one does not so much test the present to see what it holds as apply formulas and bromides of the past because the past is assumed to sustain the present. Sense of history is confused with history itself (see Stein 1983b).

In his book *Messengers of God* novelist and essayist Elie Wiesel (1976) traces the Jewish Holocaust back to the first Diaspora, the expulsion from Eden. It is as though everything is retroactively presaged—as myth has a habit of doing with its retrospective connections, condensations, explanations, and falsifications. Wiesel wryly protests the severity of God's treatment of Adam: "Poor man: punished for nothing. And he wasn't even Jewish." Moreover, Wiesel, who makes of the survivor syndrome endless allegorical works of art that compete with the reality they commemorate (and keep alive), chooses *Isaac*, son of the first Jew, Patriarch Abraham, to call "the first survivor." With Abraham and Isaac the Holocaust paradigm was set; just as with Eden, the paradigm of unmerited expulsion and diaspora was irrevocably set in motion.

Wiesel utters in a Jewish idiom what is in fact the human condition. He voices the narcissistic protest that insists that the universe is here for us, that it owes us our existence in (preoedipal?) Paradise, that we are at its center and deserve thereby to be taken care of. Jewish ethnocentrism of specialness is but a single ethnoreligious example of a species-wide narcissistic anthropocentrism that believes and hopes that deity and universe are on its side. However, by virtue of inherent maturational processes (separation-individuation) within the human animal, coupled with the early defeats that reality confers on infantile omnipotence and omniscience, whether or not our ancestral "tribe" had an Eden and an expulsion in its origin myth, we are all "Jews."

Wiesel and much of Jewish tradition have denied the accusation of oedipal "original sin," namely, disobedience to the Father. Abandonment, banishment, exile come undeserved—despite an equally traditional litany of guilt. Job has lived up to all religious obligations; what God has visited upon him is patently unfair. But then, the Voice out of the Whirlwind does have the last say: Who are oedipal mortals to question the unknowable and awesome will of the Father? Self-justifying myths of noble origin notwithstanding, what unites Jews with all mortals is the unavoidability of "original sin," of the loss of innocence, repeated anew with each generation. To speak, as does traditional Christian theology, of "original sin" as a historical event whose consequences we must forever suffer because of our descent and thereby our inherent unworthiness is to commit the selfsame error Freud (1913) made in *Totem and Taboo* (and later corrected), namely, the "projection of the Oedipal conflict into the purely mythological past history of mankind" (cf. La Barre 1968b:65), a Lamarckian displacement of recurrent personal history and guilt onto a past deed for which one is not culpable. What begins ontogenetically as infantile fantasy is subsequently repressed and returns in the acceptable phylogenetic form of "racial memory." Such idiosyncratic or cultural absolution is a defensive means of exonerating oneself and/or one's tribe. One bows contritely to the unalterable past and to its ineradicable persistence in the present.

This is precisely the form of the *theological* excuse that Jewish tradition has conferred on Abraham and Isaac and on subsequent tradition. It is not our oedipal conflict resolution that has made us what we are but the will of God. La Barre writes:

Father Abraham seems to stand as the symbol of some great pre-historic revolution in religion—the abjuring of human sacrifice for animal victims. Behind the legend of Abraham and Isaac lies the old Semitic practice of child-sacrifice, surviving in Phoenician Moloch-worship into historic times. . . . The later interpretation that, through his conflicting commands, God was merely testing the faith of Abraham, even to the sacrifice of his cherished son, rescues God from the theological dilemma of inconstancy over the centuries, but hardly enhances God's moral dignity. Historically the supposed wishes of "God" did change; but psychologically, and with better eternal human consistency, the "inconstancy" of God on Mount Moriah is better seen as the *ambivalence* of Abraham in counter-oedipal conflict over his son, for fatherly love of sons is by no means unwavering. On the deepest level, the *Akedah* or "binding" of god and man, father and son in society, must rest on that initial *religio*, the oedipal bargain between father and son in the human incest taboo. On Mount Moriah, Abraham became not merely the "Father of faith"—literally of Judaism, Christianity and Islam—but, symbolically, the father of all human society. "And he shall turn the heart of the father to the children, and the heart of the children to their fathers," says Malachi 4:6. The Father (Abraham himself projected) tells the father to kill his son; but, again, the Father tells him not to. [1972:558–59]

Following Freud, Schlossman notes that "puberty rites are used to strengthen the taboos against incest and parricide, and tighten the bonds between father and son" (1966:341). Initiation rites attempt to reconcile inherent antagonism between generations, to create intergenerational solidarity and a mutual commitment to the well-being of society. However, the very severity of initiation rites attests to the intensity of conflict and to the need for the father to *bind* the sons to their will: to make obedient men out of potentially rebellious boys. The need for ritual attests to the depth of the problem that society, through its elders, attempts to solve (magically) once and for all. Through the sons' identification with the (father) aggressor, the fathers need fear less a rebellious aggression from the sons; such aggression is repressed, displaced, and sublimated.

Death and Resurrection, as a common initiation-rite theme, expresses the father's insistence that the initiate submit and symbolically die as a mother-identified son and be reborn as a father and ally of the father generation. Yet, despite the intensity of such counteroedipal ritualization, envy and fear persist in the fathers, who, as Walsh and Scandalis (1975) brilliantly argue, unconsciously arrange for the sons to be placed in jeopardy as potential victims of the acts of external enemies through displacement of the fathers' unconscious (and unconscionable) wishes. Society (i.e., the prerogatives of the fathers) is protected through the sacrifice of many of its young males, either in ritual or in the self-defense of the *patria* in warfare. The success of ritualization is tenuous and temporary at best—hence the need for subsequent and continuous reaffirmation through more ritual. Ritual everywhere instructs and reaffirms to all participants what should be remembered and what should be forgotten. When ritual enactment is the only acceptable form of memory, access is closed—because it is forbidden to the very knowledge that could resolve the underlying conflicts.

Judah Halevi cried, "Israel is the martyr-people; it is the 'heart of the nations,' feeling every pain and disorder of the great body of mankind" (La Barre 1972:588). To understand this exclamation is to understand the meaning of being a Jew. George Santayana's dictum that those who forget the past are condemned to relive it is raised to epic proportions. But its meaning is reversed: remembrance of the past (Yizkor) becomes preparation for its terrible recurrence. The past is asseverated as a guide to the present and the anticipated future. The template of "the lessons of history" assures continuity of the myth of the past in the present. Every "test" passed is penultimate to the final test that is awaited. It is only a matter of time until the timeless prediction (and decree) is confirmed; disconfirmation only postpones the inevitable; it does not create radical disbelief. An obsessively documented litany of discrimination against Jews is continuously updated.

But why the belief that something dreadful must happen to Jews? Jews ask "why us?"—but why the questions, unless there is certainty about victimization, not only that it will occur but that it should, because somehow it is deserved? (see Glazer 1975; Ozick 1974; Podhoretz 1976; Stein 1978; Wiesel 1974). Worry and chronic dread have characterized Jewish future orientation. It is hoped that what is feared will not happen, but it is certain to happen. The imminent coming of the next pogrom or the next attempted "final solution" is more certain than Messianic Redemption. In one short story Isaac Bashevis Singer, in fact, speaks of Death as the Messiah. No calamity is unthinkable; rather, it is expectable.

After the completion of the earlier version of this chapter, Rabbi Azriel Fellner brought to my attention two essays most apposite to the present discussion: "American Jewry—The Ever-Dying People," by Marshal Sklare (1976) and "Faith and the Holocaust: A Review of Emil Fackenheim's *God's Presence in History*," by Michael Wyschogrod (1971). Sklare argues, citing Simon Rawidowicz's early essay "Israel: The Ever-Dying People," that each generation of Jews everywhere feels that it is the last, that the people of Israel are incessantly preparing for the end that in fact never arrives. Wyschogrod concludes that "for believing Israel, the Holocaust is not just another mass murder but, perhaps, the final circumcision of the people of God" (1971:293). This circumcision has exacted an unspeakably greater offering than that which Schlossman (1966) discusses. But, as I have suggested, an ever-dying people, offering itself to the Father-God, will never have a "final circumcision." Golden ages or periods of calm are mere interludes between Holocausts. No solution is ever final.

In Jewish cultural psychology there is no single Day of Judgement at the end of time. Franz Kafka wrote, "Only our conception of Time makes it possible for us to speak of the Day of Judgment by that name; in reality it is a summary court in perpetual session" (1946:169). The demand for sacrifice can come at any time. So heavy is the burden of guilt that when anything goes wrong in the world Jews are certain they will be blamed—and feel a keen sense of responsibility even if the ominous finger is not pointed from without. To bear the burden of being a Jew is to assume an awesome importance. It is to be the Chosen representative of God the Father on his earth, to do his will, to possess a delegated power no others can attain. But it is also to assume an importance derived from the magical omnipotent *powerlessness* of the victim-son.

Within Jewish tradition introspection is highly valued; it is a cornerstone of Jewish "inwardness," of which Sigmund Freud is a modern exemplar. Yet tradition does not acknowledge the practice of projection onto non-Jews of those "alien thoughts" incompatible with the normative inwardness and righteousness. (It is one of the revolutionary breakthroughs of the *father* of psychoanalysis that Freud did not allow himself the protective luxury of such self-deception.) Judaism uses Christianity projectively, mirroring the Christian use of Judaism. Victim and victimizer, exploited and exploiter, are both necessary in their mutual exploitability for the sadomasochistic embrace. Could it be that the Jewish people have survived, not *despite* persecution (as official culture avers) but *because* of it? Victimization itself has become a way of life (see, for instance, Saul Bellow's early novel *The Victim* [1947], Hannah Arendt's *Eichmann in Jerusalem* [1963], and Robert Alter's *The Masada Complex* [1973]). Fear of persecution vies with and is exaggerated by the need for persecution. To celebrate victim-as-hero is to ensure that there will be future victims. To persevere through courting destruction is to gamble psychopathically with the future—one's own and that of one's progeny. Persecution confirms the sacrificial meaning of Jewish existence. In a sense, the individual, in being bound to tradition, is "sacrificed" for the sake of the persistence of group identity.

Rose writes of "the convoluted hypothesis that the Jewish community is held together by the threat of anti-Semitism, that each time emancipation seems close to fulfillment, some new persecution 'saves' the Jews from total disappearance" (1973:17); thus the paradox of survival through persecution, self-preservation through the persistent threat of annihilation. If it is true that external oppression is necessary to preserve the Jewish people, then forces within Jewish culture sustain and precipitate conditions whereby such costly self-preservation is achieved. In the long run the memory of slavery and the anticipation of victimization are more attractive than emancipation, freedom, and survival itself (see Ebel 1978, 1980a, 1985, 1986).

We might pose the ethical question of one's right to impose the burden of the past, with its implication of a particular future, on one's children. But an *ethical* question of choice is absorbed in an *ethnic* question of continuity. The burden must be transmitted, as part of the self-chosenness of being a Jew. The issue of ethics is itself part of the rationalization of concern for the future of one's children, covering the deeper mistrust of what one's children may do in that future. One protects oneself, claiming to have only their best interest in mind. There are, it seems, only two alternatives; victim or victimizer; none other is considered. Moreover, the entire process of ensuring Jewish continuity is based on contradictions that must be denied and on the requirement that the entire process is shrouded in sacred mystery and duty. What are some of the deeper realities that tradition attempts to obscure?

To begin, one might pose a simple, straightforward question: Why is the father so frightened of his son? It is a fact of human development that parents see the child, toddler, adolescent, or offspring of whatever developmental stage not only as the child is but as he is *re-experienced* by the parents. Parents see themselves *in* their child. The father who sees in his son the potential man who might challenge and displace and kill him has had his own childhood oedipal conflict reawakened and must cope with it—and does so partly through the child. He, the father, is now his son, challenging *his* father. But he is also the father, envious of his son, wishing to destroy him, preventing later challenge by preemptive attack. We have learned from the Freudian method of psychoanalytic investigation that when a fear is voiced seemingly in excess, behind it lies a wish that has been repressed and phobically denied to defend against the conscious recognition of it. The wish to murder one's son and, through identification with the son, the wish to murder the father are, in fact, the deeper sources of the fright and dread.

In binding over his son, the father is saying: "Unless we (fathers) subdue them (the sons), they will kill us." The father must force the son to become like the father, the two bound together in a tradition that protects each against the other and against the wishes of each. Through identification with the father, born of guilt, the father is able to avert a conspiracy of son(s) against him. The son's identification with the father is nonetheless uneasy, because biblical example confirms his own private and familial fantasy: the father was prepared to go through with the murder and sacrifice of his son. Theologians say that *God* had commanded Abraham to make the sacrifice to test his faith and that, in fact, by providing a substitute offering (the ram), God thereby declared the older sacrifice of firstborn males null and void. Psychodynamically, however, God's voice was Abraham's own—in every Jewish generation from Abraham through the present; the substitute represented the son, and the ritual, a displacement of the father's intention.

Further complicating the Jew-Christian Father-Son problem is that, while Jewish tradition identifies with and takes the part of the Father, ambivalence is not absent. Ambivalence toward the son is simply clearer. The wish to be rid of the Father, the demanding Lawgiver, is in part reflected in the seeming excess of laws, prescriptions, proscriptions, taboos that traditionally circumscribed literally every human act. This psychologically obsessive and compulsive attention to detail has the quality of "undoing": it attempts to reverse, compensate for, or make restitution for unconscionable deeds and "alien thoughts" (since thought is equated with intentionality of committing the deed). Tradition must accumulate a veritable mountain of "Thou shalt's" and "Thou shalt not's" only when those who create and continuously re-create that tradition must defend against some unspeakable (and unconscious) deed(s) or wish(es). Ritual piles upon ritual, as each attempt to cope with the underlying anxiety is never sufficient to dispel it, creating in its stead secondary and tertiary sources of anxiety concerned with the perfect performance of the ever-increasing rituals.

I suggest that this holds in the Judaic tradition from the pre-Mosaic period through the official codifications of the Law and

through the dominance of the Mitnagdim (anti-Hasidic propo-
nents of rabbinic Judaism during the eighteenth and nineteenth centuries) and persists in modern secular form in science and scholarship (see, however, Bakan 1965). The search
for the right teaching, teacher, formula, law, or guru—literally, *ortho doxos*—is interminable. Scrupulous attention to
"legalistic detail" tries to cope with the rebellion of the son
against the father. Freud(1939) pursued this theme in his spec-
ulative study *Moses and Monotheism*. Whether or not one accepts Freud's thesis that it was the ancient Hebrews who killed
Moses the lawgiver, a specific historical act, I find it necessary
to accept the deeper, more timeless proposition that sons
imagine themselves rising up against their powerful fathers—
later to atone for it by religious expiation. In attempting to
discern and follow the letter of the law, one tries to alleviate
the guilt. On a less theoretical or abstract level, one need only
recall the eighteenth-century Hasidic movement as (in part) a
rejection of rabbinic power and Talmudic learning, or the attraction that the Haskalah (Enlightenment) and the opening of
the ghetto and shtetl doors *from without* had for young Jews
seeking to escape the oppressiveness of Jewish traditionalism.

Jews and Christians as Mirror Images

Christianity views Jesus as the Lamb of God who sacrifices
himself to God the Father. There was no substitution, no vicarious sacrifice. Institutionalized Christianity quickly superimposed the additional interpretation that, although Jesus
came into the world to die and although his crucifixion was
preordained, it was the Jews who killed Christ. The Jewish
people represent the feared father who kills the son (or Son)
with whom Christians identify (in addition to the father), and
who serves as a mediator with the distant and punitive father.
Christians, of course, share the universal conflict of fathers
and sons and cope with it in the form of an alternate oedipal
paradigm, projecting onto the Jews the source of their existential problems. Hence such mottoes as "The Jews killed
Christ," "The Jews are just asking for it" (i.e., to be perse-

cuted); and hence the bewilderment and anger Christians often feel—and explosively express toward Jews—concerning the Jewish "denial of Jesus." The latter reawakens their own doubt whether there really is an intermediary between themselves and the omnipotent Father. The persistence of the Jews is a persistent challenge to their own beliefs. After all, would not *everyone* want to be saved from the wrath of the Father by the kind, gentle Son (not to mention the Holy Mother, so important in Latin, Byzantine, and Oriental Catholicism)? Evidently not.

For present purposes I omit the heterodox, subversive, antinomian, and countervailing undercurrent of mysticism that sought to breach the abyss and overcome the distance through merger with the Godhead—a Godhead that was in imagery and function as much maternal as paternal. The uncompromising severity of Jewish, Christian, and Muslim orthodoxies with their omniscient, omnipotent, and unrelentingly demanding deity led to subterranean, rebellious mystical movements within each tradition (Kabbalah, Gnosticism, and Sufism, respectively) as a means of counterbalancing the official religion that demanded much but gave little (cf. Scholem 1961). One could carry this a bit further and note, following Freud (1930) in *Civilization and Its Discontents*, that rebellion and neurosis are inevitable consequences of the normative pressure for cultural conformity; our neurotics, psychotics, rebels, and prophets tell us in the extremism and deviance of their behavior what is present but repressed and disguised in the normal members of society.

I do not have the competence to enter the fray over biblical scholarship concerning the historicity of Jesus, or over the historical "responsibility" of the Jews or anyone else for the death of Jesus (cf. Cohn 1971). I do not advocate historical nihilism but rather suggest that, following Erikson (1968), what is "real" is phenomenologically or experientially subordinate to and in fact defined by what is "actual." People act on the basis of what they believe to be true, what they need to believe. Ethnic history is a myth about what the world is felt to be like, such feeling and conception fusing with the world. Just as for the Jews, slavery, persecution, victimization, homelessness, suffering, and the like are archetypal, timeless themes, so for Christians the legend of the life of Jesus is relevant to their lives irrespective of whether it "really" happened two millennia ago.

As a brief aside, I suggest that corrective historical documentation, while valuable in itself, is powerless to dispel deeply needed and deep-seated stereotypes which cannot be altered by new evidence. Discussing the "causal misperception" involved in stereotyping, Campbell writes:

It has to do with the relationship between the content of the stereotype and the hostility felt toward the outgroup. The naïve ingrouper perceives the different characteristics of the outgroup as causing his hostility. . . . He feels that were it not for these despicable traits, the outgroup would be loved. The outgroup's opprobrious characteristics seem to him to fully justify the hostility and rejection he shows toward it. The social scientist sees the opposite causal direction: Causally, first is the hostility toward the outgrouper, generated perhaps by real threat, perhaps by ethnocentrism, perhaps by displacement. In the service of this hostility, all possible differences are opportunistically interpreted as despicable, and the most plausibly despicable traits are given most attention. . . . Remedial education in race relations focused on denying or disproving stereotypes [for instance, correcting historical distortions as in Jewish and Christian history] implicitly accepts the prejudiced ingrouper's causal conception rather than the social scientists' and is undermined where actual group differences are found. [1967:825]

To apply Campbell's insight to Judeo-Christian relations, one might say that, while at the *conscious* level Jews and Christians certainly perceive themselves and the other as distinct "ingroups" and "outgroups," at the *unconscious* level they simultaneously occupy *both* positions. That is, they are bound up in a reciprocal adversary system of mutual stigmatization based on a shared father-son conflict that neither can acknowledge.

If, as the psychologically insightful theologian Eckardt (1974) has argued, Christianity retains a vested interest in the "Jewish rejection of Christ," since, without it, Christian ideology would crumble, then one might argue that Jews have an equally vested interest in the denial of Jesus as the Messiah which sustains that ideological edifice. If, as Eckardt suggested, Christianity is erected on a Big Lie—that the Jews rejected and killed Christ—which in a sinister way prepares for and justifies persecutions, then one might argue that Jews have too long protested their innocence with respect to an act whose historic factuality is irrelevant but whose recurrence in each generation is built into the very fabric of being human.

If prejudice against Jews is "the symbolic reenactment of the crucifixion of Jesus," wherein Christians have "fought for almost two thousand years to get Jesus off our backs," if, in accusing the Jews of spurning and crucifying Christ, "the charge represents our own below-conscious wish to kill Christ and to dispose of him once and for all" (Eckardt 1974), and, finally, if anti-Zionism and anti-Israelism are Christian acts of self-destruction, then one could plausibly argue that Jewish anti-Christian sentiment is a mirror image of Christian accusations. Jews, as father-representatives, retain their commitment to the father and the binding over of the son for sacrifice (or at least vulnerability and victimization) and thus attest to the persistence of the mythic-historic past in the present.

The Jesus that Christians have sought to get off their backs is not Jesus-the-Son but the demeaning conscience or superego of Jesus that represents the will of God-the-Father. We recall with some horror that that very angry young man Adolf Hitler, symbolic of adolescent rebellion and rage against all fathers (real and symbolic) (cf. Erikson 1963b), referred to conscience itself as a "Jewish blemish." Just as I see as simplistic the Christian allegation that "the Jews are asking for it," so I cannot single out the Jews for special responsibility for the existence of conscience.

But in the stereotype lies a grain of truth. Jews have long prided themselves on being the conscience of humanity, indeed, of possessing a superior conscience. This has boded good and ill. Conscience can serve as a guide or as an inner oppressor: as guide, it balances permission with restraint, instinctual expression with sublimation; as inner oppressor, it forbids severely, circumscribing all of life with taboos and inhibitions and penances. Overweening conscience produces self-righteous moralism that is hasty to point out defects and infractions of morality in others, infractions which one would like to get away with but must repress. In a sense, not only do Jews set an example for the world, but the Christian (and, more broadly, Gentile) world persists in setting a negative example for the Jews; that is, they represent what a good Jew *is not*. The moral Jewish world is contrasted with the immoral non-Jewish world.

It is difficult enough to try to be the conscience of another person, let alone that of the whole world; one not only is the watchdog of the morals of others but must constantly keep oneself under surveillance, leaving little time or energy for much else. Not unexpectedly, those who are constantly reminded of their inadequacies and failings, of their sins of omission or commission, begin to feel persecuted rather than chastened, victims of another's conscience, and, again not unexpectedly, will wish to free themselves of this burden. What is true clinically is equally true for intergroup relations. For Jews to assume the role of moral arbiter of humanity's bad conscience is to stand not *with* others but *against* them, reminding them of Jewish moral superiority and, by extension, of Gentile moral inferiority. It is a subtle form of Jewish anti-Gentilism. The doctrine of the Jews as the Chosen People is often expressed as haughty pride, if not arrogance: Jews are morally and otherwise superior to non-Jews (smarter, more tolerant, more inventive, more successful, more ethical, etc.).

It is difficult for any son to identify with the father who "lords it over him" by displaying his unreachable and unsurpassable attainments. The splendor and magnificence of the father leaves little conflict-free room for the son's initiative. And it is even more difficult for a son to identify with a father who demands fastidious obedience to the point of the son's allowing himself to be sacrificed (or his manhood severely restricted) for the sake of the father—while the father protests that it is for the son's own good. However we may wish to evaluate Saint Paul clinically or theologically, it must be admitted that his sense of sin and guilt associated with patristic Judaism was overwhelming; only by adopting the *immanent* sacrificial *and* risen Son Jesus as his guardian spirit could he cope with the *transcendent* Father and his Law.

Jews have insisted that there is no mediation with the omnipotent Father. One must *capitulate*, submit, in order to be saved or deemed redeemable. The abyss cannot be bridged. Christianity, however, has insisted that if life is to be endurable the chasm *must* be bridged. That bridge is Jesus, whom God himself sent as *his* emissary to intercede for mankind, the Father himself reaching out toward his sinful children and offering to redeem them. I hasten to add that in medieval Catholicism, Byzantine Orthodoxy, or Calvinism much of the idealized reassurance of assistance through Jesus the Son (at the behest of God the Father) was made secondary by the return of the (repressed) patristic psychology and theology associated with the very "Old Testament" Judaism that was now vilified and had purportedly been superseded. *This* Christian Father God was a transcendent, distant, exacting, vengeful father, a severe judge, not the "good father" who forgave more than he exacted. The point is, however, that Judaism *openly* identifies with the Father whom one must confront face to face in the bleakness of direct relation.

If "no Jew can contemplate the murder of the Father and his replacement by the son" (La Barre 1972:597), no Christian can contemplate the murder of the Son and his replacement by the Father. That is, no Jewish son could allow himself to partake in patristic divinity save as servant of God, while no Christian father could allow himself to imagine being one who crucified Christ the son. Jews stand as defender of the prerogatives of the (transcendent) father, obeying his command to sacrifice the son; Christians stand as champion of the (immanent) vulnerable, crucified son, seeking ways of circumventing the constricting Law of the Father.

The relation between Judaism and Christianity can perhaps be summarized in a "formula" which identifies significant attributes of the respective religions and at the same time explains why these very attributes have been seized upon for purposes of stereotyping, exclusion, and conflict. The formula reads: Jews *overtly* identify with the Father and *covertly* identify with the son; Christians *overtly* identify with the Son and *covertly* identify with the Father. The overt aspect dominates official and consciously recognized religious life and the values of ordinary daily life; the covert aspect dominates the unconscious life, being largely denied, repressed, dissociated, and projected. For example, Christians angrily accuse the Jews of killing Christ, of crucifying "our Lord," etc. Christians, consciously identifying with the Son, vehemently deny that *they* have evil wishes and intentions toward their children, especially their sons. They deny identification with the father who, at least in fantasy, would like to do away with his potential competitor(s). They project, dissociate, and displace their own internalized father onto the Jews who, through projective identification, come to embody and personify those abhorrent attributes which a good Christian cannot acknowledge as being part of the self. Christians do not murder their sons: only Jews do—from Jesus to the Host Desecration and child-murder accusations that have haunted Jews for centuries. Christians project their oedipal and counteroedipal wishes onto Jews, thereby becoming innocent. They accuse Jews of doing what they unconsciously wish they could do; attribution to Jews is an externalization of what cannot be consciously accepted, but what also cannot be lived without. Jews play the role of the father and Father for the Christians. Here the "grain of truth" is distorted and exaggerated by the stereotype of Jews which makes them into unidimensional murderers, molesters, and prototypes of evil.

Jews respond to the accusation that "the Jews killed Christ" by denying it; the Romans were responsible for the Crucifixion, and, besides, Jesus was not the real Messiah in the first place. Christians and Jews claim innocence for the prototypic crime. While Christians deny allegiance with the Father against the Son, Jews deny (project, etc.) alliance with the Son against the Father. Jesus is, after all, a false prophet, a false Messiah, worthy of neglect, nothing better. It is the duty of Jews to obey God's Law, to accept the burden and gift of Chosenness. Jews are a "nation of priests," abiding by the Mosaic Covenant—a covenant that has *not* been superseded. The function of Rabbinic-Talmudic pilpul (a sacred exegesis that has taken the modern-secular form of scientific disputation) is to explicate the will of God through studied attention to his text.

The Jewish-father and Christian-son distinction extends even to the different conceptions of the Messiah. Jews, of course, regard Jesus as a false Messiah and await what might be called a secular-worldly Messiah in the tradition of Moses or the Macabbees to rescue the Jews. While the Jewish Messiah is conceived as a *representative* of God, certainly not God himself, the Christian Messiah is the Father himself become Son who then offers himself to the Father. While I need not debate the obvious logical contradiction of the latter, its psychological message is, as the passage in the New Testament goes: "God so loved the world that he gave his only begotten Son." The Christian Messiah is simultaneously God himself and the Son who was sent by the Father as the Prince of Peace to *mediate for man* the problematic relation between man and God, to help man overcome the awesome distance. Because of the different psychologies involved, Jews must reject Jesus because he was not a "father figure" and Christians must accept Jesus because he was a "son" and not (exclusively) a "father" (cf. Reid 1972).

Jews are not rebellious sons; they are obedient sons. Yet obedient sons must suppress and abort their own rebellions and, in becoming fathers, suppress the rebellion of their own sons, as well as the rebellion of *those who symbolize identification with the Son rather than the Father.* Christians thereby come to play the role of the errant and heretic son and Son for the Jews. The "grain of truth" is reciprocally magnified so that Christians become unidimensional prototypes of rebellion, rage, revenge, and persecution. While Jews identify with the Father, they certainly do not wish to be perceived as wrathful, unyielding, exacting the very lives from their sons (and that of others' sons). Jewish tradition emphasizes that God is one of "justice and mercy," "full of lovingkindness." Abraham may have wished to rid himself of his son Isaac, but tradition rewrites the motivation so that it comes from without as a command from God. Jews consciously identify with the "good father" while often acting according to the introjected dictates of the archaic "bad father." Christians are adept at noticing the latter and then identifying the Jews exclusively as the "bad father" rather than as both.

In a superficial sense one might say that Christian theology is more psychologically honest in its admission that we are all sinners against both the Father and the Son, while Judaism concerns itself only with sins against the Father. But Christianity then disqualifies and rejects its own insight by projecting its own guilt and sinfulness onto Jews, who bear the entire burden of evil thoughts and deeds against the Son. Judaism, however, disqualifies its own protestation of innocence when it exhumes the parable of Abraham and Isaac to allegorize Jewish history and justify its persistence through the binding over of future generations. It can be endlessly debated what the Jews did or did not do to Jesus. But we do know how Jewish tradition, inside and outside formal religion, approaches the father-son relationship. From expulsion from the mythic Eden through the annual recitation of sins of the Days of Awe, Jews confess an abundance of sins against the Father. As remorseful and patient children they ask for forgiveness of the mighty Father. But there is no acknowledgment of sinfulness toward their children. God's commandments and the legends of his relation to mankind are able to mask human intentionality.

In a tragic symbiosis Jews as "Christ killers" and Christians as "Jew baiters" and persecutors fulfill one another's stereotypes and expectations, as mythic history continues to recur. Jews avenge the father, while Christians avenge the son. Jewish and Christian mutual disparagement and mistrust are in fact acts of self-debasement and self-destruction. Each group hates that aspect of itself that it sees in the other. Each nevertheless needs the other to symbolize what is repudiated or exorcised from the self. No "final solution" can ever entirely exterminate those very people who are necessary to maintain one's own self-definition. Those who are "superior" need others who are "inferior" to sustain their feelings of superiority. And in a macabre way, Jews and Christians need each other to represent what one's own are not. Jews make the Christians as much "Goyim" as the Christians make Jews feel like "jews."

Both compete, as in sibling rivalry, for God's favoritism, for the countenance and affection of God the Father, each claiming divine chosenness, each claiming to be the genuine "Israel" (with Christianity as the "New Israel"). As competing "children of God," each sees the other as fallen into error and wrong belief. Jews and Christians both are oedipal animals, something we inherit by virtue of being human. Jews and Christians differ in how the father-son conflict is resolved and symbolized, a major mechanism of which is Christian-Jewish enmity. But is there any way out of the conflict, the vicious circle of respite, waiting, and persecution? Surely the answer is not the simple reversal of "conversion" or "assimilation," which would mean choosing the side of the redeemable son rather than that of the punitive father. Nor would a "new" Christian salvation be achieved by identification with the powerful father rather than the masochistic-Pauline identification with the vulnerable, though "saved," son. Rather, the solution lies in something of a "union of opposites" wherein the Christian would not need the Jew to hate, the Jew would not need the Christian to hate, and each would not suffer with self-hate. Surely genital male maturity cannot be derived either from phallic power borrowed from (and thus still possessed by) the father or from the son's regression to (feminized) masochism and powerlessness. To be a man in Freud's dictum of "love and work" seems possible in neither tradition.

Conclusion

La Barre writes: "It is useless to hate the past; a man can only struggle to recover from it, and to modify as we can what time has made of us. Will Jews ever have outlived the usefulness of taught anger and memorized anguish? Or are they chosen forever to be the lightning rod of other men's miseries?" (1972:587). As I have suggested, the chosenness is not a wholly passive but often an invited affliction. If to be a Jew is to be a victim, what happens if the victim psychology (and pathology) is no longer there? Is the "lightning rod" the only thing to sustain a Jewish identity? And perhaps the most terrible question: What is there to justify a continued separate Jewish identity? And similarly: If the Christian no longer needs the Jew to embody all of the Christian's dissociations, what justification for the persistence of a separate Christian identity? Can reciprocal projection give way to mutual identification, toward a common future in which "forgiveness," "tolerance," and even an ideology of "ecumenism" are no longer necessary? Can the traditionally homologous ego splitting and "culture splitting" become superfluous because what was once phobically dissociated is reintegrated in ego and ethos alike?

La Barre writes that "only a Greek could have written *Prometheus Bound,* and only a Jew the *Book of Job.* The one advances the claims of the power-seeking son, the other the power and majesty of the father. But in the dialogue of father and son, the omnipotence and narcissism of both must yield if moral maturity is to arise in either human estate" (1972:590). If fathers could trust themselves enough not to fear their sons or the sons of others, there might no longer be the need to bind over the son. Conversely, if sons could trust themselves enough not to fear what they fantasize doing to the father, there might be no need to make restitution to the father and subsequently wish to rebel further. In Dietrich Bonhöffer's sense, we should "come of age" and relinquish our childhood and the religions that help sustain and perpetuate it. To become one's own *authority* as a *man* is no longer to need the authoritarian defense of identification with *God* or with a *Son of God.*

Erikson (1964) discussed the concept of "mutuality" as a relationship in which each member enhances the strengths (rather than exploits the weaknesses) of the other and in so doing enhances his own identity toward a common future identity. In my own psychoanalytic "mythology" I find the relationship between Hans Sachs and Walther Von Stolzing in Richard Wagner's opera *Die Meistersinger* to be exemplary of the mature father-son relationship. The wise elder shoemaker Sachs is dean of the Mastersingers, but he does not jealously guard his supremacy and demand strict adherence to traditional musical convention and rules. He supports his young protégé Walther, who clearly has new musical ideas; he helps

Walther polish and discipline himself, without acting as the unreachable disciplinarian. He sees in Walther the future of music (just as he himself is the gifted consummation of its past), a future with which he also identifies. He is thus an ally of that future, not its obstacle and enemy.

Sachs is, shall we say, the "good father." Sixtus Beckmesser, whom Wagner unmistakably identifies with the critic Edward Hanslick as the stereotypic Jew, represents the "bad father," the father who jealously guards what he has, who tries to gain from others by illicit means, and who insists that the young abide rigorously by the cumbersome old rules. Beckmesser is a stickler for "the letter of the law." While I find Wagner's virulent hatred of Jews to be repugnant, I think it a mistake to discount his entire diatribe. We must look behind the abusive language for what is symbolized and, for him, personified by "the" Jew. The Jew embodies the image of the legalistic, exacting, conniving, distant, oppressive, retributive, vengeful father who will not allow his "son" to become a "man" without relinquishing his individuality. In the relationship between Sachs and Walther, I discern the mutuality between generations that transcends the inevitable inequalities and conflicts built into the oedipal animal. Despite Wagner's pan-Teutonic ideology, the intimately personal relationship between Sachs and Walther transcends the issue of Christian and Jew and strengthens the bond of mutual identification between father and son (cf. Lipman 1976).

Christian anti-Semitism and Jewish anti-Christianism are defenses that prevent each from becoming more fully human. They are symptoms of our incompleteness and our struggle with the half we have rejected at such terrible cost. Only one who is whole can allow wholeness (indeed, otherness) in another. The answer is reintegration. We are all fathers and sons, both. The fateful question for Jew and Christian alike is whether we shall persist in sustaining our venerable pseudo-identities by living parasitically off of the projected and lived-out identities of others.

CHAPTER 5

Us and Them: Group Identity and the Need for Enemies

> We play the survival game with confidence since we know in pious certainty that a cosmic Papa will return our marbles when we lose. Extinction is not for keeps. We rush into death because we know we do not die. [La Barre 1984:132]

> Why do you kill me? What! Do you not live on the other side of the water? If you lived on this side, my friend, I should be an assassin, and it would be unjust to slay you. . . . But since you live on [the other] side, I am a hero. . . . Three degrees of latitude reverse a jurisprudence. . . . A strange justice that is bounded by a river! [Blaise Pascal, quoted in Shafer 1982:135]

This final chapter proposes a psychodynamic theory of group identity and of intergroup (including international) relations. Though these two processes are often considered separately, I believe that they can be shown to be inextricably tied. They are, in fact, two facets of the same underlying group dynamic and structure. A "case study" of Soviet-American relations is used to illustrate the emotion-laden division of labor between adversary societies. In our dangerous nuclear age the urgent need for all human beings to develop a sense of the earth that transcends all parochial group boundaries—ethnic, religious, national, ideological—collides with the universal propensity to compartmentalize the social world into "all-good" and "all-bad" people, places, and things. This latter propensity is the legacy of the very nature of human infancy and of growing up in a family. One's senses of belonging, loyalty, security, safety, cohesiveness, and well-being all decisively influence how far—or how narrowly—one draws one's boundary of social responsibility.

In this chapter I discuss some of those developmental invariants that structure the perception of psychogeographic space within groups and between them. Such factors must be taken into account as we enter an era in which global sensibilities are more than a lofty aspiration—one thinks of Beethoven's Ninth Symphony—but have become a matter a survival. And in considering this disparity, we encounter the discomfiting realization that people have throughout history chosen to protect their sacred group character at the expense of losing their very lives and jeopardizing the lives of those they love as well as those they hate. If we are to survive as a species, we must transcend our tendency to split the social world into overvalued allies ("our friends") and devalued adversaries ("our enemies"). At the same time we must be keenly aware of how natural it is to revert—regress—to such bipolar absolutism when we feel threatened.

The Boundary of Identity and Social Responsibility

As human beings, how far does our sense of responsibility toward others extend? It is safe to say that universally in every tribe the boundary of one's sense of responsibility coincides with the limiting boundary of the cultural group, a group to which Erikson gave the name "pseudo-species" (1968). Yet globally our cultures, those extensions into "group" of our very characters and of our sense of security, have come to jeopardize our survival. With the dawning of the nuclear age at the close of World War II, a special urgency was added to the already nascent consciousness of the unity of the human species itself.

If we are ever to end war, we must first ask why war has been so compelling throughout human history. Why has it been exceptional *not* to regard the fellow across the border as a loathsome if not disposable monster? Those of us who labor in behalf of wider, global social responsibility must inquire into what drives men and women—not unlike ourselves—toward cataclysmic irresponsibility. Egregious irresponsibility such as war does not just happen: the forging of collective fantasy precedes and sets the stage for the act that literally enacts it.

The American national mood of callousness and pugnacity is most recently evident by such indicators as the 1984 Olympic bravado with underlying smugness; the box-office success of such violent films as *Rambo;* the popularization in articles, books, and treatment approaches of "tough-love" child-rearing styles; the proliferation of ever-briefer, more focused, and "tougher" individual, family, and group therapies; the return to popularity of the GI Joe doll and military toy paraphernalia around Christmas, 1983; the appearance in the design of many 1984- and 1985-model cars of a hiked-up, exaggerated, menacing rear end; the popularity among women's fashions of blouses and jackets that are heavily shoulder-padded, emphasizing a more muscular, if not also intimidating (phallic woman?) body image; and the near ubiquity among young children and adolescents of khaki fatigues and camouflage shirts, vests, trousers, and shorts (see Stein 1982a, g for a more detailed discussion of cultural styles, body image, and militarism). Yet despite all this excited intensification on one side, we—or any other group—cannot have the purge and rebirth through violence we call war in the absence of a well-cultivated historical enemy who will adequately oblige us with corresponding fantasies and acts of its own. Such a danse macabre between historic enemies is a virtually universal intergroup choreography.

Group mythologizing conflates fantasy with reality while claiming to illumine truth through fantasy. We often utilize myth to disguise and displace the meaning of what we do. In a speech of March 1, 1985, President Ronald Reagan characterized the Nicaraguan Contras as "Freedom Fighters," the "moral equivalent of our Founding Fathers" and the fighters of the "French Resistance" during World War II. We recall that, in the mid-1960s, President Lyndon B. Johnson made the symbolic equation of South Vietnam with the mission-fortress Alamo in San Antonio, Texas, where in 1836 a handful of Americans were besieged and killed by the Mexican army (for a poignant analysis of this myth as disguise for wish to be punished for oedipal guilt of the death of President John F. Kennedy, see Beisel 1985). Human history is littered with the casualties of living out sacred myth. Cultural "reality" is heir to dream (La Barre 1966). It is a diurnal "the dreaming," a universal Alchuringa time (see La Barre 1984). How can we possibly negotiate internationally when our perception of others and feeling about them so condense with fantasy and wish, when others are for all purposes *indistinct* from our myth of them? Negotiation becomes mere echo; perception becomes mirroring.

Consider the following hypothetical clinical situation. I ask the reader to imagine with me that we are therapists. Suppose that in our day-to-day clinical encounters one of our regular patients is a young man who endlessly obsesses about someone with whom he is associated but cannot get along, with whom he has been in conflict for decades. Over the course of time in therapy the patient insists that this person cannot be trusted, refers to the prospect of "mutually assured destruction" (MAD), "weapons gaps" between his and the other's potency, conjures a new defensive arsenal named "Fratricide," begins to speak apprehensively sometime later of a hitherto unrealized "window of vulnerability" and perhaps of the need to develop "first-strike" capabilities rather than take the chance of being attacked, characterizes this opponent as inhabiting some sinister "evil empire," talks somewhat fatalistically about how an inevitable clash may in fact be biblically prophesied as "Armageddon," and proceeds to try to persuade us of his need for an elaborate, impregnable defense at all costs. Suppose, too, that this patient goes on to enumerate for us the contents of a valued arsenal, some of which are named for omnipotent mythological male gods: Thor, Jupiter C, Atlas, Trident, Vanguard, Minuteman, Poseidon, to name but several. The patient later informs us of yet a new weapon ready for deployment, one named with two "hard" consonants "MS." Our patient dubs this newest weapon "the peacekeeper" but talks with a twinkle in his eye and acts with a bravado that makes us wonder whether "peacekeeper" is euphemism for its opposite.

While the good listener is always attuned to reality issues

that might condense with fantasy ones or might provoke old hurts to be reawakened, I would imagine that if the above *language* were consistently used by a patient (who conceivably could have been female) in virtually any clinician's office one would have little difficulty considering paranoia, or at least a "focal psychosis," in one's differential diagnosis. One hardly has to be a trained or committed Freudian to be able to discern patently paranoid themes in this "patient's" personal folklore (themes that sound like those ghastly "miracles" in Freud's long study of D. P. Schreber [1911]). If we will only listen, people are telling their "intrapsychic story," leaving the deep "footprints of the unconscious" (a felicitous image I owe to Dr. Maurice Apprey) everywhere they go.

It is when we begin to apply these same rules to human behavior in groups—from the "small groups" of medical grand rounds or union meetings to the dimensions of international politics—that we hear the outcry that we are engaging in "wild analysis." For to question these groups that embody not only our cultural beliefs, values, and loyalties but also our very sense of personal cohesion and psychic survival is to summon those defenses that are the most developmentally primitive and therefore more powerful and dangerous to reality adaptation. Yet "culture" is merely an extension of "character," and any dichotomy between them not only is false (Spiro 1951; La Barre 1984) but is an intellectualized defense against recognizing their inextricable linkage.

For several years I have supported Physicians for Social Responsibility and the Center for Defense Information, regarding both as constant voices of reality in our nuclear wilderness. Yet neither organization has addressed the dimension of shared group irrationality as part of the "facts" that they wish to convey to the American people. Omitted from the prospective horrific body counts, climatic change, and medical futility in the wake of nuclear war is a recognition of those deeper and abiding universal psychological issues—not limited to the cultural patternings of Soviets and Americans—that make nuclear war thinkable if not attractive rather than singlemindedly repugnant. Reaction formations may temporarily keep us from acting on our own feared violent fantasies, but they do not help us account for them; nor do they help us do anything with them but fight to suppress them further.

The World as Body and the Narcissism
of Group Differences

For all human beings the emotionally directed construction of the world—natural as well as social—begins with the experiences of growing up in a body (La Barre 1951, 1968a). "The ego," wrote Freud in *The Ego and the Id*, "is first and foremost a bodily-ego; it is not merely a surface entity, but it is itself the projection of a surface" (1923:26). Just as the ego uses the body as a battlefield upon which to play out, displace, and project dangers and wishes too great to incorporate into itself, the ego likewise uses society and nature as a surface upon which to project and represent itself. Thus world-destruction fantasies play out on the surface of the world internal fantasies about the annihilation of the body. We often experience the vicissitudes of the body *as* vicissitudes of the world (see La Barre 1972), especially as we—individually or collectively—regress deeply. Erikson writes that "ideological space-time perspectives . . . must alleviate what anxiety remains from the bodily ontogeny of each" (1974:91). These ideologies underlie "the need to know where we come from and where we stand, where we are going, and who is going with us" (1974:91; see also chap. 1 above).

Much of intergroup, including international, conflict is heir to the *unconscious leap from the mind to society* based on the *fantasy of society-as-body* (organism) (see chap. 1 above). Members of cultures, along a range from the concrete to the metaphoric, experience and speak of their society as a virtual personified "body" (the body politic) from which they feel inseparable (nay, indistinguishable; see Koenigsberg 1975). Society is often spoken of reverentially as "mother" or "father," and it is from this body that all pain, all badness, is split off and made distal by locating it outside the social body upon which all life is felt to depend (see Bakan 1968 for a study of how somatic pain is made distal to the self). We summon aggression into play to protect the social body and fend off if not attack in others outside that body what we cannot tolerate to incorporate within ourselves (see chap. 1 above).

In *Civilization and Its Discontents*, Freud wrote:

> It is clearly not easy for men to give up the satisfaction of this inclination to aggression. They do not feel comfortable without it. The advantage which a comparatively small cultural group offers of allowing this instinct an outlet in the form of hostility against intruders is not to be despised. It is always possible to bind together a considerable number of people in love, so long as there are other people left over to receive the manifestations of their aggressiveness. I once discussed the phenomenon that it is precisely communities with adjoining territories, and related to each other in other ways as well, who are engaged in constant feuds and in ridiculing each other—like the Spaniards and Portuguese, for instance, the North Germans and South Germans, the English and Scotch, and so on. I gave this phenomenon the name of "the narcissism of minor differences," a name which does not do much to explain it. We can now see that it is a convenient and relatively harmless satisfaction of the inclination to aggression, by means of which cohesion between the members of the community is made easier. [1930:114]

It is also clear from history that this group narcissism often exercises aggression that is far from "relatively harmless" to those beyond the pale of the group boundary—not to mention the suffering brought upon the group itself, as in warfare, while safeguarding group cohesion.

In the leap from the mind to society, society—one's own and others—can come to be perceived, felt, and acted toward in terms of idealized or disparaged parts of the self, aspects of the id-ego-superego structure, participants in the primal scene, and family relations (parents, children, siblings, etc., as in the "family of nations"). That these are not psychoanalytically "imposed" interpretations (the common accusation) but part of a culture's folklore about itself and others can be amply demonstrated by listening to people talk about their image of their own nation and that of their country's opponents or, alternately, by reading the newspapers and listening to the imagery used in leaders' speeches. As Dundes writes (1985) with reference to the book *Dreams in Folklore,* which Freud and the classicist Oppenheim wrote in 1911 (published in 1958):

Freud shows how symbolic equations as reported or explicated in dreams which occur in folktales correspond exactly to the "Freudian" interpretations of everyday dreams. In other words, much of Freud's interpretation of dream symbols upon examination turns out to articulate symbolic equations already in some sense "known" by the folk. [1985:116].

And, I would further add, the tradition of *Homo monstrosus*—that universal notion of the bizarre, misshapen, unintelligible tribes who live beyond "our" borders (Malefijt 1968)—would seem to confirm the universality of the group-shared psychodynamic process that, beneath formal differences in manifest content, attempts to resolve the conflict of identity by creating exaggerated images of differences in adversaries. Furthermore, the deeper the regression, the less the representation of the enemy resembles a distinct human being, and the more the enemy becomes an unredeemable, persecutory "it" (as in the Western image of the "Jap" in World War II, the Nazis' image of "the Jew," and so forth). Today in America we are witnessing a similar dehumanization of the Soviets through a renewed process of zoomorphization, i.e., the Russian as menacing, ferocious, devouring bear.

In his epochal book *Cyprus: War and Adaptation,* Volkan notes that throughout human history "psychological dangers have been condensed with the actual perils being guarded against" (1979:77). To cross borders may thus represent transgressing the incest barrier (Falk 1974), and ". . . it may symbolize internal boundaries also—the discharge of impulses from the id through the barrier of the ego and the superego" (Volkan 1979:77). Crossing ethnic and international borders carries with it the danger and opportunity in self-knowledge of journeying toward the unknown region of oneself. One may thereby become more open to acknowledging the true otherness of another who had previously served primarily as an embodiment of idealized or devalued aspects of oneself. It is odd and paradoxical that the journey outward in *space* is in fact a journey home, inward in *time*—a home we feared to visit (see chap. 2 above). Culture, though, is often something we construct to aid us in avoiding that painful inward odyssey. Volkan writes:

It has been observed in clinical practice (Giovacchini 1967) that some patients with character disorders make the environment compatible with their excessive use of externalization. The very environment they construct themselves is frustrating in order that they may justify their defenses and maintain their total ego orientation. [1979:67]

Human beings in groups—from small groups to national groups—can be seen, not only by analogy but in fact, to do likewise. In *Muelos: A Stone Age Superstition About Sexuality,* La Barre (1984), following Casper Schmidt, M. D., makes the useful distinction between individual neurosis or psychosis and group "archosis," "a massive and fundamental misapprehension of reality" (1984:130).

Two decades ago, in his paper on Soviet-American relations, Henry wrote that "in order to be accepted in a culture one must accept or adopt an uncritical attitude toward its customs and its fears" (1963:122). The specific danger of cultural archoses lies in the fact that we uncritically value them rather than question them: they are our shared, inviolate reality that makes reality testing tantamount to heresy. Neurosis and psychoses are signs that something has gone awry (ego-dystonic), while archoses are *ego-syntonic* for group members, which means that people will find them reassuring, anxiety-diminishing, and guilt-reducing. If at the level of ideology archoses are each group's hotly defended dogma, at the level of personal dynamics archoses are each group's shared character disorder. They are all the more dangerous because we use them to lull ourselves into believing that they make us more secure.

If I may transpose Heinz Hartmann's felicitous phrase—the "average expectable environment" (1958)—from the extrauterine mother-infant relationship to that of intergroup or intercultural relations, we must inquire into what constitutes an *average expectable cultural environment*. To answer this question, we must ask in all seriousness *what constitutes a good-*

enough enemy. Here adequacy must be defined in terms of the *accessibility* of both separateness and object constancy, and the quality of *embodying* all that one has *negated* in oneself. A "good enough enemy" is a separate object that is used as a reservoir to store and absorb all of one's own negated elements.

Such an enemy is precisely one that is both *heir* to all "environmental failure" in the early family environment and *selected* by one's parents and wider group to represent (by displacement, externalization and projection) all intolerable persecutory material from those early object relations. "The enemy" is experienced as embodying all that one *must* rid oneself of yet simultaneously *cannot* do. This formulation, I believe, helps us understand the process in both its retrospective and its prospective dimensions. A good enough enemy is one capable of stabilizing the internal group world by serving as an available repository for group externalizations.

Scholars, not unlike political and military strategists, spend entirely too much time and effort divining the nature and characteristics of the adversary and devote virtually no time or effort into exploring the *relationship* between adversaries together with the investment of each participant (and all) in that relationship. This proclivity, however deplorable in its consequences, is surely understandable: while many complicated and sophisticated ideas are condensed into the concept of "enemy," at a fundamental level our enemy is our pretext. To address the relationship, and our (as well as their) tacit collusion in that relationship, is to deprive ourselves of that vital pretext.

Us, Them, and the Projective Face of the Enemy

The significance of "the other" for the emotional stability and definition of one's own group was grippingly portrayed by the Greek poet Constantinos Cavafy (Konstantinos Ḵabphes) in his celebrated poem "Expecting the Barbarians." As the arrival of the barbarians seems imminent, the entire society is mobilized. The assembled populace becomes disappointed and confused when the barbarians fail to arrive. The poem concludes with what is at once a lament and a bitter realization that the people are at a loss without any barbarians, for the barbarians had become "a kind of solution" (1976:19). Every cultural group rails against the "barbarians" across the border—or those within the border who are sullying its internal goodness and purity.

We who would pursue peace must understand how all warriors decry bloodshed while courting and indulging it and how the pursuit of war most often underlies (and undermines) the official pursuit of peace. To achieve peace we should pursue an understanding of why international hatred feels so compelling. Otherwise, those who "fight for peace" (a phrase that betrays ambivalence) will have as *their* historic adversary those compatriots who are fiercely nationalistic and militaristic, just as the larger nation has identified as *its* currently historic enemy the U.S.S.R. It is truly difficult to pursue peace without fighting with *someone*.

In a February, 1985, public letter from Admiral Gene R. La Rocque appear these lines: "So when people ask me who we can trust, I say: We can trust any country to go all out for what's in its own best interests. And it's in the best interests of both the United States and the Soviet Union to avert a nuclear war." Were we all rational men and women, there could be no argument, and the solution not only would be simple but would have been found long ago. Yet a group's perception of what is in its best interests is often highly contaminated with shared unconscious agendas that shape the pursuit of those interests.

It is, I believe, only as we can begin to acknowledge—emotionally as well as intellectually—that the historic enmity between the United States and the U.S.S.R. and the increasing danger of nuclear war are group *solutions* and not altogether problems blocking the realization of self-interest that we can approach national and international solutions that have a chance to work. As long as Americans rely on the Soviet Union to embody and act out our own disavowed and disembodied evil, and as long as they rely on us to do likewise, we shall reciprocally fail to serve those "best interests" of survival, mutuality, and prosperity. For how can one negotiate with any enemy who is not fully seen as separate from oneself or one's own inner contents?

A number of writers have commented on the human proclivity to subdivide the human species into "us" and "them." Under universal conditions of growing up the residues of inner splits are directed by oneself with the aid of one's parents and teachers onto images of outgroups, thereby stabilizing one's own and one's group's cohesiveness. Further under the destabilizing conditions of regression (often prompted by culture change; see La Barre 1971), what had been residual may now come to the forefront and come to function more as a delusion than as a mere belief.

Figure 7 grimly depicts the fantasy of the complete, literal bifurcation of the world in the United States of the 1980s. While in one sense this split of "us" (= good) and "them" (= bad) is indeed depicted as President Ronald Reagan's personal vision, it is also, to a considerable degree, a national group fantasy personified by and coordinated and realized in Reagan's presidency. This image of the world cracked and split is widespread. I am reminded, for instance, of the cover of *Time* magazine of March 24, 1986, depicting a placid rural scene that is menacingly cut in two by a stark vertical crack (a bolt of lightning?) descending from the top of the page to the top of a flagpole near the bottom center of the page. The utter and irreparable sundering of inner worlds characterizes the chaos of many schizophrenics' regressed experience. For cultural "normals" this same experience is felt not as internal but as external, that is, in terms of the psychogeography of the world instead of the psychogeography of the body. In less regressed, extreme times what cartoonist Conrad depicts as the absolutism of "Reagan's World" is a less totally bifurcated, albeit potent universal image of "us" and "them" that characterizes the experience of self and other in all human groups.

In 1961, Bronfenbrenner described as "mirror image" those similar reciprocally distorted representations of conflicting groups. Haque and Lawson summarize a number of studies of

Paul Conrad

Fig. 7. © 1986, Paul Conrad for the Los Angeles Times. Distributed by the Los Angeles Times Syndicate. Reprinted with permission.

international conflict that "indicate that the opponents tended to attribute similar desirable traits to themselves and similar undesirable traits to each other (Enemy)" (1980:108). Frank likewise wrote of the ubiquitous "image of the enemy" (1967, 1968, 1980):

This image is remarkably similar no matter who the conflicting parties are. Enemy images mirror each other—that is, each side attributes the same virtues to itself and the same vices to the enemy. "We" are trustworthy, peace-loving, honorable and humanitarian; "they" are treacherous, warlike and cruel. [1980:951]

This "image of the enemy" is everywhere one of every group's most treasured possessions. Not the comforting teddy bear to be kept close, but the uncomfortable inner monsters that must be expelled and kept outside oneself, Volkan calls this adversary object choice "suitable targets for externalization" (1976). The very fundamental and universal notion of *group boundaries*—which separate in psychogeographic space the identity of every "us" from every "them"—rests on an equally fundamental and ubiquitous misperception that is at once paradoxical, ironic, and dangerous. For, alas, *those groups from which we most passionately distinguish ourselves are those with which we are most inseparably bound.*

The enemy, whom we are certain is a despicable "other," is in fact endowed and littered with parts cast out from the self. The "enemy" is in many instances an *inner representation become flesh*. The "boundary" is thus a sacred illusion and delusion, defended to the death to keep the "good" inside and the "bad" outside. Each partner in this deadly dance needs the other to complete itself. We Americans have our monocular "Russia watchers," and the Soviets have their "America-watching" counterparts so that, by directing all of our respective acuity *outward*, we can avoid the painful look inward. In fixed gaze over the political and ideological fence we continue to look for the enemy in the wrong place. And if symbiotic partners in this trance have arranged for reality to confirm fantasy, the reason for this blur is no less an inner one. Having contrived this state of affairs since 1917, how could we (or they) reliably test reality, know the other's motivations, and thereby distinguish a *real* threat from an imagined one? Despite our gleaming technology we are, it seems, no better off than the inhabitants of Plato's cave. So steeped in externalization and projection is our foreign policy that we do not realize the extent to which our enemies' projectiles are in fact our own boomerangs.

Erikson (1968) has characterized these polarized images and polarizing tendencies in terms of the "positive identity" and "negative identity," wherein the positive and valued attributes are those of one's own group, while the negative and devalued ones are attributed to outgroups. Pinderhughes (1979) approaches this same dichotomizing in terms of two types of bonding: libidinal, or affiliative, bonding to the ingroup and aggressive bonding to the outgroup. In a comparative study of interethnic relations Spicer (1971) infers a principle of "opposition." At a conference of the Group for the Advancement of Psychiatry in April, 1983, Volkan titled his presentation "The Need to Have an Enemy." In a series of papers I have explored the psychodynamics of the historical enmity between Jews and non-Jews (Stein 1978, 1984, and chap. 4 above); Russians and West Europeans (Stein 1976, and chap. 3 above); Soviets and Americans (Stein 1982a, 1985b); the creation of a cohesive white ethnic movement identity out of opposition to a negated WASP image (Stein 1979; Stein and Hill 1977a, b); and the antagonistic relations between such professional identities as physician's associate and physician, clinical psychologist, and psychiatrist (Stein, Stanhope, and Hill 1981); family medicine and other medical specialties (Stein 1981b); and the medical and business sectors of the health-care system (Stein 1983d). Spatial "otherness," in fact, is universally heavily contaminated by the debris of various exteriorizing defenses (see chap. 1 above).

Sociologist Max Weber introduced the concept of ethnic honor: ". . . belief in a specific 'honor' of their members, not shared by outsiders, i.e., the sense of ethnic honor" (1961:307). The split between honor-shame or dishonor, good inside–bad outside is a universal and generic group-identity and boundary issue. Discussing Robert LeVine and Donald Campbell's work on ethnic boundaries (1972), Reminick notes that "boundedness of a social group more easily achieves a functioning network of reciprocal obligations" (1983:50). Self-definition is largely achieved by contrast with one (or those) whom one is decidedly *not*. It is achieved by inclusion and exclusion.

In an allegorical account of "The Day the Soviet Union Disappeared," psychohistorian Henry Ebel (1983) refers to the "indispensable bogeyman" who enables people "to *focus* their sense of paranoid endangerment." This pastiche of perspectives should enable us to account for the essentially undifferentiated facelessness of the enemy during our most regressed moments—that is, our inability to see the Soviets as human. This approach likewise helps us account for the seemingly insuperable obstacles to the achievement of human siblinghood (despite Schiller and Beethoven). As long as the enemy is seen as wearing the mask that we have superimposed onto it, we inevitably must see a face we despise when we look upon the enemy. The enemy, in essence, wears our disavowed features: that is the psychic function of the enemy.

We cultivate our enemies. They do not merely emerge menacingly on the horizon as though products of spontaneous generation—although the unconscious surely believes that this is how they come about. We tend our externalized demons as diligently as we do our revered deities. That is, perception "confirms" projection. Often the "right" enemy must also be *perceived* to be powerful enough so as to constitute a "real" threat. A good enough enemy may be felt to endanger the very survival of one's own group, or it may be felt to be the source of humiliation for one's group; in either event the enemy must be experienced as capable of succeeding in its menace.

Interestingly, during 1983, President Reagan depicted the Soviet Union as "the focus of evil" in the modern world, a statement that condenses both the ambiguity over precisely whose evil is under scrutiny together with the identity of precisely where the evil is to be perceived and attributed. Such a "focus" is employed to deflect all ego-dystonic affects from relationships (together with their internal representations) in which one feels they would be intolerable if not disruptive. The ability to focus one's anxiety also makes one feel safer; as a group solution to the free-floating anxiety of everyday life the availability of a common enemy not only allows one to know where to look for danger but prescribes precisely where one should look.

The Psychological "Fit" Between the United States and the Soviet Union

Anyone who examines the history of the Soviet-American relationship must be struck by the chronicity of the enmity (see, for instance, Parenti 1969). The late Jules Henry began his essay "The United States and the Soviet Union: Some Economic and Social Consequences of a Twentieth-Century Nightmare" with the sentence, "The most important single fact in American history since the Revolution and the Civil War is the pathogenic fear of the Soviet Union" (1963:100). And since 1917 the Soviet Union has likewise woven the United States into the fabric of a millennium of invasion, encirclement, subjugation, and threat. Each has woven the other into its persecutory delusion, one which, propelling action on the historical stage, makes the delusion come true. Not only is each an objective threat to the other, but the availability of each as a subjective menace to the other is indispensable to the emotional "national security" of each.

National ideologies of both the United States and the Soviet Union are founded on revolution against monarchies (and *their* sprawling empires). Each too has profound ideological aversion to counterrevolutionary ideas and projects the lure of the ancien régime onto its currently historic enemy. The erstwhile group identity now repudiated yet not eliminated becomes the face of the enemy across the sea. Soviets and Americans alike view each other as that parentally autocratic threat to those freedoms for which the revolution had been fought. Yet each revolution later reinstated strong, centralized authority in new guises. In disdaining the enemy, one further counter-cathects the forbidden wish that the image of the enemy represents: reaction formations shore up the externalizations. "Russians" are simultaneously Americans' own feared lawlessness, unfettered aggression, *and* autocracy. At yet another level of analysis one can identify the "symbiosis" of American anticommunism and Soviet anticapitalism, "communism" being the American counterdependent bogey, and "capitalism" being the Soviet counterindividuative menace. (Might this account for the American revulsion toward and fascination with George Orwell's *1984?*) Each embodies the threat that masks the disavowed wish.

There are yet other fateful equivalences that fuel Soviet-American psychological complementarity. What Nina Tumarkin (1983) calls the Soviet "fear of disorganization" finds as its complement the United States' fear of totalitarianism. The Soviets, who prefer an *external* locus of control, fear the presence of *too little* outer authority, while Americans, who espouse an *internal* locus of control, fear the presence of *too much* external authority. In a shared language of metastatic cancer, both peoples fear the "corruption" of the body politic by infiltration from the adversary. While, as Tumarkin argues (1983), the Soviets view themselves as "bad little children" in relation to the United States which they view as the "bad parent" (punitive), one could likewise argue that the United States almost too eagerly accepts the delegated role of scolding, ridiculing parent and at the same time experiences the Soviets to be ominous parental figures who threaten their often adolescent-style freedom (see Erikson 1963c). It should be quickly added that, while at the level of secondary process this appears to be a contradiction, at the level of the unconscious an object can symbolize apparent opposites (parent-child), and there are no negatives to prevent the alternation or condensation of images.

Now, as Spiegel (1971), Devereux (1967), and Stein (1985d) have written, no culture's values are altogether self-consistent. Russians piously bow to czarist and Soviet authority and seek security and stability yet admire the defiant spirit of the Cossacks. Americans prize individualism, self-reliance, and egalitarianism yet maintain undiminished fascination with autocratic bosses of politics and industry. As Devereux writes: "Every highly cathected pattern or belief has (in the *same* culture) also a less elaborated (and/or latent) contrary manifestation ('man's best friend'—'dirty dog')" (1978:381). "Man affirms on one level what he denies on another level" (1978: 397). What makes for the dangerous "fit" between the United States and the USSR is that what is highly cathected by one is counter-cathected by the other—and projected outward as a despised attribute of the enemy.

It must be emphasized that not only are disavowed aspects of the self *allocated* to others but each partner must develop a permanent *relationship* with these others—for only in the relationship is one continuously *completed* by and in the "other." From Freud we long ago learned to suspect a disavowed because forbidden wish to be present where a great fear or prohibition exists. It is trite to say that we hate our enemies, though the hatred is unmistakable. It is more psychodynamically apt to say that we need to hate our enemies—and likewise to have enemies to hate—so that we not despise and (we likewise fear) destroy ourselves.

To take the point further: Americans prize "freedom," a freedom which the Soviets are perceived as menacingly and unremittingly trying to take away. The USSR serves as the image of what might be called the Great Depriver. It is as if to say: "We don't wish to lose our independence; they are the ones who seek to make us feel dependent." Religiously devout Americans—increasingly secularized—can split off those antinomian, irreverent impulses and accuse atheist "Russian Communists" (who are contending with resurgent Orthodoxy at home) of conspiring to undermine American religion. As Americans look longingly at the putative paternalism and maternalism of Japanese corporations and reinstate religious fundamentalism and political authoritarianism at home, we keep our illusion of precious freedom by accusing the Soviets all the more of seeking to take it away. We enlist the Soviets to help us manage our ambivalence toward *our own culture*.

Manifestly, the statement that "you can't trust the Russians" describes the "Russians" (Soviets). But, while "Russians" are the object, the verb is "trust," and the subject is ourselves. There is more: what seems at first to be a *description* is in fact an *admonition* not to trust the "Russians." Such an exercise reveals the sentence to be a statement about ourselves in the guise of being an objective assessment of "Russians." The "Russians" are one in a long lineage of historical threats to that "freedom" which Americans so stridently, yet so ambivalently, value. And, in parallel fashion, "Americans" are one in a long lineage of historical threats to that "security" which "Russians" seek—while yearning for that disavowed freedom they associate with the rebellious Cossacks and menacing Asian marauders. In mistrusting the "Russians," we mistrust our own authoritarianism—while at home we pursue political, religious, and moral "fundamentalism"! Americans are certainly not the first to accuse our enemy of our own motives.

On repeated newscasts I have heard the following formula articulated by American officials: "The Soviets only respect force. Therefore you have to show force." This is a statement of how we view the Soviets in the guise of a statement about the Soviets. It reveals our own projected wish and fear of going out of control. It justifies our use of force or our increase in "defense" budget. "We" are inseparable from "them" in our self- and object representations: at the unconscious level "we" seek to control ourselves through controlling "them."

In recent years American officials and the public once again invoke the refrain that "the Russians [Soviets] have no regard for human life." Yet the fact that the Soviets are in virtually perpetual mourning for their loss of twenty millions during World War II—a loss that condenses with a millennium of invasion—passes unnoticed here in the United States. And as if to underscore the externalizing nature of the moralistic accusation, the prevalent "cut-slash-chop" morality in America has set in motion a draconian social policy that is anything but compassionate toward those who lack the money to purchase their health and their future. The defense mechanisms operating here are once again the exteriorizing ones that diminish anxiety and guilt by making the historic enemy the embodiment of all of our own evil or unresolved ambivalence.

The oft-repeated slogan "The Russians have no regard for human life" is a stereotype in the guise of an observation. The implicit logic reads, "Since the Russians disregard human life, therefore we may disregard theirs." Their violence becomes a necessary precondition or releaser of ours (tightly rationalized, to be sure): their moral holiday justifies ours. Since the Soviet function is to serve as an American projective target (and conversely), we studiously avoid understanding how the Soviets *do* regard life apart from our stereotype.

Our obsessive dread that the "red tide" of the Russians will overtake us is psychologically our fear (itself containing a wish) that what they represent to us will overrun and overwhelm us. For Americans and the Soviets, the more each fears the threat of being overwhelmed by what the other represents, the more each feels compelled to shore up if not expand its boundaries to protect the vulnerable core. Each craves security that requires psychic boundaries, for if *either* expanded to become the world (merger fantasy), there would no longer be any danger from *outside*, because there would at last no longer be an outside or other. The danger would then exist where it is most feared: *inside* the group.

Resistance in the psychoanalytic sense to peace or rapprochement with the Soviets can be comprehended to be a fervent defense of our externalizations and projections. From an eminently practical viewpoint those engaged in international diplomacy must not only contend with the real and imagined threats which the enemy poses but also address *the threat which the prospect of an enduring peace would pose* to participants to international conflict.

From an international "systems" perspective, when peace-making (e.g., rapprochement) efforts are too likely to begin to *succeed*—and thereby remove the availability of the adversary as container and target for externalizations and projections—peace-making efforts *must* fail so that the intergroup and intrapsychic status quo ante can be reinstated. Stated differently, current intragroup stability is purchased at the price of destabilizing intergroup relations. The disparity between our reality needs and our fantasy ones could not be starker, for while at the level of reality the security of the Soviet Union is crucial to the security of the United States, at the level of fantasy the *in*security of the Soviet Union is indispensable to the psychological security of the United States.

Mourning, Transcendence, and Rapprochement with One's Enemies

For this truth must be before us: Whatever America hopes to bring to pass in the world must first come to pass in the heart of America. [Eisenhower 1953]

The perspective I have offered in this chapter and throughout this book places me far closer to the Stoics than to any utopians. For it is clear that, our most fervent wishes for international peace notwithstanding, all things are not possible for the human animal. In the nuclear age we are suicides—the dead whom we kill—in a triple sense: the enemy who embodies parts of ourselves; our sons whom we send out to be killed and to kill others' sons, a sacrifice of youthful vigor to the angry conscience; and lastly, ourselves, for in a nuclear war we consume ourselves irrespective of where the bombs and missiles fall. In our imagination we are beginning to see the spectre of nuclear war as our own psychic boomerang.

Unambivalent love—whether for a person, a family, a work group, a church, or a nation—proves to be a dangerous illusion. For unacceptable feelings, wishes, and ideas that cannot be included in that love must surface somewhere. And they do so with force majeure in that carefully guarded condensation which Frank calls the "image of the enemy" (1980). How ironic is the fact that we *do* evil so that we will not *see* and *feel* ourselves to *be* evil. We repeat to avoid remembering (Freud 1914). The beginning of change that still pays its due to human nature is a virtual confession of our unacceptable wishes despite those beliefs, nay, convictions, that we are in full charge of our faculties and actions. We give heed to the voice of reason only when we begin to acknowledge and accept the clamor of unreason that is part of us all, *and* have the strength of character to exercise that instinctual renunciation that permits us to inspect and feel that din without acting upon it to diminish the pain.

In recent years I have become interested in what I would call "problems which cannot be solved within their current framework," this despite the conscious good intentions and, presumably, good will of all participants. From difficult doctor-patient dyads to inflexibly patterned family systems and finally to international relations that always threaten to escalate into something more out of control, I have become convinced that the same underlying processes govern these very different social structures and are implied in both etiology and perpetuation of conflict irresolution. What is more—and this has gotten me into frequent difficulty as allegedly "disloyal"—I have come to conclude that the question we usually ask, namely, "Which side should I take in the dispute?" only further contributes to the problem in the guise of appearing as a solution.

Bateson, for instance, discussed the conflict between the "imperialist" Romans and the "downtrodden, exploited colony" of Hebrews in Palestine around the time of Christ. He concluded:

I do not care, here, about defending the Romans or defending the Palestinians—the upper dogs or the underdogs. I want to consider the dynamics of the whole traditional pathology in which we are caught, and in which we shall remain as long as we continue to struggle with that old conflict. We just go round and round in terms of the old premises. [1972a:433]

My only cavil with Bateson's courageous formulation is that I think that "premises" are in fact a derivative, secondary cognitive structure, resting on primitive splitting of self- and object representations along affective lines, externalization, together with higher-level defense mechanisms (such as identification with the aggressor—in Bateson's example the ambition of the downtrodden to become themselves the imperialists whom they now envy and despise). In other words, the ideas contained in political or religious ideologies can be seen as themselves symbols or derivatives that express and play out unconscious emotional issues. It seems to me that one who can truly mediate or serve as conciliator is foremost one who can internally encompass—integrate—both or all sides of the conflict and who *therefore* can imagine a framework alternative to the present historic repetition compulsion (Stein 1983b).

The beginning of hope for our species lies, paradoxically, with our acceptance—however grudging and partial—of the tragedy of the human condition, in our painful grieving for our group defeats rather than trying to wrest victory from the hungry jaws of defeat, to recover honor from feelings of shame. In his essay "The Cuban Missile Crisis: An Anniversary," Norman Cousins writes of both Kennedy and Khrushchev:

A nation had not only its interests to uphold but its pride. A nation went to war before risking the appearance of weakness. Nuclear war was not unthinkable; the only thing that was unthinkable was a departure from one's conception of the national honor. The survival of the species was a "soft" question. The "hard" question concerned the national security. . . . [In the United States] the resolution of the missile crisis was widely interpreted as proof that if only we would stand firm we would always come out ahead. Very little was said about the fact that if both countries had been guided by that notion, both would have been destroyed. [1977:4]

In groups as in individuals, the dawning of liberation lies in the dawning consciousness of the sense of inexorable, linear, irreversible, biological time—that the lost cannot be retrieved through the humiliation or devastation of the enemy or through territorial "reclamation." Liberation begins with an understanding of what we need and use our reliable enemies for.

We in the West insist that simple, quick, immediate, mechanical solutions can be found for every kind of problem—social, medical, and political, as well as technological. Likewise we steadfastly believe that complex issues can be solved by virtually "throwing" money at them. Intergroup and international conflict, however, are not amenable to quick "fixes." To pursue new, alternate solutions, we must first come to recognize that what have heretofore been accepted as virtually sacred cultural solutions are themselves contributory to the problem.

The problem of human aggression—not simply American or Soviet, Israeli or Palestinian, Turkish or Greek aggressiveness—will not disappear. Such lofty philosophical aspirations as internationalism, cosmopolitanism, and universal peace can be realistically pursued only if we can acknowledge that part of the process of being human is the search for an enemy to embody, temporarily or permanently, disavowed aspects of oneself. These issues must be constantly addressed in the very process of political negotiation, for, in that respect at least, every historic enemy is very much like ourselves. And here the role of the leader becomes a pivotal one—for it is not at issue *whether* groups will regress under stress but *what the leader can and will do with that regression* that he or she becomes appointed to deal with in the group's behalf. Abse and Ulman cogently argue that groups

typically share enough unconscious psychological currents to become cohesive under the direction of an adequately charismatic political leader, who, if healthy himself, will use collective regression in the service of the ego, but who, if not altogether sound, will in the long run probably decompensate and exploit the reactivation of common infantile desires and even reflections of primeval phylogenetic experience. [1977:50]

While in some respects the leader is created by the group in that transitional zone between self and object (see Dervin 1984), the more or less mature leader can address and channel that regression without exploiting it. Specifically, he or she can help the group mourn and thus not need to act to contrive a situation that would make it appear as though the loss had not occurred. Such a leader would be therapeutic in the sense of fostering greater integration rather than in the more spuriously (but ego-syntonic for the group) therapeutic maneuver of promising to safeguard those inner splits for which he or she was, in whatever way, "elected" to office. We cannot, however, expect our leaders—presidents, congressmen, etc.— to do that difficult work if we are not willing, in our various professions, to do that work *with* them. Current workshops and lectures on psychoanalysis and international diplomacy conducted within the State Department are only a beginning of a much wider educational *and* listening process that needs to be undertaken. It is, I believe, only through efforts of this type that American statesmen will discover the need to understand the Soviets as a *representation* as well as a political-military *reality*—and, I would hope, to recognize the diplomatic-strategic implications of that differentiation.

In his conclusion to his book *Beyond Culture*, Edward Hall writes:

Possibly the most important psychological aspect of culture—the bridge between culture and personality—is the identification process. This process, which works admirably when change is slow but wreaks havoc in times of rapid change such as we are currently experiencing, is most certainly a major impediment to cross-cultural understanding and effective relations among the peoples of the world. Man must now embark on the difficult journey beyond culture, because the greatest separation feat of all is when one manages to gradually free oneself from the grip of unconscious culture. [1977:240]

Physicist Freeman Dyson urges that we view nuclear weapons not in terms of their intrinsic destructive or supposedly strategic qualities but in terms of

how different our view of nuclear weapons might have been if Hitler had in fact got them first. . . . Hitler's bombs would neither have changed the grand strategy of the war nor lessened our determination to fight it to a finish. What would have been changed is our post-war perception of nuclear weapons. Forever afterward we would have seen nuclear weapons as contemptible, used by an evil man for evil purposes and failing to give him victory. The myth surrounding nuclear weapons would have been a myth of contempt and failure rather than a myth of pride and success.

It is important for Americans to go through the mental exercise of looking at nuclear weapons as if they *had* been Hitler's weapons rather than ours, because this exercise enables us to come closer to seeing nuclear weapons as they are seen by Soviet citizens. To understand Russian strategy and diplomacy, it is necessary for us to distance ourselves from our own myths and to enter into theirs. An understanding of Soviet views is the essential first step toward any lasting amelioration of the danger in which the world now stands. [1984:88]

A difficult but necessary beginning in conflict resolution is to imagine what it would be like to be "the enemy," to try to feel the world from *their* childhood and history, and from *that* position ask how one might feel about and perceive and wish to act toward one's own group (now identified as "the enemy"). One would further ask how the availability of "the enemy" (that is, one's own group) serves as something of a solution that has the force of necessity. One may then "return" to one's group and pose the identical questions about oneself.

How, though, are we to accomplish this seemingly insurmountable feat of imagining ourselves into other cultures? The answer, I believe, lies in the process of grieving for what has been historically lost to one's group and to one's private circle of intimates rather than in attempting to undo history and restore it as if it had never occurred. "To be able to mourn is to be able to change," writes Pollock (1977:29). In a paper on the Middle East, Volkan writes that "man cannot accept change without mourning for what is lost to the past. . . . It is through mourning that we accept changes within ourselves and within others, and become able to face reality about our unfulfilled hopes and aspirations" (1984:5–6).

Our human identity as a species lies beyond the culture principle (Stein 1977). Transcendence of groupisms can be accomplished only, and always incompletely, as we are able to relinquish and integrate the inner splits between "goodness" and "badness" that have led us throughout history to dichotomize between idealized and disparaged groups, of which the tragic history of Soviet-American relations is but a single thread. Only by *grieving* our own imperfectability and mortality can we permit ourselves and others to be ambivalently but fully "human all too human" and not people the social and supernatural world with saints and demons.

A profound step from the American side toward rapprochement with the Soviet Union would be an open acknowledgment—say, by an American president—of the hurts and vulnerabilities that pervade Russian and Soviet history. For instance, were President Reagan to lay a wreath at the Soviet Tomb of the Unknown Soldier or at the Pisgaryov Cemetery at Leningrad, such an act would be recognized by the Soviet people as honoring their over twenty million dead from World War II and from the centuries of invasion and occupation which that war now represents.

To grieve for the dead of the enemy is to have compassion for their suffering. It is to identify with them, to stand, if only briefly, with them rather than against them. It is to strive, however imperfectly, to understand the world from their viewpoint. It is to begin to include the adversary in one's own world rather than to banish them from it. To mourn for the Soviet dead conveys a wish to the living that they be alive rather than dead, that they be part of a shared world. It expands the compass of the very term "our."

Mourning Russian and Soviet history as well as our own liberates us to transcend the one-dimensional image of "Russians"—an image further distorted when we zoomorphize the Soviet Union into a menacing bear—and to begin to see them as humans with whom we share a common vulnerability and destiny. In giving recognition to Soviet hurts and fears of renewed agony, we extend ourselves across the psychological barrier that separates and polarizes us. In effect, we reduce the emotional distance between us. The promise of reconciliation through the expression of common grief contrasts with the intensification of mistrust and defensiveness based on a world view of persecution, violation, and revenge.

Such a crossing of the boundaries of national identity by honoring the identity and historical sensibilities of the enemy can begin to reduce the enemy's defensiveness and with it international tension. One thinks immediately of Egyptian President Anwar Sadat's historic visit to Israel in 1977. The Soviets likely would begin to experience the United States as a more complex symbol as well. For the nation that *menaces* them would also be the one that seeks to *reassure* them (one could only wish that a similar atmosphere of compassion had been present during the drafting of the fateful Treaty of Versailles).

The capacity to withstand the ever-present temptation and wish to humiliate the enemy—to visit upon them our own humiliations and thereby avenge history,—and instead to extend to them the recognition of a shared humanity and the assurance of a place on the planet is itself an act of international rapprochement. It transcends cliches about "moral equivalence."

Certainly no single presidential gesture such as honoring the Soviet dead from World War II will magically thaw the latest round of the cold war. I am talking not about misguided notions of cause and effect but of a change in a relationship. Mutual distrust and competition in which all weapons are perceived as offensive do not easily or quickly dissipate. But such a symbolic act would mark a touching beginning that departs dramatically from militaristic business as usual. It is difficult to attack someone or some group who has just made you feel understood rather than under siege and in need of defending yourself. To experience others' pain in their presence is to invite a reciprocal attempt from them to include us. Both become less driven to retaliation or preventive attack. To grieve both one's own and other's losses is to at last allow the dead to be dead; it is to accept time as irreversible and to allow for a truly new beginning. It is to mourn the past and to begin to forge a common future less haunted by the past.

The way back from the abyss of glory and extinction is to confess our mortality so that neither we nor our historic adversaries need to rush to hurl each other over the abyss. To survive we must forsake the thrall of soul's timelessness and be able to accept the pain of biological time. If we can accept that we have but one life, we will be less eager to imperil it by the promise of rebirth through violence. Perhaps the final, and most fundamental, "instinctual" renunciation is that of rebirth, where cleansing requires a bloodbath.

The difficult path to peace lies first in the *emotional disarmament of grief work,* for only through it do we come to understand what the face of the enemy is—and ours as well— behind our protective cultural masks. For in grieving we bear witness to the anguish we had transposed into hate. Only through grief work can we permit our adversaries to possess their own history-worn faces instead of our masks of scorn and indignity. From the moment he became premier in the spring of 1985, Mikhail Gorbachev has quickly been likened in the American press to the martyred John F. Kennedy, and Gorbachev's stylish wife to Jackie Kennedy. Over twenty years after our new frontiersman's death we ask what right the Soviets have to their Kennedy when we were so abruptly deprived of ours. We are not finished with Kennedy's death, nor with that of his brother Bobby, assassinated in 1968, nor with that of the Reverend Martin Luther King, Jr., all embodiments of that American dream which then held great promise. In successive years of black rage, white ethnic rage, and now American rage, we have taken flight from sorrow too deep to feel. Our "intelligence" agencies collect libraries worth of information about every move of the Soviets. But it takes another kind of intelligence to recollect where we were and what we felt on November 22, 1963, "the day the music died," as Don McLean's popular dirge "American Pie" lamented.

The second Beatitude in Matthew (5:4) reads: "Blessed are they that mourn: for they shall be comforted." Through the difficult grieving over what we cannot become or reverse lies the foundation for the only good enough identity there is. It is an identity capable of recognizing in oneself and others the tragedy of the condition all human beings suffer. Everywhere and always we are the enemy we kill and kill again. In the recognition of our shared humanity—a recognition that transcends, if always imperfectably, the creation of enemies and the merger fantasy that "we are all the same"—dawns the further insight that our responsibility extends to our species rather than withdraws to our tribal caves.

Human history traces the erratic expansion of identity and loyalty from family and local band to ever-larger social units (Sagan 1985). A sense of the earth is still a novel idea indeed. With the dawning awareness of our planetary identity comes a feeling of indebtedness to the future of our species and to the planet that is our home.

References

Abse, D. W., and R. B. Ulman. 1977. Charismatic Political Leadership and Collective Regression. In R. S. Robins, ed. *Psychopathology and Political Leadership*. New Orleans: Tulane University Press.

Adams, K. A. 1981. Arachnophobia: Love American Style. *Journal of Psychoanalytic Anthropology* 4(2): 157–97.

Alter, R. 1973. The Masada Complex. *Commentary* 66 (July): 19–24.

Anderson, R. T. 1971. The Acculturation of Russia. In *Traditional Europe: A Study in Anthropology and History*. Belmont, Calif.: Wadsworth.

Ardrey, R. 1961. *African Genesis*. New York: Atheneum.

———. 1966. *The Territorial Imperative: A Personal Inquiry into the Animal Origins of Property and Nations*. New York: Atheneum.

Arendt, H. 1963. *Eichmann in Jerusalem*. New York: Viking Press.

Arensberg, C. M. 1955. American Communities. *American Anthropologist* 57(6): 1143–62.

Bachrach, L. L. 1981. *Human Services in Rural Areas: An Analytical Review*. Monograph Series, No. 22, July. Washington, D.C.: Project Share, A National Clearinghouse for Improving the Management of Human Services, Department of Health and Human Services.

Bakan, D. 1965. *Sigmund Freud and the Jewish Mystical Tradition*. New York: Schocken.

———. 1968. *Disease, Pain, and Sacrifice: Toward a Psychology of Suffering*. Chicago: University of Chicago Press.

Balint, M. 1959. *Thrills and Regressions*. London: Hogarth Press.

Banfield, E. C. 1958. *The Moral Basis of a Backward Society*. Glencoe, Ill.: Free Press.

Barth, F., ed. 1969. *Ethnic Groups and Boundaries*. Boston: Little, Brown.

Bateson, G. 1972a. Conscious Purpose Versus Nature. In *Steps to an Ecology of Mind*, pp. 432–45. San Francisco, Calif.: Chandler.

————. 1972b. *Steps to an Ecology of Mind*. San Francisco, Calif.: Chandler.

Bedrosian, M. 1983. Armenians in America: Reclaiming Pockets of Diversity. Paper presented on the panel Ethnic Communities at the Eleventh Annual Conference on Ethnic and Minority Studies for the National Association for Interdisciplinary Ethnic Studies, Ontario, Canada, April 14.

Beisel, D. R. 1980a. Chamberlain and the Munich Crisis. Paper presented at the panel on France and Britain in the Development of the Second World War, Third Annual Convention of the International Psychohistorical Association, New York City, June 12.

————. 1980b. The Group-Fantasy of Early German Nationalism, 1800–1815. *Journal of Psychohistory* 8(1): 1–19.

————. 1981. International Affairs as a Family System: The Case of World War II. Paper presented at the Fourth Annual Convention of the International Psychohistorical Association, New York City, 11 June.

————. 1982a. European Group Fantasies Before the Second World War. Paper presented at the Fifth Annual Convention of the International Psychohistorical Association, New York City, 11 June.

————. 1982b. Reply to commentaries on The Group-Fantasy of German Nationalism, 1800–1815. *Journal of Psychohistory* 9(3): 345–53.

————. 1985. The Vietnam War: A Beginning Psychohistory. *Journal of Psychohistory* 12(3): 371–93.

Bellow, S. 1947. *The Victim*. New York: Vanguard Press.

Binion, R. 1976. *Hitler Among the Germans*. New York: Elsevier.

Bion, W. R. 1955. Language and the Schizophrenic. In M. Klein, P. Heimann, and R. Money-Kyrle, eds. *New Directions in Psycho-Analysis*, pp. 220–39. New York: Basic Books.

————. 1959. *Experiences in Groups*. New York: Basic Books.

Black, J. L. 1973. M. P. Pogodin: A Russian Nationalist Historian and the "Problem" of Poland. *Canadian Review of Studies in Nationalism*. 1(1): 60–69.

Blos, P. 1962. *On Adolescence: A Psychoanalytic Interpretation*. New York: Free Press.

Blum, J. 1961. *Lord and Peasant in Russia: From the Ninth to the Nineteenth Century*. Princeton, N.J.: Princeton University Press.

Bowen, M. 1978. *Family Therapy in Clinical Practice.* New York: Jason Aronson.

Boyer, L. B. 1979. *Childhood and Folklore: A Psychoanalytic Study of Apache Personality.* New York: Library of Psychological Anthropology.

———. 1986. On Man's Need to Have Enemies: A Psychoanalytic Perspective. *Journal of Psychoanalytic Anthropology* 9(2): 101–20.

Bronfenbrenner, U. 1961. The Mirror Image in Soviet-American Relations: A Social Psychologist's Report. *Journal of Social Issues* 17:45–56.

Bruhn, J. G. 1965. An Epidemiological Study of Myocardial Infarctions in an Italian-American Community: A Preliminary Sociological Study. *Journal of Chronic Disease* 18:353–65.

Bryner, C. 1939. Alexei Homyakov and Russian Nationalism. *Slavia* (Illustrovane Novisti) 14(11–12): 1–17.

Campbell, D. T. 1967. Stereotypes and the Perception of Group Differences. *American Psychologist* 22 (October): 817–29.

———, and R. A. LeVine. 1968. Ethnocentrism and Inter-Group Relations. In R. P. Abelson et al., eds. *Cognitive Congruity Theories.* Skokie, Ill.: Rand McNally.

———, and ———. 1972. *Ethnocentrism: Theories of Conflict, Ethnic Attitudes, and Group Behavior.* New York: John Wiley and Sons.

Cavafy, C. 1976. Expecting the Barbarians. In *The Complete Poems of Cavafy,* trans. R. Dalven, pp. 18–19. New York: Harcourt Brace Jovanovich/Harvest edition.

Cohn, H. 1971. *The Trial and Death of Jesus.* New York: Harper and Row.

Cooke, A. 1973. *America: A Personal History of the United States.* New York: Alfred A. Knopf.

Cousins, N. 1977. The Cuban Missile Crisis: An Anniversary. *Saturday Review,* 15 October, p. 4.

deMause, L. 1977. Jimmy Carter and American Fantasy. In L. deMause and H. Ebel, eds. *Jimmy Carter and American Fantasy: Psychohistorical Explorations,* pp. 9–31. New York: Two Continents/Psychohistory Press.

———. 1979. Historical Group-Fantasies. *Journal of Psychohistory* 7(1): 1–70.

———. 1982a. *Foundations of Psychohistory.* New York: Creative Roots.

———. 1982b. Symposium on "The Fetal Origins of History." *Journal of Psychohistory* 10(2): 213–48.

Dervin, Daniel. 1984. Group-Fantasy Models and the Impostor. *Journal of Psychohistory* 12(2): 240–50.

Devereux, G. 1955. Charismatic Leadership and Crisis. In G. Roheim, ed. *Psychoanalysis and the Social Sciences*, 4:145–57. New York: International Universities Press.

———. 1967. *From Anxiety to Method in the Behavioral Sciences.* The Hague: Mouton.

———. 1975. Ethnic Identity: Its Logical Foundations and Its Dysfunctions. In G. DeVos and L. Romanucci-Ross, eds. *Ethnic Identity: Cultural Continuities and Change*, pp. 42–70. Palo Alto, Calif.: Mayfield Publishing Co.

———. 1978. The Works of George Devereux. In G. D. Spindler, ed. *The Making of Psychological Anthropology*, pp. 364–406. Berkeley and Los Angeles: University of California Press.

———. 1980. *Basic Problems of Ethno-Psychiatry.* Translated by B. M. Gulati and G. Devereux. Chicago: University of Chicago Press.

———, and E. M. Loeb. 1943. Antagonistic Acculturation. *American Sociological Review* 8:133–48.

De Vos, G. A. 1973. Role Narcissism and the Etiology of Japanese Suicide. In *Socialization for Achievement*, Chap. 17. Berkeley: University of California Press.

———. 1974. Cross-Cultural Studies of Mental Disorders: An Anthropological Perspective. In G. Caplan, ed. *Child and Adolescent Psychiatry, Sociocultural and Community Psychiatry*, vol. 2, chap. 36. In S. Arieti, editor-in-chief. *American Handbook of Psychiatry.* New York: Basic Books.

Donne, J. 1624. *Devotions XVII.*

Douglas, M. 1970. *Purity and Danger.* New York: Penguin.

Dundes, A. 1985. The American Game of "Smear the Queer" and the Homosexual Component of Male Competitive Sport and Warfare. *Journal of Psychoanalytic Anthropology* 8(3): 115–29.

Dunn, S., and E. Dunn. 1963. The Great Russian Peasant: Culture Change or Cultural Development. *Ethnology* 2:320–38.

———, and ———. 1967. *The Peasants of Central Russia.* New York: Holt, Rinehart, and Winston.

Dyson, F. 1984. Cutting Nuclear Myths Down to Size (review of K. Tsipis, *Arsenal: Understanding Weapons in a Nuclear Age*, Simon and Schuster; and J. Schell, *The Abolition*, Alfred A. Knopf). *Science 84* 5(5): 88, 90.

Ebel, H. 1978. A Dialogue with the Prosecutor. *Journal of Psychohistory* 6(2): 301–307.

———. 1979. Personal communication, 20 August.

———. 1980a. Being Jewish. *Journal of Psychohistory* 8(1): 67–76.

———. 1980b. How Nations "Use" Each Other Psychologically. *Journal of Psychoanalytic Anthropology* 3(3): 283–94.

———. 1980c. Mitteleuropa. Manuscript quoted with permission.

———. 1980d. Psychiatrist Traces the Painful Emergence of Geography from Body Fantasies. *Behavior Today*, 21 April, 5–6.

———. 1983. The Day the Soviet Union Disappeared. Manuscript quoted with permission.

———. 1985. The Psychohistory of an Enduring National Identity. *Journal of Psychoanalytic Anthropology* 8(2): 157–75.

———. 1986. Adapting to Annihilation (review essay on Y. H. Yerushalmi, *Zakhor: Jewish History and Jewish Memory*, 1982; and D. G. Roskies, *Against the Apocalypse: Responses to Catastrophe in Modern Jewish Culture*, 1984). *Journal of Psychoanalytic Anthropology* 9(1): 67–89.

Eckardt, A. R. 1974. *Your People, My People: The Meeting of Jews and Christians*. New York: Quadrangle/New York Times Book Co.

Eisenhower, D. 1953. First Inaugural Address, 20 January.

Erikson, E. H. 1963a. *Childhood and Society*. Rev. ed. New York: Norton.

———. 1963b. The Legend of Hitler's Childhood. In *Childhood and Society*, 2d ed., pp. 326–58. New York: Norton.

———. 1963c. Reflections on the American Identity. In *Childhood and Society*. New York: Norton.

———. 1964. *Insight and Responsibility: Lectures on the Ethical Implications of Psychoanalytic Insight*. New York: Norton.

———. 1965. Youth: Fidelity and Diversity. In *The Challenge of Youth*. New York: Doubleday/Anchor.

———. 1968. *Identity, Youth, and Crisis*. New York: Norton.

———. 1974. *Dimensions of a New Identity*. New York: Norton.

———. 1977. *Toys and Reasons: Stages in the Ritualization of Experience*. New York: Norton.

Fabrega, H. 1969. Social Psychiatric Aspects of Acculturation and Migration: A General Statement. *Comprehensive Psychiatry* 10:314–26.

Fador, N. 1950. Varieties of Nostalgia. *Psychoanalytic Review* 37: 25–38.

Falk, A. 1974. Border Symbolism. *Psychoanalytic Quarterly* 43: 650–60.

Federn, P. 1952. *Ego Psychology and the Psychoses.* New York: Basic Books.

Fisher, S. 1963. A Further Appraisal of the Body Boundary Concept. *Journal of Consulting Psychology* 27(1): 62–74.

———. 1970. *Body Experience in Fantasy and Behavior.* New York: Appleton-Century-Crofts.

———. 1972. Influencing Selective Perception and Fantasy by Stimulating Body Landmarks. *Journal of Abnormal Psychology* 79(1): 97–105.

———. 1973. *Body Consciousness.* Englewood Cliffs, N.J.: Prentice-Hall.

———, and S. E. Cleveland. 1956. Body-Image Boundaries and Style of Life. *Journal of Abnormal and Social Psychology* 52: 373–79.

———, and ———. 1958. *Body Image and Personality.* Princeton, N.J.: Van Nostrand.

Forizs, L. 1980. Assimilation of Sociocultural Phenomena into Object Relationships. *Journal of Psychoanalytic Anthropology* 3(3): 243–57.

Frank, J. D. 1967. *Sanity and Survival.* New York: Random House.

———. 1968. The Face of the Enemy. *Psychology Today* 2(6): 24–29.

———. 1980. The Nuclear Arms Race—Sociopsychological Aspects. *American Journal of Public Health* 70(9): 950–52.

Freud, S. 1900. The Interpretation of Dreams. In *The Standard Edition of the Complete Psychological Works of Sigmund Freud,* vols. 4–5. London: Hogarth Press, 1953.

———. 1901. The Psychopathology of Everyday Life. In *The Standard Edition of the Complete Psychological Works of Sigmund Freud,* vol. 6. London: Hogarth Press, 1960.

———. 1911. Psycho-Analytic Notes on an Autobiographical Account of A Case of Paranoia (Dementia Paranoides). In *The Standard Edition of the Complete Psychological Works of Sigmund Freud,* 12: 9–82. London: Hogarth Press, 1958.

———. 1913. Totem and Taboo. In *The Standard Edition of the Complete Psychological Works of Sigmund Freud,* 13: 1–162. London: Hogarth Press, 1955.

———. 1914. Papers on Technique: Remembering, Repeating and Working-Through. In *The Standard Edition of the Complete*

Psychological Works of Sigmund Freud, 12:145–156. London: Hogarth Press, 1958.

———. 1915. Mourning and Melancholia. In *The Standard Edition of the Complete Psychological Works of Sigmund Freud*, 14:243–58. London: Hogarth Press, 1957.

———. 1920. Beyond the Pleasure Principle. In *The Standard Edition of the Complete Psychological Works of Sigmund Freud*, 18:7–64. London: Hogarth Press, 1955.

———. 1923. The Ego and the Id. In *The Standard Edition of the Complete Psychological Works of Sigmund Freud*, 19:12–66. London: Hogarth Press, 1961.

———. 1928. Dostoevsky and Parricide. In *The Standard Edition of the Complete Psychological Works of Sigmund Freud*, 21:177–94. London: Hogarth Press, 1961.

———. 1930. Civilization and Its Discontents. In *The Standard Edition of the Complete Psychological Works of Sigmund Freud*, 21:64–145. London: Hogarth Press, 1961.

———. 1939. Moses and Monotheism: Three Essays. In *The Standard Edition of the Complete Psychological Works of Sigmund Freud*, 23:7–137. London: Hogarth Press, 1964.

———, and D. E. Oppenheim. 1911. *Dreams in Folklore*. New York: International Universities Press, 1958.

Gans, H. J. 1962. *The Urban Villagers: Group and Class in the Life of Italian-Americans*. New York: Free Press.

Geffen, Rabbi J. S. 1975. A Question of Jewish Existence. *Torch* (published by the National Federation of Jewish Men's Clubs), Fall, pp. 6–7.

Giovacchini, P. L. 1967. Frustration and Externalization. *Psychoanalytic Quarterly* 36:571–83.

Glazer, N. 1975. The Exposed American Jew. *Commentary* 59 (June): 25–30.

Glenn, M. L., and B. Dym. 1983. Spatial Representation of the Family. *Family Medicine* 15(3): 93–95.

Goffman, E. 1963. *Stigma: Notes on the Management of Spoiled Identity*. Englewood Cliffs, N.J.: Prentice-Hall.

Gonen, J. Y. 1975. *A Psychohistory of Zionism*. New York: Mason/Charter.

———. 1978. The Israeli Illusion of Omnipotence Following the Six Day War. *Journal of Psychohistory* 6(2): 241–71.

———. 1980. The Day of Atonement War. *Journal of Psychohistory* 8(1): 53–65.

Gorer, G., and J. Rickman. 1962. *The People of Great Russia: A Psychological Study.* New York: Norton; originally published 1949.

Hall, E. T. 1959. *The Silent Language.* New York: Doubleday.

———. 1977. *Beyond Culture.* Garden City, N.Y.: Anchor Press/Doubleday.

Hallowell, A. I. 1955. *Culture and Experience.* Philadelphia: University of Pennsylvania Press.

Hamilton, J. W. 1981. Review of C. F. Keys, ed. *Ethnic Adaptation and Identity: The Karen on the Thai Frontier with Burma* (Philadelphia: Institute for the Study of Human Issues, 1979). *American Anthropologist* 83:952–55.

Haque, A., and E. D. Lawson. 1980. The Mirror Image Phenomenon in the Context of the Arab-Israeli Conflict. *International Journal of Intercultural Relations* 4:107–15.

Hartmann, H. 1958. *Ego Psychology and the Problem of Adaptation.* New York: International Universities Press; originally published in German, 1939.

Hazelton, L. 1979. *Israeli Women.* New York: Simon & Schuster.

Henry, J. 1963. The United States and the Soviet Union: Some Economic and Social Consequences of a Twentieth-Century Nightmare. In *Culture Against Man,* pp. 100–23. New York: Random House.

Hippler, A. E. 1974. Some Alternative Viewpoints of the Negative Results of Euro-American Contact with Non-Western Groups. *American Anthropologist* 76:334–37.

———. 1979. Comment on "Development in the Non-Western World." *American Anthropologist* 81(2): 348–49.

———. 1981. The Yolngu and Cultural Relativism: A Response to Reser. *American Anthropologist* 83(2): 393–97.

Hook, R. H. 1979. Phantasy and Symbol: A Psychoanalytic Point of View. In R. H. Hook, ed. *Fantasy and Symbol,* pp. 267–91. New York: Academic Press.

Hurst, L. T. Y. 1951. Displacement and Migration. *American Journal of Psychiatry* 107:561–68.

Inkeles, A. 1966. The Modernization of Man. In M. Weiner, ed. *Modernization.* New York: Basic Books.

Irvine, W. 1955. *Apes, Angels, and Victorians.* New York: Time.

Kafka, F. 1946. *The Great Wall of China.* New York: Schocken Books, 1970.

Kane, J. 1983. Where's Oklahoma? *Ten* (KTOK, Oklahoma's Radio Magazine, Oklahoma City) 1(1): 8.

Kernberg, O. F. 1975. *Borderline Conditions and Pathological Narcissism*. New York: Jason Aronson.

Khantzian, E. J. 1985. Bridging the Old and the New. *Ararat* 26(3): 2–6.

Klein, M. 1946. Notes on Some Schizoid Mechanisms. *International Journal of Psychoanalysis* 27:99–110.

———. 1955. On Identification. In M. Klein, P. Heimann, and R. Money-Kyrle, eds. *New Directions in Psycho-Analysis*, pp. 309–45. New York: Basic Books.

———. 1976. *Narrative of a Child Psychoanalysis*. New York: Dell.

Kluckhohn, C. 1944. *Navaho Witchcraft*. Boston: Beacon Press.

Koenigsberg, R. A. 1975. *Hitler's Ideology: A Study in Psychoanalytic Sociology*. New York: Library of Social Science.

Kohn, H. 1960. *Panslavism: Its History and Ideology*. Rev. ed. New York: Vintage Books.

Kohut, H. 1966. Forms and Transformations of Narcissism. *Journal of the American Psychoanalytic Association* 14:243–72.

———. 1971. *The Analysis of the Self*. New York: International Universities Press.

———. 1972. Thoughts on Narcissism and Narcissistic Rage. *The Psychoanalytic Study of the Child* 27:360–400.

———. 1977. *Restoration of the Self*. New York: International Universities Press.

Korzybski, A. 1941. *Science and Sanity*. New York: Science Press.

Kostka, E. 1966. Review of Hans Lemberg, *Die Nationale Gedankwelt der Dekabristen* (1963). *Slavonic and East European Journal* 10:366.

Kren, G., and L. Rappoport. 1980. *The Holocaust and the Crisis of Human Behavior*. New York: Holmes and Meier.

La Barre, W. 1951. Family and Symbol. In G. Wilbur and W. Muensterberger, eds. *Psychoanalysis and Culture: Essays in Honor of Geza Roheim*, pp. 156–67. New York: International Universities Press.

———. 1966. The Dream, Charisma, and the Culture-Hero. In G. E. Von Gruenbaum and R. Caillois, eds. *The Dream and Human Societies*, pp. 229–35. Berkeley and Los Angeles: University of California Press.

———. 1968a. *The Human Animal*. Chicago: University of Chicago Press.

———. 1968b. Personality from a Psychoanalytic Viewpoint. In E. Norbeck, ed. *The Study of Personality*. New York: Holt, Rinehart, and Winston.

———. 1969. *They Shall Take Up Serpents: Psychology of the Southern Snake-Handling Cult.* New York: Schocken Books.

———. 1971. Materials for a History of Studies of Crisis Cults: A Bibliographic Essay. *Current Anthropology* 12(1): 3–44.

———. 1972. *The Ghost Dance: The Origins of Religion.* New York: Dell.

———. 1975. Anthropological Perspectives on Hallucination and Hallucinogens. In R. K. Siegel and L. J. West, eds. *Hallucinations: Behavior, Experience, and Theory,* pp. 9–52. New York: John Wiley & Sons.

———. 1978. Psychoanalysis and the Biology of Religion. *Journal of Psychological Anthropology* 1(1): 57–64.

———. 1984. *Muelos: A Stone-Age Superstition About Sexuality.* New York: Columbia University Press.

Lampert, E. 1965. *Sons Against Fathers: Studies in Russian Radicalism and Revolution.* New York: Oxford University Press/ Clarendon.

Langbaum, R. 1973. Thoughts for Our Time: Three Novels on Anarchism. *American Scholar* 42(2): 227–50.

La Rocque, Admiral G. R. 1985. A Personal Message from Admiral Gene R. La Rocque (open letter). Washington, D.C.: Center for Defense Information.

Leach, E. 1964. *Political Systems of Highland Burma.* Boston: Beacon Press.

Lesse, S. 1974. *Masked Depression.* New York: Jason Aronson.

LeVine, R. A. 1965. Socialization, Social Structure, and Intersocietal Images. In H. C. Kelman, ed. *International Behavior: A Social-Psychological Analysis.* New York: Holt, Rinehart and Winston.

———, and Donald T. Campbell. 1972. *Ethnocentrism: Theories of Conflict, Ethnic Attitudes, and Group Behavior.* New York: John Wiley & Sons.

Levinsohn, F. L. 1977. A Sign from G-d. Manuscript, quoted with permission.

Lévi-Strauss, C. 1963. *Structural Anthropology.* New York: Basic Books.

———. 1968. *The Savage Mind.* Chicago: University of Chicago Press.

Lipman, S. 1976. Wagner Comes to Broadway. *Commentary* 61 (January): 67–70. [See also letters and rejoinder, *Commentary,* July 1976 issue].

Lippmann, W. 1922. *Public Opinion.* New York: Macmillan.

Loeb, E. M., and G. Devereux. 1943. Antagonistic Acculturation. *American Sociological Review* 8:133–48.

Loewald, H. W. 1981. Regression: Some General Considerations. *Psychoanalytic Quarterly* 50:22–43.

Loewenstein, R. M. 1951. *Christians and Jews: A Psychoanalytic Study.* New York: International Universities Press.

Loizos, P. 1982. *The Heart Grown Bitter: A Chronicle of Cypriot War Refugees.* New York: Cambridge University Press.

Lorenz, K. Z. 1970. *On Aggression.* New York: Bantam.

Lukasevich, S. 1968. Review of Georges Luciani, *Panslavisme et solidarité slave au XIXe siècle: La Societé des Slaves Unis (1823–1825)* (1963). *Slavonic and East European Journal* 12:120–22.

Mack, J. E. 1979. Foreword. In V. D. Volkan. *Cyprus: War and Adaptation—A Psychoanalytic History of Two Ethnic Groups in Conflict,* pp. ix–xxviii. Charlottesville: University Press of Virginia.

Mahler, M. 1963. Thoughts About Development and Individualism. *Psychoanalytic Study of the Child* 18:307–24.

———, and M. Furer. 1963. Certain Aspects of the Separation-Individuation Phase. *Psychoanalytic Quarterly* 32:1–14.

———, with M. Furer. 1968. *On Human Symbiosis and the Vicissitudes of Individuation.* Vol. 1, *Infantile Psychosis.* New York: International Universities Press.

———, F. Pine, and A. Bergman. 1975. *The Psychological Birth of the Human Infant: Symbiosis and Individuation.* New York: Basic Books.

Malefijt, A. de W. 1968. Homo Monstrosus. *Scientific American* 219(4): 113–18.

Malia, M. 1961. *Alexander Herzen and the Birth of Russian Socialism.* Cambridge, Mass.: Harvard University Press.

Marmot, M. 1975. Acculturation and Coronary Heart Disease in Japanese Americans. Ph.D. dissertation. Berkeley: University of California.

Meissner, W. W. 1980. A Note on Projective Identification. *Journal of the American Psychoanalytic Association* 28(1): 43–67.

Mezey, A. G. 1960. Psychiatric Aspects of Human Migrations. *International Journal of Social Psychiatry* 4:245–50.

Minuchin, S. 1974. *Families and Family Therapy.* Cambridge, Mass.: Harvard University Press.

Modell, A. H. 1963. Primitive Object Relationships and the Predisposition to Schizophrenia. *International Journal of Psycho-analysis* 44:282–92.

Monas, S. 1965. Review of E. Lampert, *Sons Against Fathers: Studies in Russian Radicalism and Revolution* (1965). *Slavic Review* 24:725–26.

Muller, H. 1957. "Holy Russia," Byzantine and Marxist. In *The Uses of the Past.* New York: Oxford University Press.

Murphy, H. B. M. 1965. Migration and Major Mental Disorders. In M. B. Kantor, ed. *Mobility and Mental Health*, pp. 5–29. Springfield, Ill.: C. Thomas.

Nann, R. C., ed. 1982. *Uprooting and Surviving: Adaptation and Resettlement of Migrant Families and Children.* Boston: D. Reidel.

Naroll, R. 1983. *The Moral Order: An Introduction to the Human Situation.* Beverly Hills, Calif.: Sage Publications.

Niederland, W. C. 1956. River Symbolism, Part 1. *Psychoanalytic Quarterly* 25:469–504.

———. 1957. River Symbolism, Part 2. *Psychoanalytic Quarterly* 26:50–75.

———. 1959. Further Remarks on River Symbolism. *Journal of the Hillside Hospital* 8:109–14.

———. 1971a. The History and Meaning of California: A Psychoanalytic Inquiry. *Psychoanalytic Quarterly* 40:485–90.

———. 1971b. The Naming of America. In M. Kanzer, ed. *The Unconscious Today: Essays in Honor of Max Schur.* New York: International Universities Press.

Novick, J., and K. Kelly. 1970. Projection and Externalization. *Psychoanalytic Study of the Child* 25:69–95.

Ozick, C. 1974. All the World Wants the Jews Dead. *Esquire*, November, pp. 103–107, 207–10.

Parenti, M. 1969. *The Anti-Communist Impulse.* New York: Random House.

Perin, C. 1977. *Everything in Its Place: Social Order and Land Use in America.* Princeton, N.J.: Princeton University Press.

Pinderhughes, C. A. 1979. Differential Bonding: Toward a Psychophysiological Theory of Stereotyping. *American Journal of Psychiatry* 136:33–37.

Podhoretz, N. 1976. The Abandonment of Israel. *Commentary* 62 (July): 23–31.

Pollock, G. H. 1977. The Mourning Process and Creative Organization. *Journal of the American Psychoanalytic Association* 25:3–34.

Porshnev, B. F. 1973. Opposition as a Component of Ethnic Self-Consciousness. Paper presented to the 9th International Congress of Anthropological and Ethnological Sciences, Chicago, August–September.

Raditsa, B. 1967. The Disunity of the Slavs. *Orbis* 10(4): 1082–90.

Raithel, G. 1979. Philobatism and American Culture. *Journal of Psychohistory* 6(4): 461–96.

Reid, S. 1972. Moses and Monotheism: Guilt and the Murder of the Primal Father. *American Imago* 29:11–34.

Reik, T. 1948. *Listening with the Third Ear: The Inner Experience of a Psychoanalyst.* New York: Farrar, Straus.

Reminick, R. A. 1983. *Theory of Ethnicity: An Anthropologist's Perspective.* Lanham, Md.: University Press of America.

Roheim, G. 1943. *The Origin and Function of Culture.* New York: Nervous and Mental Disease Monographs, no. 69.

Rose, P. 1973. Review Essay. *Contemporary Sociology* 2:14–17.

Ruud, C. 1974. Pre-Revolutionary Russian Nationalism. *Canadian Review of Studies in Nationalism* 1(2): 276–86.

Ryan, S. 1980. Petain and Vichy: Abandonment, Guilt, "Love of Harlot," and Repetition Compulsion. *Journal of Psychohistory* 8(2): 149–58.

Sagan, E. 1985. *At the Dawn of Tyranny: The Origins of Individualism, Political Oppression, and the State.* New York: Alfred A. Knopf.

Schanche, D. A. 1983. News report on eruption of Mt. Aetna. *Fort Worth* (Texas) *Star-Telegram*, 13 May.

Schilder, P. 1950. *The Image and Appearance of the Human Body.* New York: International Universities Press.

Schlossman, H. H. 1966. Circumcision as Defense: A Study in Psychoanalysis and Religion. *Psychoanalytic Quarterly* 35: 340–56.

———. 1969. Review of Shalom Spiegel, *The Last Trial. American Imago* 26:87–89.

Schmidt, C. 1982. The Use of the Gallup Poll as a Psychohistorical Tool. *Journal of Psychohistory* 10(2): 141–62.

Scholem, G. 1961. *Major Trends in Jewish Mysticism.* New York: Schocken Books.

Searles, H. F. 1960. *Nonhuman Environment in Normal Development and in Schizophrenia.* Monograph no. 5 in Series on Schizophrenia. New York: International Universities Press.

———. 1963. The Place of Neutral Therapist-Responses in Psychotherapy with the Schizophrenic Patient. *International Journal of Psycho-Analysis* 44:42–56.

Seguin, C. A. 1956. Migration and Psychosomatic Disadaptation. *Psychosomatic Medicine* 18:404–409.

Shafer, B. C. 1954. *Nationalism: Myth and Reality.* New York: Harcourt, Brace.

———. 1982. *Nationalism and Internationalism: Belonging in Human Experience.* Malabar, Fla.: Robert E. Krieger.

Simos, A. T. 1981. Cyprus and Cuba: An Episcopal Fantasy. *Journal of Psychoanalytic Anthropology* 4(2): 223–38.

Sklare, M. 1972. Jews, Ethnics, and the American City. *Commentary* 53(4): 70–77.

———. 1976. American Jewry—The Ever-dying People. *Mainstream*, June–July, pp. 17–27.

Snyder, L. L. 1974. Review of Boyd C. Shafer, *Faces of Nationalism* (1972). *Canadian Review of Studies in Nationalism* 1:287–88.

Spicer, E. H. 1971. Persistent Cultural Systems. *Science* 174: 795–800.

Spiegel, J. 1971. *Transactions: The Interplay Between Individual, Family, and Society.* New York: Science House.

Spiro, M. E. 1951. Culture and Personality: The Natural History of a False Dichotomy. *Psychiatry* 14:19–46.

———. 1967. *Burmese Supernaturalism.* Englewood Cliffs, N.J.: Prentice-Hall.

Srole, L. 1980. Mental Health in New York: A Revisionist View. *Sciences* 20(10): 16–20, 29.

Stanton, D. M. 1977. The Addict as Savior: Heroin, Death, and the Family. *Family Process* 16(2): 191–97.

Stein, H. F. 1974a. Freedom and Interdependence: American Culture and the Adlerian Ideal. *Journal of Individual Psychology* 30:145–58.

———. 1974b. Where Seldom Is Heard a Discouraging Word: American Nostalgia. *Columbia Forum* 3(3): 20–23.

———. 1975a. American Judaism, Israel, and the New Ethnicity. *Cross Currents* 25(1): 51–66.

———. 1975b. Ethnicity, Identity, and Ideology. *School Review* 83(2): 273–300.

———. 1976. *Peter and the Wolf,* A Musical Tale of Individuation and the Imagery of the New Soviet Man: A Psychoanalytic Exploration of Russian Cultural History. In W. Muensterberger, A. Esman, and L. B. Boyer, eds. *The Psychoanalytic Study of Society,* 7:31–63. New Haven, Conn.: Yale University Press.

————. 1977. Identity and Transcendence. *School Review* 85(3): 349–75.

————. 1978. Judaism and the Group-Fantasy of Martyrdom: The Psychodynamic Paradox of Survival Through Persecution. *Journal of Psychohistory* 6(2): 151–210.

————. 1979. The White Ethnic Movement, Pan-ism, and the Restoration of Early Symbiosis: The Psychohistory of a Group-Fantasy. *Journal of Psychohistory* 6(3): 319–59.

————. 1980a. Bowen "Family Systems Theory"—The Problem of Cultural Persistence and the Differentiation of Self in One's Culture. *Family* 8(1): 3–12.

————. 1980b. Culture and Ethnicity as Group-Fantasies: A Psycho-Historic Paradigm of Group Identity. *Journal of Psychohistory* 8(1): 21–51.

————. 1980c. *An Ethno-Historic Study of Slovak-American Identity.* New York: Arno Press/New York Times Press.

————. 1980d. Medical Anthropology and Western Medicine. *Journal of Psychological Anthropology* 3(2): 185–95.

————. 1980e. Review essay of Arthur Kleinman's *Patients and Healers in the Context of Culture* (Berkeley: University of California Press, 1980). *Journal of Psychological Anthropology* 3(2): 197–204.

————. 1980f. Wars and Rumors of Wars: A Psychohistorical Study of a Medical Culture. *Journal of Psychohistory* 7(4): 379–401.

————. 1981a. Alistair Cooke's "America": A Study in Cultural Consensus and Popular History. *Journal of American Culture* 4(4): 34–44.

————. 1981b. Family Medicine as a Meta-Specialty and the Dangers of Overdefinition. *Family Medicine* 13(3): 3–7.

————. 1982a. Adversary Symbiosis and Complementary Group Dissociation: An Analysis of the U.S./U.S.S.R. Conflict. *International Journal of Intercultural Relations* 6: 55–83.

————. 1982b. The Annual Cycle and the Cultural Nexus of Health Care Behavior Among Oklahoma Wheat Farming Families. *Culture, Medicine, and Psychiatry* 6(1): 81–99.

————. 1982c. Autism and Architecture—A Tale of Inner Landscapes. *Continuing Education for the Family Physician* 16(6): 15–16, 19.

————. 1982d. The Contest for Control: A Case of Diabetes Mellitus in Psychosomatic, Familial Health Care, and Cultural Contexts. *Journal of Psychoanalytic Anthropology* 5(2): 173–96.

————. 1982e. Ethanol and Its Discontents: Paradoxes of Inebriation and Sobriety in American Culture. *Journal of Psycho-analytic Anthropology* 5(4): 355–77.

———. 1982f. "Health" and "Wellness" as Euphemism: The Cultural Context of Insidious Draconian Health Policy. *Continuing Education for the Family Physician* 16(3): 33–44.

———. 1982g. Neo-Darwinism and Survival Through Fitness. *Journal of Psychohistory* 10(2): 163–87.

———. 1982h. Physician-Patient Transaction Through the Analysis of Countertransference: A Study in Role Relationship and Unconscious Meaning. *Medical Anthropology* 6(3): 165–82.

———. 1982i. Wellness as Illusion. *Delaware Medical Journal* 54(11): 637–41.

———. 1983a. The Case Study Method as a Means of Teaching Significant Context in Family Medicine. *Family Medicine* 15(5): 163–67.

———. 1983b. Historical Understanding as Sense of History: A Psychoanalytic Inquiry. *Psychoanalytic Review* 70(4): 595–619.

———. 1983c. The Influence of Counter-Transference upon the Clinical Relationship and Decision-Making. *Continuing Education for the Family Physician* 18(7): 625–30.

———. 1983d. The Money Taboo in American Medicine. *Medical Anthropology* 7(4): 1–15.

———. 1983e. Psychoanalytic Anthropology and the Meaning of Meaning. In B. Bain, ed. *Sociogenesis of Language and Human Conduct,* pp. 393–414. New York: Plenum.

———. 1983f. Toward a Psychoanalytic Bioanthropology: A Retrospective Study of the Contribution of Weston La Barre. *Journal of Social and Biological Structures* 6(3): 249–64.

———. 1984. The Holocaust, the Uncanny, and the Jewish Sense of History. *Political Psychology* 5(1): 5–35.

———. 1985a. Culture Change, Symbolic Object Loss, and Restitutional Process. *Psychoanalysis and Contemporary Thought* 8(3): 301–32.

———. 1985b. Psychological Complementarity in Soviet-American Relations. *Political Psychology* 6(2): 249–61.

———. 1985c. The Unfolding: A Clinical Tragedy in Two Acts, or—When Life Is Like a Night at the Opera, Chapter 6. In H. Stein and M. Apprey, *Context and Dynamics in Clinical Knowledge.* Monograph vol. 1 of H. F. Stein and M. Apprey, eds. Series in Ethnicity, Medicine, and Psychoanalysis. Charlottesville: University Press of Virginia.

——. 1985d. Values and Family Therapy. In J. Schwartzman, ed. *Families and Other Systems: The Macrosystemic Context of Family Therapy*, pp. 201–43. New York: Guilford Press.

——. 1987. Farmer and Cowboy: The Duality of the Midwestern Male Ethos—A Study in Ethnicity, Regionalism, and National Identity. In H. F. Stein, and M. Apprey, *From Metaphor to Meaning: Papers in Psychoanalytic Anthropology.* Monograph vol. 2 of H. F. Stein and M. Apprey, eds. Series in Ethnicity, Medicine, and Psychoanalysis. Charlottesville: University Press of Virginia.

——, and D. Fox. 1985. Work as Family: Occupational Relationships and Social Transference. In H. F. Stein, and M. Apprey, *Context and Dynamics in Clinical Knowledge.* Monograph vol. 1 of H. F. Stein and M. Apprey, eds. Series in Ethnicity, Medicine, and Psychoanalysis. Charlottesville: University Press of Virginia.

——, and R. F. Hill. 1973. The New Ethnicity and the White Ethnic in the United States: An Exploration in the Psycho-Cultural Genesis of Ethnic Irredentism. *Canadian Review of Studies in Nationalism* 1(1): 81–105.

——, and ——. 1977a. *The Ethnic Imperative: Examining the New White Ethnic Movement.* University Park: Pennsylvania State University Press.

——, and ——. 1977b. The Limits of Ethnicity. *American Scholar* 46(2): 181–89.

——, and ——. 1979. Adaptive Modalities Among Slovak- and Polish-Americans: Some Issues in Cultural Continuity and Change. *Anthropology* 3(1–2): 95–107.

——, W. D. Stanhope, and R. F. Hill. 1981. P. A. and M. D.—Some Parallels with Clinical Psychology and Psychiatry. *Social Science and Medicine* 15E: 83–93.

Steinglass, P. 1981. The Alcoholic Family at Home: Patterns of Interaction in Dry, Wet, and Transitional Stages of Alcoholism. *Archives of General Psychiatry* 38: 578–84.

Stierlin, H. 1976. *Adolf Hitler: A Family Perspective.* New York: Psychohistory Press.

Stolorow, R. D., and G. E. Atwood. 1979. *Faces in a Cloud.* New York: Jason Aronson.

Szaluta, J. 1980. Apotheosis to Ignominy: The Martyrdom of Marshal Petain. *Journal of Psychohistory* 7(4): 415–53.

Taylor, A. J. P. 1978. *The Origins of the Second World War.* New York: Fawcett.

Time. 1983a. Concern for Galileo, 23 May, p. 58.

Time. 1983b. Outbreak of Comet Fever. 23 May, p. 56.

Tumarkin, N. 1983. Invited presentation at the Second Annual Esalen Institute Symposium on the Psychology of the U.S.-Soviet Relationship, Esalen Institute, Big Sur, California, 3–7 October.

Volkan, V. D. 1972. The Linking Objects of Pathological Mourners. *Archives of General Psychiatry* 27: 215–21.

———. 1976. *Primitive Internalized Object Relations.* New York: International Universities Press.

———. 1979. *Cyprus: War and Adaptation—A Psychoanalytic History of Two Ethnic Groups in Conflict.* Charlottesville: University Press of Virginia.

———. 1981. *Linking Objects and Linking Phenomena: A Study of the Forms, Symptoms, Metapsychology, and Therapy of Complicated Mourning.* New York: International Universities Press.

———. 1984. Psychological Formulations Developed at the Conferences on the Middle East. Manuscript.

Walsh, M. N., and B. G. Scandalis. 1975. Male Initiation Rites and Modern Warfare as Related Expressions of Unconscious Cross-Generational Aggression. In M. A. Nettleship et al., eds. *War: Its Causes and Correlates.* The Hague: Mouton.

Weber, M. 1961. The Ethnic Group. In Parsons and Shils et al., eds. *Theories of Society.* Vol. 1. Glencoe, Ill.: Free Press.

Weinberg, A. A. 1961. *Migration and Belonging.* The Hague: Martinus Nighoff.

Whyte, M. K. 1970. Rural Russia Today. *Trans-action* 7: 26–32.

Wiesel, E. 1974. Ominous Signs and Unspeakable Thoughts (editorial). *New York Times,* 28 December.

———. 1976. *Messengers of God: Biblical Portraits and Legends.* New York: Random House.

Winnicott, D. W. 1953. Transitional Objects and Transitional Phenomena: A Study of the First Not-Me Possession. *International Journal of Psychoanalysis* 34: 89–97.

———. 1967. The Location of Cultural Experience. *International Journal of Psychoanalysis* 48: 368–72.

Wyschogrod, M. 1971. Faith and the Holocaust: A Review of Emil Fackenheim's "God's Presence in History." *Judaism* 20: 286–94.

Yakauer, A. 1980. The Pseudo-Environment of National Defense. *American Journal of Public Health* 70(9): 949.

Youmans, E. G. 1977. The Rural Aged. *Annals of the American Academy of Political and Social Science* 429: 81–90.

Zinner, J., and R. Shapiro. 1972. Projective Identification as a Mode of Perception and Behaviour in Families of Adolescents. *International Journal of Psycho-Analysis* 53: 523–30.

Zonis, M. 1984. Self-Objects, Self-Representation, and Sense-Making Crises: Political Instability in the 1980s. *Political Psychology* 5(2): 267–85.

Zwingmann, C. A. 1973. The Nostalgic Phenomenon and Its Exploitation. In C. A. Zwingmann and M. Pfister-Ammende, eds. *Uprooting and After*, pp. 19–47. New York: Springer-Verlag.

Index

231